After Stalingrad

After Stalingrad

*Seven Years as a Soviet
Prisoner of War*

Adelbert Holl

Pen & Sword
MILITARY

First published in Great Britain in 2016 by
PEN AND SWORD MILITARY
an imprint of
Pen and Sword Books Ltd
47 Church Street
Barnsley
South Yorkshire S70 2AS

ISBN 978 1 47385 611 0

Printed and bound in England by
CPI Group (UK) Ltd, Croydon, CR0 4YY

Typeset in Times by CHIC GRAPHICS

Pen & Sword Books Ltd incorporates the imprints of
Archaeology, Atlas, Aviation, Battleground, Discovery,
Family History, History, Maritime, Military, Naval, Politics,
Railways, Select, Social History, Transport, True Crime,
Claymore Press, Frontline Books, Leo Cooper, Praetorian Press,
Remember When, Seaforth Publishing and Wharncliffe.

For a complete list of Pen and Sword titles please contact
Pen and Sword Books Limited
47 Church Street, Barnsley, South Yorkshire, S70 2AS, England
E-mail: enquiries@pen-and-sword.co.uk
Website: www.pen-and-sword.co.uk

Contents

Preface

When I became a prisoner of war of the Russians twenty-two years ago in Stalingrad, as a young soldier I was full of confidence and belief in our leadership at the time.

I served my time as a prisoner of this establishment and wrote the following unvarnished report immediately after my return home.

I have been able to study extensively the failure of those who wanted to be our examples since my return home and have come to the bitter realisation of their shameful misuse of our most sacred feelings.

This account is not intended to give rise to any false myths, nor to arouse any false hatred, but rather to serve as an explanation. My wish is for the youth of the world to be spared such a senseless war through wise statesmanship.

My quiet thoughts are for the families of all the dead who lost their lives in this frightful war.

Adelbert Holl
Duisburg, June 1965

Chapter 1

Prisoner!

'Captain, they are coming!' With these words the sentry burst into the long dugout.

Everything was quiet for a moment. Now the time had come that I would never have believed possible but which in the last three days had become an irrefutable certainty.

My thoughts returned to the moment when I had stood before my sector commander and, in a last burst of defiance, refused the order to withdraw with my last remaining combat capable men. The wounded were to be left behind in the old position, which went against our code of 'All for one and one for all'.

Second-Lieutenant Augst was now leading to our sector commander's command post the last combat capable men: about a hundred of them, scraped out of the rear services, some of whom had had no infantry training. I myself had gone back to the shelter, to my wounded comrades, escorted by twelve of my older men. We were not ashamed of our tears as I explained to the wounded, of whom there were about forty, that we were going into an unknown fate. We had done our duty as soldiers, but fate had been stronger than us. I told them of their country's gratitude for their service in Stalingrad, and shook their hands. Most of these men had been with the division since the beginning of the war. I was certain of one thing: if the Russians so much as bent a hair of one of the wounded in my presence, he would learn something! I had with me my 08-Pistol with two full magazines and a bullet in the breach – 17 rounds of ammunition, 16 for Ivan and the last one for me. In addition, I still had two hand-grenades in my possession.

It had been a hot time for us defending the north-western corner of 'Fortress Stalingrad'. The main front line ran in an east–west direction directly past us to the right-hand corner in the south, enabling the Russians to attack us from three sides. Nevertheless all their attempts to break through had been unsuccessful.

Some seconds passed full of stress. What would the Russians do? I sat on the extreme corner of the dugout on the edge of the slope in which the dugout was located. It was Second-Lieutenant Augst's command post and simultaneously served as the collecting point for the sick and wounded. Nevertheless for days now the hospital had been not accepting any more patients, as it was completely full, so the wounded had had to remain forward on the front line.

I was not identifiable as an officer in my camouflage uniform. The pistol was secured to my knee. Now must I decide whether it would be a short final fight, or captivity? What is that? I did not know, and gave myself no time as something nagged at my nerves. Ivan would soon come and he would be sorry if he mishandled my wounded comrades!

There was movement in the front part of the room. 'They are here!' I sat motionless and noted what was going on around me. There were seconds of high concentration and stress. Suddenly I heard Russian voices and saw a Red Army soldier with a cocked submachine gun in his hands. His face was that of a normal Russian: broad, bloated, unimpressive. He issued orders that my Company Sergeant-Major Josef Pawellek immediately translated. Pawellek was from Upper Silesia and had learned some Russian during the months of the Russian campaign. The orders went: 'Lay down your weapons immediately! Abandon all resistance! Fall in outside in front of the dugout!'

My attitude in front of the enemy soldiers was somewhat hostile. I asked Pawellek to ask what would happen to the wounded. 'They remain here if they cannot move themselves. They will be looked after.' We had to line up in front of the bunker. I got up from my seat and wanted to go outside, but Pawellek's voice stopped me: 'Captain, take these two bread bags with you, I have got them extra for you. We could well need them!' Almost mechanically I took what was handed to me without noticing what was in them. It was as if I was in a dream. I followed the others, seeing as I was going out the distress of those left lying on the stretchers – and I was outside.

Numbed, I followed Sergeant-Major Pawellek, and we trailed

behind our comrades, disappearing behind a hill. A Russian soldier, also armed with a submachine-gun, stopped us. He asked something. I heard again and again the words 'Urr' and 'Chleb', but understood nothing. Pawellek spoke to him. Suddenly he addressed me: 'Captain, the Ivan wants a watch and will give us bread for it. I have two watches. Shall I give him one?' It was all the same to me. Pawellek gave the Red Army soldier a wristwatch that he took from his jacket pocket. The Russian took it and put it on, then said something to Pawellek and indicated with his hand the direction in which the others had gone. Pawellek was furious, but the Russian scornfully pointed the muzzle of his submachine-gun at him. We went on without having obtained any bread.

As we walked on I became aware of something hard in my trouser pockets. I immediately remembered the two hand-grenades and the pistol. Once I had established that there was nobody watching in the vicinity, I dismantled my old pistol and strewed the parts and the hand-grenades out of sight in the snow.

The route led us back to our old sector, which lay to the left of that of Second-Lieutenant Augst and his men.

Here we saw the column of prisoners gathering together. Men were coming out of all the holes. A peculiar feeling came over me as we assembled precisely over my old command post. I had still been there only nine hours ago. It was now between 9 and 10 o'clock in the morning. The bodies of those Russians who had fallen in our sector had already been removed. There had been a lot of them. What would the Russians have done if they had captured us here, in our old sector? The dugouts and foxholes in which we had been sitting only a short time before had been carefully combed through.

A particularly large Russian, who wore a black emblem on his snow shirt and was apparently an officer, was making an announcement. I understood nothing of what he said, but the movements of the other prisoners indicated that we were to fall in. My few old comrades pressed around me. We wanted to stay together if possible. There were three men especially who had been with me for years: Sergeant Dr Alfred Rotter from the Sudetenland, Sergeant Josef Pawellek from Oppeln County in Upper Silesia and Sergeant Heinrich Grund from Erdmannsdorf in Saxony.

GORODISCHTSCHE: THE COLLECTING POINT FOR PRISONERS FROM THE NORTHERN CAULDRON

The columns slowly got under way. There were about two or three hundred men. Some of them were equipped with rucksacks, others had knapsacks or bread bags. We cautiously made our way down the icy slope until we came to the bottom of the Gorodischtsche valley. The head of the column stopped until the last prisoners caught up with them.

Now it was easier going forward. We had already crossed the frozen stream and reached the point where the nose of the hill jutted out. I had always wondered what lay behind it, but I had never expected this. Behind the nose, some 10 to 20 metres apart, stood some super-heavy Russian mortars. I counted twelve of them only 400 metres from my former position.

A path ran through the valley, leading us on in a westerly direction through the mortar position. Further away from us was another column of prisoners, to which we gradually made our way. Once we reached them, we stopped.

Until then I had not spoken a word to my comrades. They too were silent. What was going on in their heads? I thought it must be just about nothing, being so numbed and dull. For me it was as if I had a plank in front of my head, as if there was a dark void inside my brain.

A Russian asks a question and it is translated. He wants to know if there are any officers among us. As I go to step forward, my men hold me back. 'Be quiet, Captain!' Rotter whispered. 'We want to stay together, otherwise we will be separated.' He was right: I did not want to be separated from my comrades, especially on this journey into the unknown!

Further ahead of us another German officer has stepped forward. He receives an order which is translated for him. Moving to the head of the column of prisoners, he gives the order to move on. The column starts off again towards the west. Wherever one looks there are columns of prisoners.

How long we have been tramping through the snow, I do not know. Was it minutes? Was it seconds? It is all beyond my comprehension, so incredible. Until now we have been fighting, dishing out blows and naturally also receiving blows, and now we are trotting along in an apparently endless column of prisoners.

Another halt. We have stopped in front of a staff headquarters. I don't know what will happen now. I cannot believe my eyes: a woman, a Red Army soldier with a strongly painted face, vanishes into one of the offices. Around me comrades are trying with difficulty to get some food cans warmed up. The cans contain ready to eat meals. I wonder how they got the food. We have not seen such cans for a long time now. We look on with gnawing stomachs as the others eat. I think of yesterday evening when we shared among forty-eight men, including myself, 4 kilograms of bread, three-quarters of a can of Schokakola, and 3 grams of fat. Fortunately Pawellek had killed our bunker cat during the night and cooked it. The second back leg provided a small morsel for each of my faithful men this morning.

Near me a senior corporal of artillery is bent over, weighed down by a plump haversack. I can see this haversack is full of crisp bread. How did that man get this crisp bread? The men standing around him ask him to give them some. He refuses. What a dog! Is there a soldier anywhere who does not know the moral duty of sharing? 'Now give the others something!' I tell him. A cheeky, impudent face looks at me. 'What's up with you? You can kiss my arse!' I boil inside but control myself and turn away. Rotter says to the senior corporal: 'Behave yourself! That is a captain.' I hear his reply as I walk away: 'That is nothing to me, we are all just prisoners of war now!' I am ashamed; I had never experienced anything like it before and could never have believed it possible.

We had already been standing there for an hour and a half, as the so-called control was proceeding very slowly. Those who had been through it called out to us that everything would be taken from us, especially attractive items such as rings, watches, fountain pens, propelling pencils and cigarette lighters. I have nothing apart from my wristwatch, which only goes by the minute. 'Listen, we must try to join the others over there without going through the controls, and then we can get through quicker.' By keeping a good look out we could run over to the already checked group, and if we pushed further forward we would soon be marching on. As I had meanwhile discovered, all the prisoner of war columns that had passed through the controls were going on towards Gorodischtsche without specific supervision.

Our plan worked. At a suitable moment we ran across to the other group. Slowly, without anything unusual happening, we went on. Ahead of us the already checked troop of about 300 men was moving off. We hurried to join them. Thank goodness, at last we were making progress. The standing around had become a torment for me especially as I was the only man wearing standard Wehrmacht boots, there having been too few felt boots to go round the whole company.

Our marching column was becoming fragmented, pulled apart by the poor state of the road. One man who had been lightly wounded tried to get on a passing Russian sledge but the driver hit him with his whip until he fell off. He managed to hold on for a short distance until his strength gave out and then lay unconscious in the road. A former medical orderly saw to the hapless man.

The day was one of full sunshine. It must have been afternoon. The village of Gorodischtsche could be seen in the distance. Long columns of prisoners were converging on the village from all directions. We looked for a shortcut from the great bend in the track that we had already covered for 400 metres, hoping to save about 500 metres walking. If only we had not done this! When we parted from the crowd we were stopped on this stretch by a young lieutenant and his gang. A thorough search ensued. Anything that pleased them and caught their eye was taken from us.

I was surprised that, despite the various checks, we still had something that the Red Army soldiers found useful. What did they really think of us? Every prisoner who had a water bottle was told to produce it. The lieutenant seemed drunk as he brandished his pistol and shouted: 'Wodka jest?' His comrades also sniffed at the water bottles and bellowed like oxen. I thus understood that they only wanted vodka. When had we last seen any alcohol? It was already weeks ago. Finally they let us go on.

We reached the edge of the village of Gorodischtsche. Wherever I looked there were prisoners and more prisoners. How many there were it was impossible to say. I recalled having been here three months earlier as a soldier. There was nothing to eat, or to drink. There was no identifiable organisation or system for dealing with the prisoners, but there was talk about marching on to a specific camp. We let ourselves be swept along in the mass of humanity. We had already been here in the village for hours. It was dark when the almost endless stream of soldiers reached the western edge of

Gorodischtsche. The village itself was stuffed full of benumbed prisoners.

THE FIRST STAGES: BARBUKIN, BOL-ROSSOSCHKA

Going forward gradually became easier. I was far too numbed by all the experiences I had been through to think clearly. I moved along with the column like a sleepwalker. The road was bad, the darkness hiding the potholes, so I staggered on to the left and then to the right, pushed this way and that by the stumble of a comrade. I was covered in sweat from the irregular marching.

How long had we been marching already? I did not know. In the distance ahead of us appeared a few isolated lights. I had no idea what they could be, but I heard someone say: 'That must be Gumrak.'

The sound of an approaching vehicle made us step aside. It was a heavy Josef-Stalin tractor with two heavy guns attached, the crews sitting on them despite the cold. No ostentation, no baggage, only ammunition, just as we should have done.

We gradually came nearer to the lights. The presence of the railway line confirmed to me that this was Gumrak. Destroyed vehicles and guns had already been collected alongside the railway line. The traffic here was livelier. Here and there the door of a dugout opened and the light of the gleaming lamps shone out. Further on there was no light near us or in the distance. Only the long dark worm of the railway line accompanied us, and the firmament cast its cold pride over us as we struggled along. From time to time there was a brief halt as the guards waited for the column of prisoners to close up again. Like my comrades, I used these moments to lie down in the snow with my blanket under me. I was very tired. The lack of rest in the last two weeks was having an effect, but we could not stay lying down for long as our bodies cooled quickly in the biting cold, the relentless frost creeping over us, rising unceasingly from below. Only after walking for several hundred metres does the blood start to circulate again and the body to warm up.

The night seems endless. My stomach demands attention and its rights, not having had any proper attention for days. But I still have nothing. When will I get something to eat again? I breathe out. I can see a narrow strip in the east heralding the approaching dawn. It will soon be day and the world will look somewhat different. The guards have also said that there will be something to eat in the foreseeable future. Some know this place. They think that we are marching to Barbukin and will be accommodated there.

We have arrived in Barbukin. We stop in the valley, perhaps better described as a hollow. Scattered weapons and equipment indicate that there was a fight here once. The guards vanish into one of the holes in the ground. A solitary wooden house marks where a lively village had stood a few weeks ago. We look for some shelter from the wind, huddle together, freezing. Suddenly there comes: 'Come and get your food!' We join a group that takes two men at a time. There is a loaf of bread for every twenty men and half a salt herring each.

What is wrong with the bread? It is as hard as stone! Someone says: 'This bread is frozen!' It has to be cut with a pointed instrument as we no longer have knives.

I get my piece, which is ice-cold and hard. I try carefully to bite into it without success. Disappointed and with a hungry stomach, I stick it in my trouser pocket. Perhaps it will thaw a bit with time. I gulp the cold fish down with truly great hunger. My lips burn with the salt but I do nothing about it. The February sun looks down glaringly on us, but has no effect. But marching on we get warm again. When we stop for a moment we immediately become ice cold. It is better marching along on our new route. Snowploughs have been putting things in order here and metre-high walls of snow border the road.

Several individuals are showing noticeable signs of fatigue. We have now been nearly a day and a half on our legs without proper rest, not to mention the ceaseless fighting of the past days. I too am tired, but I carry on.

We finally come to a valley at noon. It is the Bol-Rossoschka valley. Our column stops and stands for a long time. A Russian officer who has suddenly appeared asks for German officers. Several step forward out of the column, those in camouflage uniforms having concealed their insignia. The Russian repeats his question. My men try to hold me back. I struggle with myself, not knowing what the Russians have in store for the officers. But should I deny being an officer? Might someone, if I was known to be an officer, say that I kept quiet about my rank out of fear? No! I said farewell to my comrades with a heavy heart and went to the already paraded and separate group. Where and when would we see each other again?

Wherever we looked there were dugouts. We were led to one of them and had to crawl into it through the hole. There were about sixty of us, but movement ceased when barely half of us were inside the dugout. Muffled voices came from within saying that it was full and there was no more room. The Russians then helped with their rifle butts and several minutes later we were all in this hole in the earth.

We stood pressed tightly together, as no one could sit down. Those who were at the end of their strength were unable to fall. The earthen walls were pitiless, dominating our area and allowing no expansion. The cries, groans and complaints were gradually followed by a pathetic silence. The only window hole was covered by a hanging tent preventing the icy snow from entering. The room was in complete darkness.

Was it hours? Was it days? Who could estimate the time passed in such a situation when seconds became eternity! Suddenly the door was torn open and we were ordered to get out. If only there had not been the packs of some of the prisoners! So the getting out of this tight space took twice as long. We were led in rows to a cauldron in which something had been cooked for us. Fortunately I still had my mess tin. I saw some prisoners eating out of rusty tin cans. Romanian prisoners were the cooks here. They did not behave well. What had they put in the pot? Unpeeled potatoes, mostly rotten and completely black. Despite our hunger, we were forced to throw out most of them. The rest of the meal was a mixture of venison, unpeeled oats and other jumbled cereals. For the first time in three days our stomachs had something warm again.

Then it was back to the hole in the earth. As we scrambled to get in, I noticed some prisoners hacking away at horse carcases. Once inside, the same complaining, pushing and jostling led again to the same apathetic silence. Some of those standing seemed already alarmingly in need of attention. I wondered where my comrades had been put.

Could hours become such an agonising eternity? Previously I would have thought it impossible but it was happening. I was almost indifferent. I had done my duty and what would happen now only heaven knew.

THE ROAD OF DEATH

If I am not mistaken, today is the 6th of February. A Red Army soldier orders us to fall in. It is still early in the morning. There are already about three hundred men paraded outside. The appearance of some of them shows that they have already suffered a lot. Some individuals display hunger and weakened bodies. We are given some pieces of hard bread, plus a small glass jar of preserved meat. I can hardly believe my eyes. Meat, but for eight men! There is not enough for one! As the hard bread is issued, we can see how the really hungry are out of control and behave badly and in an undisciplined way. We fall in. A prisoner translates one of the guard's orders. It is a warning: Anyone who tries to escape will be shot! We march off further to the west. I will make my way along whatever happens. We are lucky that the god of the weather is being kind to us: the sun is shining and there is no wind.

We have been marching directly westwards for three hours without a break. Then a plan occurs to me. Hopefully we will be crossing the Don. I lie down on my blanket for a nap and take my eighth of a scrap of preserved meat. Wonderfully tasty but laughably little!

Again we are ordered to fall in. I get up, sling the blanket over my shoulder and turn round. Could it be possible? In front of me is the old accountant of the 5th Company of Infantry Regiment 24 from Preussisch Eylau, Franz Neumann. His eyes too widen with astonishment, having recognised me immediately.

'So Franz, how did you get here?'

'I could ask you the same question!'

'I was taken prisoner in the northern part of Stalingrad on the morning of the 2nd February.'

'And I was with my division as Senior Paymaster right on the Volga.'

'This is a surprise. We last saw each other in August 1939 before marching into Poland. You were a senior NCO and I was still a corporal.'

We now march on together, the column having long since started off. Franz and I did not notice the time passing. We talked about the old days and what had happened in the time we were apart. He had attended the paymaster school in Hannover and I had done a training course at Döberitz. This was how each of us had got his job. Captivity was hard luck but now we could deal with this uncertainty together, through a lucky chance that had brought us together years later. Unfortunately Franz had a sick stomach, but we would manage. We would cope somehow.

It was already getting dark as we entered an unknown village. Red Army soldiers were still looking for watches, rings, cigarette lighters and similar items to exchange for worthwhile articles for themselves.

A repulsive sight for me is the women in uniform. There is nothing noticeably feminine about them, the war having also left them colourless. I avoided going near them. The village children, covered in rags, joined in with some of the soldiers in calling out: 'Gitler Kaput! Gitler Kaput!'

Our chief guard has already gone several times looking for accommodation for us. He does not want to lose us during the night. His efforts are unsuccessful. After more than an hour's waiting we were driven on westwards. Dear God, how much longer will this go on? The guards themselves apparently have no idea of the way. Always on and on. Many of the men are tottering not marching, for they are completely exhausted. But always, when the last ones get a bit behind, the guard covering the rear calls 'Dawai!' and some indiscriminate blows with a rifle butt ensure that the one fighting exhaustion quickly goes a few steps further on. I keep going at the regular pace I learnt as an infantryman. I have been linking arms with Franz for a long time already. The previous days have left him in a very bad way. If only those at the head of the column were not going so fast it would be easier for those at the back and the Russian guards would not harry them so much.

'Go slower in front!' My voice rang out loudly, but without success. This is enough to make me sick! Several of the young ones begin to complain about those marching in front. If it goes on like this there will be a catastrophe! The guard in front is urging haste in order to reach a village, the weak ones thus straggling behind. The whole group is being torn apart, and the guards behind mercilessly strike those unable to keep up with the pace.

I have already seen several bodies lying on the road, naked and stiff, completely stripped, like signposts on the road of death. The further west we go, the more we see of those who slipped away.

Ah, they have stopped in front. The last of the prisoners come staggering in. We are standing before a long auxiliary bridge. Next thing we are standing on the bank of the Don. I am pleased. The further west we go, the closer I am to the front line and the easier my escape attempt.

The guards on the wooden bridge make it clear that we have to cross it. We move on. It occurs to me that four and a half months ago I crossed this river in the opposite direction filled with a victorious feeling. If I had only known where were being taken and how long the way still was!

Meanwhile we climbed up the Don Heights on the west bank, but our column had already extended to a few hundred yards.

One of the weakest appeared to have given up. I can still hear him saying to the guard: 'I can't go on any more!' The guard said something in Russian and hit him with his rifle butt, but to no avail. A shot tore through the quiet of the night. A soldier's life ended on the endless road of captivity, the road of death.

Yes, it is a road of death. We cannot escape from our route any more, passing the dark dead that lie ghostlike in the snow's white surface. At times they are half-covered in whiteness as the wind blows snow over them. They lie stretched out, most stripped down to their shirts. Does the sight of the dead affect the guards?

A second shot startles the night out of its ghostly silence. Something must have happened! The head of the column is no longer in sight so big is the gap. Those shits at the front are afraid of the guards! My strength is also flagging. For some time now my task has been to get moving again those who stumble out of the group and sink up to their hips in the snow. If we leave them stuck there, a shot in the night will finish them. Some of our younger comrades who still have sufficient initiative also lend a hand. It is endless - just when one has got a completely exhausted man back on his legs and walked along with him for a bit, another one sits down suddenly in the snow and the whole thing has to be gone over again.

I no longer think about the many corpses lying on the roadside. By increasing my marching speed I get to the head of the bulk of the marching column; setting a quieter pace, I no longer concern myself about those marching in front who are no longer in sight. Some of the more anxious ones try to speed up the pace again but I confront them: 'I am setting the pace now!'

What time can it be? No one knows. Time seems to be standing still. After a while something dark appears before us. It is the head of the marching column. They must have already taken a rest for a few minutes. The guard stands up as soon as I arrive and orders us to march on. I refuse. Most of my comrades that came with me have already sunk down. They simply cannot go on and must have a rest.

Those who have already had a rest have immediately stood up as ordered by the guards. I cannot explain what has come over me. I turn to the guard and tell him that we have to rest for a while. He is apparently not agreeable to this, as he loads his submachine-gun and aims it at me. I become angry and shout at him: 'Then shoot, you stupid idiot!' As the guard realises that his threats have no effect, he swears wildly, which I do not understand, but eventually agrees to a five minute rest. Had he fired then it would have been all the same to me. The black spots along the route indicate that death will come at some time or other. I was scornful of those marching in front who thought only of going on, whether their own comrades kept up or not.

We went on. How much longer? Day was dawning in the east. How good the world looks by day even if it is so dreary. Franz, who has been plodding along without help for some time, is considerably exhausted. I take his pack along with mine and we link arms together.

Some recognise the place and say: 'It leads to Kissel-Jakov.' It cannot be too far off, only another 4 kilometres. A few kilometres is quite a strain on this road, but we have to do it. From a hill we get a glimpse of the valley beyond and can see various buildings: Kissel-Jakov. However, will it be our destination?

We reach the village towards midday. There is endless standing around and speculation, then we are led through the village past some holes in the ground. At the far end of the village stand two wooden houses. We are driven into them and so have a roof over our heads.

IN KISSEL-JAKOV TRANSIT CAMP

The room in which we find ourselves could have been a schoolroom. Now it is full of people all concerned with finding a good place to rest. Such a crowd is like a herd of sheep without a shepherd! Despite our exhaustion, there is noise and shouting until eventually everything becomes quiet.

Franz and I have obtained a place to sleep directly under a window opposite the entrance. We are glad to have the wall to support our backs, unlike most of the men who have to sit in the middle of the room. The window is not very thick and leans inwards but that is the least problem. The room is overcrowded. Some try to stretch themselves out, but that is impossible. If one man stretches himself out, immediately his neighbour complains of being cramped. Is this going to be permanent? And who is going to be the first in the night?

It has become dark, and fatigue lies heavily on the dead-tired prisoners. Everyone now tries to find a sleeping position and even the stove has to be used. There is not a square centimetre of space not in use. The air is stuffy and moist breath freezes on the windows.

Some stupid ones fight over their places. Apparently their nerves are no longer under control. Franz and I agree that one of us will sleep for two hours, while the other stands against the wall. There is no better solution. At least one of us can stretch out for a short time. On the whole things are quieter in our immediate surroundings than in other places.

The night is endless, especially when Franz wakes me up and I have to stand for two hours at the wall. But there is no better way. The dawn is greeted with a general breathing out. It is somewhat more bearable by day than in the night when everyone tries to stretch out in their sleep. There is no proper rest here.

We have already been in this accommodation for several days and it gets more unbearable by the day. The many speeches by the camp commandant that he delivers when we are driven from the buildings for our 'morning toilet' do not change. While we are gone the rooms are searched for 'forbidden items': in other words the guards steal everything from us that they can take. Our physical condition gets worse from day to day. We cannot exist permanently on two slices of hard bread and a cup of soup, mainly gruel. Several comrades have only one topic of conversation and, because of the constant feeling of hunger, that is food. I too dream of every lovely dish that I could eat and picture them immediately available before my eyes. Franz has exchanged his boots for a loaf and a small piece of tinned meat, and I was able to exchange my wristwatch, which now only works for minutes at a time, for a loaf. This way we obtained something extra to eat for two days. But it is better this way than in other cases in which the Russians take the boots by force and beat one with a rifle butt in exchange.

Thoughts of escape occupy me most. From various conversations I gather that the front line is still 200–300 kilometres from here. It is important for me that we have already crossed the Don, but an exceptional difficulty arises from the bad condition of the roads. I will be obliged to keep to the roads, and these are watched. And how can I obtain food?

I am unarmed. If necessary I will have to kill someone in order to obtain weapons and supplies. But I cannot wait much longer as the already poor state of my health is getting worse. I have already discussed this plan with Franz. He understands me and approves it, but is in no position to take part. I find three similar-thinking comrades who want to come along: Lieutenant Jim Fürstenburger, the son of a chemist from the Saar, Second-Lieutenant Werner Imig, a headmaster's son from Wülfrath, and Second-Lieutenant Alfred Peter, a regular soldier from the Hildesheim area. Secretly, so that nothing of importance gets out, we discuss it only individually, but we have an unclear perspective of the current front line. One thing is certain: we will be away at the first opportunity!

The days go by and nothing changes. I now have another birthday behind me. It was on the 15th, when I completed the second dozen years of my life. When and how will I end this mortal existence? Without having anything to say about it, I needed this day, although it should be a happy event, to recall my thoughts of home.

A little change has occurred in our daily routine. Jim Fürstenburger has found a book in the snow – a German book! It comes from a former field hospital and is Trenker's *Der verlorenen Sohn* ('The Lost Son'). We have been sitting for days now as I read it to my attentive audience. Our thoughts turn to our German homeland so far away. Oh Trenker, if you only knew what you were giving to German prisoners on the Don Steppe so far from home! We are all experiencing the fate of this Tonio Feuersänger with him, seeing in his fate our own.

The plague of lice is getting worse. It is absolutely essential for us to go searching morning and evening, looking for the lice in our underwear and cracking them with our thumbnails. Nevertheless there are still more and more lice! Yesterday someone said sarcastically: 'We have no lice, the lice have us!' This is indeed the truth. They are an agonising plague, especially at night, such as one would never believe possible. We lie crammed together, sweating extensively, which is the right temperature for little Russian domestic animals. One notices how the lice run and bite; we feel the bite and try to catch it, then scratch at the bitten point – and once one has started scratching one does nothing else. Painful! That is why we are dog tired; our sleeping partner is already waiting as his two hours are up.

Three days ago the four of us had tried to find a better sleeping place. Our attempt failed miserably. We got up into the attic and made ourselves a tent with tent-halves and blankets. But the steppe wind whistled cruelly through the rafters and did not stop at the tent. We soon withdrew remorsefully back down again and had to stay standing outside the door, which could not be opened because of the lack of space inside. Jim said dryly: 'Better stink warm than the freezing cold!'

A SECOND DEATH MARCH

It seemed as if something was up. We had been standing for over an hour with our packs in front of the barracks. It looked as if we would be marching on. But to where? A pair of quite clever ones wanted us to know that it would be back to Stalingrad. I did not believe it. Why to Stalingrad, the city that was completely destroyed? In that case we would not have been brought here. No, we would see soon enough. The guards are running to and fro, handing out hard bread in sacks. More prisoners whom we had passed on the march here come out of the other buildings and earthen bunkers. As far as I can see, they are all officers.

Soon a column of six hundred men has assembled. I am astonished to see that my last commander, Colonel Reinisch, and his adjutant, Lieutenant Brendgen, as well as the divisional Ia. Lieutenant-Colonel Menzel, are among them. They had been living in the earthen bunkers.

At last the group starts moving. God be praised, we are not going back the same way, so we are not heading to Stalingrad! The village soon lies far behind us as we march along the ice and snow-crusted road.

The guards are very unfriendly. They do not allow us to drink when we reach a stream and cross over it on a low wooden bridge. Our thirst is very great, and some are even eating snow. I control myself as the resulting thirst would be even greater, and it would not be good for the teeth.

Franz and I march alongside each other. He worries me as his stomach trouble is worse than I had thought. But with our combined strength we will make it. As long as I am with him, I will go along with him. I think of the talk we had in which he asked me to look after his son, as he would not be going home. Annoyed that he was giving up, I ticked him off, but gave him the desired promise in order to calm him down.

Night descends quite suddenly. We trot along close behind the man in front. We stop. A light comes from a dugout. Are we to be accommodated here? It is obvious that rest is urgently needed, as some are already considerably weakened. The moon has not come up yet. The chance of flight seems feasible. I distance myself from the mass. No guards react. The outline of a collapsed hut is visible about 200 metres from our stopping place. Perhaps I would find something to drink there? I went in, now quite alone, not seeing my comrades any more, only hearing their voices. A yard lies on the far side. There seems to be no one around. Perhaps I can find something edible here. I slowly creep closer. Suddenly a door opens and is immediately closed again, the light falling for a second on the yard. I have not moved, but I have been spotted. A Russian soldier asks me something in Russian. I do not understand. I ask in German for something to drink. Back comes a torrent of incomprehensible words and the soldier's attitude indicates that I should vanish immediately. I willingly obey his demand. My departure has not been noticed by anyone, and a pistol shot would have brought my life to an end without the least resistance! I then seek to get away from the hut, keeping in the dark, listening. God be thanked, the crowd is still in the same place. I can clearly hear voices that help me to feel my way forward. Nobody notices my arrival. All are stamping their feet. An all-too-long wait in this cold is not exactly pleasant. The feet are the first to freeze. How cold could it be today? We estimated 30 to 35 degrees below zero and are happy that there is no wind.

At last the guard commander returns and talks to the other guards. Then we go on. What is this? Are they not going to give us any rest? Are we going to march all night? One of us who understands what the Russians are saying is asked to interpret. Suddenly he says: 'There is no room for us here. We have to go on for several kilometres!' How many kilometres will this be? Some of us are already staggering.

How can there be a land with such unending distances? Meanwhile the moon has appeared. It looks down on us with a milky face. Is it laughing at our pitiful figures, or is it just a scornful grin? The endless expanse disappears in the twilight from the moon. It is coming up to midnight. New hope arises. Lights are visible before us in the darkness. That will at least be our accommodation. But we are not there yet. A long road lies ahead of us, but the lights give us a goal, giving even the weakest renewed strength to keep going on together. Those who cannot walk any longer will be held upright.

It has happened at last. The lights are immediately in front of us. There are holes in the ground. We said several days ago they would be dugouts. Two houses are standing there, occupied by Russian soldiers. While I am looking around I have an anxious presentiment. Where can we be accommodated here? The guard commander vanishes. He returns after a few minutes. We go on again for several hundred metres. My anxious presentiment appears about to be fulfilled. The others also notice something, asking horrified: 'Is it possible?' Yes it is possible! Behind the village, about three hundred metres from the two houses, we are driven into an open field. There a square of 100 by 100 metres is marked out and our accommodation is ready.

A square of 100 by 100 metres, with a carpet of snow some 15 to 20 centimetres deep and 30 to 35 degrees of frost! At first we stand there as if numbed. Two guards have disappeared. They are warming themselves up. The other two remain standing diagonally opposite each other. If any of us should cross the marked line, the submachine-guns will rattle. A hollow doubt grips some. It cannot be! We have to light a fire. But what with? Dried bundles of grass, some small bits of bushes sticking out sparsely over the snow are collected. After much searching a certain amount is assembled. A couple of overzealous individuals try to cross the forbidden border to where a thick bundle of grass attracts them, but a bellowing sentry has them quickly returning to the square. Meanwhile someone has managed to get the fire going. Crouching on his knees, his mouth pressed close to the reluctant embers, he blows into the weak glow until the smoke makes his eyes run and he is quite out of breath. Another who has been looking on, thinking he knew better, tries and gives up. Still others try in vain to get the fire going by various means.

I wander around here and there like most of the others, keeping my body moving, especially my feet, not standing still for a moment, constantly stamping on the spot. It is a fight for life and death! The bitter frost walks beside every one of us, waiting for one of us to tire and fall under his spell. And one's physical strength must tire sometime! A couple of wooden logs – and all the danger will be over. But where can we get wood here? I see only moving figures. They are not identifiable in the pale moonlight. Some of those wandering about lie down for a few minutes. They take everything they have to cover themselves, but in vain. Soon the cold gets to them like a creeping fever and they stand up again with chattering teeth and shaking limbs.

Is the time standing still? Slowly, much too slowly for us, ringed with frost, the moon makes its way across the sky and we can establish that time is actually passing. I am possessed by an incredible fatigue. There is a great temptation to lie down on this white shroud. Some who can no longer stand the exhaustion have laid down pressed close together, the heap of lying bodies getting ever larger under the mass of blankets, tent-halves and whatever they can use for cover, these utterly exhausted men, some of them wounded. For weeks we have held our ground against enemy soldiers, but now, in the grip of the frost, our new enemy, we present only a pitiful sight.

Exhaustion wins, my reasoning simply switched off. I pull the blanket over me and seize a bit of tentage in the mixture of tent-halves, blankets and exhausted men. It is like a dream, with Morpheus taking me in his arms.

A nudge brings me back to reality. I am freezing. Where is my blanket? I jump up. It is no longer there. Perhaps someone has taken it by mistake. I know it exactly. The last men lying on the ground are now standing up, as 'Get ready! We are marching on!' comes. I step on a small fire and am burnt. It must have taken a real artist to get the fire going, and there is even another one! Busily men crouch over the fires and melt snow.

The guards are shouting. It is time to fall in. It is dawning in the east, God be praised! I feel as if I am changed, completely frozen through. Gradually the group gets moving. Now the misery of the past days resumes all over again. We already know its theme. At first all are pleased to be moving again, as our bodies will become warmer, but soon our exhaustion becomes noticeable and movement is painful. Who has got my blanket? Could one of those marching along have stolen it? That is impossible. We are all officers! I begin to doubt the honesty of the German officers, but I suppress these thoughts.

The sun is now rising in the east. No one responds to this natural event, which is always beautiful, but for us it means marching, marching, marching! We have already been on our way for hours without a rest or even a short break. When someone has to do his business, there is no other way than to run ahead when possible, then he has time until the next guard arrives to deal out blows with a rifle butt and he has to catch up with the column at the double. Who can endure such punishment for long? The rows of marching men, or more accurately tottering men, have drawn wide apart. The stronger ones have their hands full, for we dare not leave anyone behind. That means certain death. Most of the prisoners go on apathetically. The demands on one's strength that the marching makes are simply too much. Added to this is the slowly increasing weakening of the body through under-nourishment as hardly anyone has anything to eat. What have they given us for the next four days? I got five slices of dry bread, three sweets – the Russians say 'confectionery' – and a cup of millet to cook. Franz, who has a sick stomach, gives me another two slices, so altogether I have seven. If only the prisoners would give up eating snow! They are only stuffing their stomachs without quenching their thirst. The stress is particularly bad for the older comrades. Apparently we are about to be granted a short rest. The head of the column turns right away from the road. The men lie down, but it is more like falling down for me. So now we have also joined them. How tired I am though. If only I could sleep! The sun is slowly sinking. Night cannot be far away. Have we to get through another night like the last? Oh, go away, you stupid thoughts! Don't start thinking now, or you will go mad! Better to be dull and vegetate.

Traces of extreme exhaustion are clearly visible on most of us already. The short rest does us good, but our overtired, starving bodies demand more yet. They want to sleep! And then it comes again: 'Fall in! There is no accommodation here!' So on again! Luckily the wind is not blowing here over the steppe landscape as it was a few weeks ago.

Meanwhile the night has sunk down over the earth, but none of those stumbling along spares a glance for the diadems of the star-filled sky. We only stare ahead of us, concerned about moving forwards and not leaving any comrades behind. Things look very bleak for many of them. Some who were helping their comrades before have now become more concerned with themselves. If this could only come to an end soon!

We are now marching alongside the railway line leading to Gumrak. An empty goods train trundles past through the night. It is going the same way – why does it not take us with it? I have long since given up any ideas of flight. Should I climb on a truck and kill the crew? It is all nonsense. Under cover of a wall of snow I lie down at a bend in the track and make the attempt to see if getting away unnoticed from the marching column would be possible. The last ones have gone past, and also the guard. No one has noticed anything or taken any action. The cold creeps into my body and brings me back to reality. I stand up and hurry through the darkness after the others. It would be nonsense to flee here! I cannot take a single step from the road without sinking up to my thighs in the snow.

This night too is endless. The previous night we had to stand together in a narrow space in a great frost and now we are marching on without a break. Someone says that the next objective is Gumrak, where we can rest comfortably. I no longer believe it. The Russians have lied so far, but we have kept going anyway. If there only were none of those damned sledges on which are the Red Army soldiers' packs and some other things I do not recognise. A staff colonel doctor has with him a large trunk containing the instruments and medicines that he naturally cannot carry himself, and the trunk lies on one of the two sledges. Until now the relief of the sledge teams has gone in an orderly manner. Franz is conducting himself bravely. One has only to look at him to see that this marching is hard for him, but he carries on. Sometimes I support him, sometimes someone else. How does it actually happen that I have to pull the sledges? Until now I have succeeded in avoiding them. I have had enough to do dragging my comrades along, but now I am stuck with it. Behind us, my fellow puller and me, comes a guard, his slit-eyed yellow face disfigured by pockmarks. I do not understand what he says. I cannot understand a word. It seems like our 'further'. I think it also has something to do with 'forwards', as to reinforce these words we take blows alternately with a rifle butt in our backs. How can I get out of this? For about half an hour – or is it almost an hour – we keep pulling in this manner. If it had been any longer my strength would have gone with it. Why does this dog not drive us on with his voice instead of his rifle butt? At last! He has realised that we can do no more and has selected two other victims. Poor devils! I ensure that I get out of this Asian's sight. I am in no state to help anyone for the next hour as I stumble along like a drunkard. Won't that damned Gumrak ever come? It is already getting dark and there is nothing to be seen. How many men succumbed during the night? When one is already at the end of one's strength one hardly has an ear for other things. For every one of us there is only one thing: you have to keep moving forward, staying quite close to the stronger ones, otherwise you are lost! Another man collapses further forward in front of me. Someone says it is Colonel von der Gröben. Several young prisoners from his division hold him up and drag him along with them. At last Gumrak comes in sight. We breathe out. There are still 3 or 4 kilometres to go, but at least it is good to see it. Everyone pulls together and gives the last of their strength to reach the goal.

A RAVINE OF DEATH

At last we are in Gumrak. We are directed to a ravine for accommodation. A few weeks ago this ravine had been a dressing station. Now it is full of snow, otherwise we would not have noticed it. New Red Army soldiers have come out of their holes. They stand up on the edge of the ravine and are our new guards. I have no idea where I should go. There is deep snow everywhere. If I look up, I can see the grey-blue winter sky with the dark silhouettes of the soldiers. Someone tells us that we are to rest here for six hours. How can we?

Some stalwarts dig snow from a hole with a plank they have found, while others use their mess tins. Afterwards, like badgers in their setts, they cover themselves with everything available and try to sleep. If only I had the option of sleeping! For many of the men hunger is all-consuming as a result of the painful stress the march has inflicted, crushing their bodily strength. With the patience of angels they try to light their fires.

Franz is very exhausted. We too have to look for something to cook. While Franz flattens the snow in our part of the slope, I look for something to burn, but this too is difficult. What can one find out here on the steppe? Finally we are able to go ahead and cook. We start a fire with the steppe grass that I have managed to scrape together. Finally I lay on top the scraps of wood that I had found in the least likely corner of the ravine. With constant blowing – there is no wind in the ravine – I ensure that the fire does not go out, as then all my trouble would have been for nothing, and if we wanted to eat we would have had to start all over again. Who counts the time necessary when one's stomach wants to feel something warm again, even though it is only a handful of gruel boiled in thawed snow? I have to keep throwing in snow until the mess tin is full. The snow around the fire begins to thaw, but the ground remains solid. I stand on it. What is that? An arm appears, a whole body. Can one be so insensitive? So we crouch next to a corpse and cook our meal, as we want to live. We hardly take any notice of the dead man. It does not bother us that he is completely naked. I look around me. Everywhere is the same picture. We have been driven into a ravine that is full of dead soldiers. Whether they were German, Romanian or Hungarian, no one knows. They lie there completely naked. No one has tried to differentiate between them and they are all the same before the Almighty. The Russians simply let these men perish here. It is a ravine of the dead.

BACK IN STALINGRAD

The time must be already well advanced but which of us notices that with the continuing strain on our physical strength? We are asked if anyone is unable to march. It is said that those not capable of marching will go to a hospital, but after the experience of the last days I am sceptical, especially when I look around me in the ravine of death! Did the Russians handle the other wounded in the same way? It is easy to accept and yet I cannot believe that so many thousands were simply left to starve!

Fall in! 'We are now marching only to Stalingrad city,' it is said. 'Only another 8 kilometres.' 'We'll have a roof over our heads tonight.' The words whirl around. Some men have crept into out-of-the-way holes in the canyon of death in order to sleep protected from the cold. And it is good that the snow had shrouded most of the corpses in the ravine. Again come the tortured, painfully miserable sounds of the prisoners of war that all of us dread. It goes: 'Forward, no matter how, even if it is on all fours. Only don't stay behind!' The last guards are not waiting, they have no desire to remain long and be well behind.

When one is at the end of one's strength, then 8 kilometres may as well be 80 – it is all the same. We totter again along the road leading to Stalingrad past a couple of shot-down aircraft. Then come the first outlines of the city's rubble, but how far away is it?

Our guards changed in Gumrak. However, these new ones are as sharp and inconsiderate as the old ones, perhaps worse, if that is possible. It is hard for us to remain as close together as the commander of the Red Army soldiers, a sergeant, wants. I suddenly take a blow on my back. It was this sergeant who had hit me with a thick stick. A tremendous rage of despair comes over me. I want to take this churl who has dared to assault me by the throat. Besides I had got my share of blows with sticks last night. But common sense holds me back. I am a prisoner now and, apart from that, exhausted. Tears roll down my cheeks unceasingly. It is just as well no one can see them in the dark. Every one of us has enough to do.

We have reached the city boundary. It has long since become dark. The guards do not know where to take us. We hobble in all directions through the ruined city. Finally it seems that something suitable has been found for us. We stop in front of the ruins of a building that must have been quite imposing once. Ah, there is a cellar and the first ones have already been driven in. The process is going only slowly. I suddenly hear a voice from home and see a young second-lieutenant in front of me. We establish that we do not live far from each other, this Second-Lieutenant Haferkamp from Mulheim an der Ruhr and I. Why are those below not going on? The cellar is already full. A

Russian sentry bars the way down the steps, remaining standing at the cellar door and hitting those standing nearby with his rifle butt. We are already moving again with the pressure from those outside wanting to come in and fearing the rifle butt.

Franz and I have made it, we are inside. We do not know what happens next. We are only being pushed forward. There is a din that can only be made by those whose nerves are at an end and who lack a guiding hand.

What kind of cellar room is this? I sit down suddenly on a 200-litre drum and several other figures immediately sit down around me on the drum. This makes me think and I try to get away. Men are still pushing in from outside. Summoning all my strength, I am at last able to get further forward. Those affected release a torrent of swearing, but at last I have succeeded! I am sitting on a pile of rubble from a bomb crater that lies beyond the cellar in the next building. Where exactly I am sitting I am unable to tell as it is so dark. But this is the end. I cannot go any further. Nor can I go back, so I have to stay where I am already stuck. I sit on my bread bag with my knees drawn up. I call for Franz, but get no reply. He is further back. It is generally quieter here. The men are all too exhausted. Only now and then somebody shouts out and another one tries to stretch. I think I am dead tired. But there is no rest. It is as cold in here as it is outside, but the crush soon makes our limbs ache. I try to change my position but come into collision with someone else; I fall suddenly asleep from exhaustion, only to be soon woken up again by a kick. I do not know how long I was asleep. Pain from my pressed-together knees keeps me awake. Someone also overcome by sleep is lying on my feet. Even pulling my legs from under him does not wake him. By the door someone is already shouting; he cannot control himself any longer. But the pockmarked Usbek is inexorable. After a long time the guard commander arrives and allows five prisoners at a time to step outside. Thirst is tormenting us, but where is there water? One of us who speaks Russian negotiates with the guard commander. Finally he achieves that twenty men, led by a sentry, can collect water. I collect together five mess tins, plus mine, and once we have clambered through the mass of humanity we are outside to collect water. We pass through several streets of the ruined city that saw such bitter and incomparable fighting a few weeks ago. The guard stops to ask a sentry standing in front of a collapsed building where the watering point is and we are sent on for a few more streets. Then we ask again and are again sent further on. After marching about 3 kilometres through the city, nobody knowing exactly where, we finally come to the Volga.

Everyone who was still alive in the 'City of Death', surviving somehow in holes in the earth and hideouts that survived the tragic battle, gets their water here. Even military units living outside the city come here to tank up with water. We fill our mess tins at a hole hacked out of the ice with the liquid essential for life; we drink our stomachs full like cattle, knowing no limits in our greed. The water from the Volga is icy but I had never thought that water could taste so good. Once we have filled the mess tins, I look around a little. I want to see how the city looks from the Volga bank, and notice to my astonishment that I am quite close to the mouth of the Zariza River. It was here that I achieved my greatest military success as I thrust through to the western end of the city for the second time and broke through to the Volga. This is the third time that I am here at the mighty river, but this time as a prisoner of war fighting for his life. Strange feelings overcome me when I think back to that time. The journey back to the cellar goes much more quickly, having taken an hour and a half to get to the river.

Such a mean trick! My comrades are still stuck in the cellar. What luck that at least I was able to move about a bit instead of being crammed together in a dark hole.

The water is shared out. I reach for my bread bag and take a piece of dry bread in my hand, about a quarter of a whole slice. 'Has one of the gentlemen taken four slices of bread from my bread bag?' No answer. I speak directly to some comrades. No one has seen anything. So that is the thanks I get for fetching water for others. The thief was just considerate enough to leave a tiny piece in my bread bag. I simply cannot believe it. We are only officers here and nevertheless things are being stolen. How can it be? I will have to starve for the next two days because of the way the supply system works. It is only through luck that I still have a share of a cube of millet concentrate that another prisoner is looking after otherwise I would have nothing left.

My dark brooding is interrupted by a voice saying that a general baggage search is starting. Whoever has been searched has to go up to the yard. Now that should be jolly. There are still quite a number of prisoners who have watches, rings or various valuables that are very desirable items for the Russians. Some are now trying to hide these things wherever they can. Rings are put in the mouth, watches secured between the trouser legs; others wrap them in wool so that just a harmless knob remains. Everyone tries in his own way. I have nothing to hide as my pack is small. My wedding ring is sewn into my coat lapel. If it is discovered I will be unlucky. They will not take the comb, shaving kit and mirror.

All the cellar occupants are moving; everyone wants to be in front to see how the search goes. Eight Red Army soldiers take a prisoner each. The packs are quickly gone through and the Russians take whatever they like. It is done completely wilfully: sometimes they take pictures and tear them up, others they leave. Should the Russians find valuables that have been specially concealed, the owner gets a beating for his troubles.

I am next in line. A Red Army soldier who honours his socialist country takes me on. He begins with the body search and finally rummages through my belongings. When there seems to be some confusion, I manage to save my pictures with a diversion. But he likes my comb that is in a leather case, and my mirror. He even takes my razor from me. Unfortunately I no longer have any blades as these were already taken from me at Kissel-Jakov.

Some prisoners outside are already sitting around a little fire, which they are carefully tending. They are melting snow so the last remains of the concentrated millet gruel can be cooked. From the two cellar windows come calls for known comrades. When they go to the window they are thrown something that the Russians would otherwise confiscate. It is a chancy business for if a guard sees them they risk a beating and a renewed search for the one caught.

Everywhere small groups are sitting around small fires. Others forage for wood, everyone being anxious to prepare something, even if it is only snow water.

It has already gone noon. Suddenly comes the order: 'Fall in!' A large proportion of the men are not ready to march off. It is pitiable. Everyone knows from the experience of the previous days what it means not to be with the big ones. Something quite outrageous happens. The Surgeon-Colonel, who had the trunk with instruments and medication that had been carried on sledges until now, is in the cellar where we had been, completely defeated. He had dared to try to prevent the Russians from taking the instruments from him. 'I need them for my comrades!' he had called out, believing that the Russians would recognise his immunity as a doctor. In response he received strong blows with rifle butts on his skull. He is lying in a corner with his skull beaten in. No one dared go to him!

We go on through the ruined city to the south. What a feeling for me! I had fought here in September and October, determined to take part in the conquest of the city that bore Stalin's name. It was terrible how things turned out differently. Fortunately the whole German Wehrmacht has not come to an end!

If only the guards knew where we were, but we know better than they do. Now we are standing again at a crossroads and no guard knows which road to take. These stops are good for our weakest ones. But once again we continue on through the city that extends along the Volga for about 25–30 kilometres from north to south.

Women are driving camels pulling sledges past us. On these sledges lie the victims of the battle for Stalingrad. They lie there as stiff and as hard as wood, friend and enemy alike. It is a sad sight. The women look like phantoms from another world. Their faces reflect the horrors that must have occurred during the battle in the previous months. Now they are obliged to take the spoils of death out of the city. The animals, even those near death themselves, stretch their necks well ahead as if they want to flee from the loads behind them. I will never be able to forget this sight.

Darkness signals the approaching night and we are still within the city boundaries. As one says, it could be that we are going to Beketovka, which is still another 19 kilometres. Can we make it? Not before early morning. No, we are marching straight towards the big grain elevators near Stalingrad-South. We had fought a hard battle for them.

Our route is marked by packs of all kinds discarded by their owners as unnecessary ballast because of increasing weakness. I wonder why some had so many packs. With my two bread bags I have no need to throw away anything. In front of me a sapper, who had been very unfriendly until now, throws his pack away. We go past it without thinking, but after some time he realises that he had a packet of millet concentrate in it, but it is too late to turn back now. He will have to go hungry, along with the partner who was to share half of it.

It has long since become dark. It is coming up to midnight. If it goes on like this for many more days we can all count on our certain downfall. A large number already remain behind in Stalingrad.

Some weak lights come into view ahead of us. A deep breath passes through our ranks. It must be Beketovka. The lights come closer. But it is not Beketovka but a railway junction with several small wooden houses. Dear God, do we still have to go on? We simply cannot go any further. Rather here crammed in than lying out in the steppe snow and sleeping or perishing, but we must have a rest at any price!

Apparently there has been some discussion with the stationmaster, as we turn left off the road and totter towards the houses. Some stand still until we are finally driven into an empty one. We have to work things out as again, as in the cellar at Stalingrad, we have to lie on top of each other. Only sleep, sleep! The cries of the crazy ones do not disturb me; nor does my feet being clamped together as if in a vice. I look up once more. The dark blue sky can be seen through the partly destroyed roof.

Am I asleep or am I dreaming? A Russian with a torch has come into our room. Has he taken a comrade's boots? Hit him? Go away dreams, let me rest, I want to sleep! Where am I, though? The noise from my comrades brings me back to reality. We already have to parade outside. Day has broken. One man is running about. He has no boots. He will have to march on without any footwear. Naturally he refuses. I would have done the same. The guard vanishes and returns after a few minutes with a pair of torn canvas shoes. Good or bad, the poor chap must be satisfied with them. As someone tells me, we are only 6 kilometres from Beketovka, where we are to be accommodated in a clubhouse.

IN THE BEKETOVKA CLUB

We have made it to Beketovka after an almost three-hour march. This time we have not been lied to. We are accommodated in a club. It is a hall about the size of a medium cinema. We sit or lie down at any angle on the floor, on the benches, on the tables, on the stage, under the stage and in some side rooms as far as they are accessible to us. There is not a space in the club that a prisoner is not lying in. It is still cramped, but in contrast to the previous days quite wonderful! We get some bread quite quickly too, and it is fresh bread. There is a round loaf for every seven men. But the craziest thing is that we get a piece of sausage! Real sausage! We are told that the sausage is goat meat. It looks like German Mettwurst, only somewhat thinner in size, but it tastes wonderful. I hear voices claiming that they have never tasted a better sausage. Oh hunger, where do you lead us? There is even a little sugar.

Franz and I have found a place in the left-hand aisle close to the stage. After the running around and the handing out of the rations, we looked for somewhere to sleep. Despite our great fatigue, it is impossible. Every time we fall asleep, along comes an idiot and trips over our feet, or even our body; we might think ourselves lucky he did not hit our heads. Franz looks shockingly bad. He lies there completely exhausted and hardly eats anything. It has been a great strain on him holding out until now. I can help him along if he will only eat. His stomach seems to have completely let him down, but he must do it. It cannot remain like this for ever.

We have already been five days in the club. The lice have almost eaten us up. The sanitary conditions are appalling, with shit lying around everywhere and smelling of putrefaction. There, where a prisoner of war had sat to perform the necessary, another goes to collect snow to thaw for drinking water. Leaving the building is controlled and only allowed at certain times, so it is impossible to get pure, clean snow.

The deaths of the first prisoners to die from natural causes, if one regards stomach typhus as natural, had already taken place. I carried out the first corpse myself. We had to take him to a room, strip him and pack his clothes. How can a person deteriorate so far? The dead consist literally only of skin and bones. Will we all end up this way? I recall the scene well and like other images I will not forget it. A mosaic picture comes together piece by piece. It is called: 'The True Picture of Bolshevism.'

The men responsible for conducting the pack searches also belong to this mosaic. How many searches pass over us? And still they find something that appeals to them and is taken from us, as it is apparently forbidden for us to have such items. In fact these items find their way into the Russians' pockets.

Today is the 1st of March 1943. We were woken up early and told to prepare to march off. It is said that we are going to be loaded up to get to a base camp, where everything will be better and we will live like normal people again. Most take this news with scepticism. We had been lied to so often during the few weeks of our captivity that it was all the same to us, but with diminishing bodily strength. The number of those who have been left along the way is not inconsiderable.

Now we have to parade in front of the club and the order comes: 'All those feeling especially sick and who cannot undertake a long train journey step forward, including all sappers!' Franz wants to step forward.

'Don't you feel in a position to make a long journey, Franz?'

'No, Bert, it is no use me going along. Hopefully they will put us in a hospital and there I should get something else to eat. I'm going in the wagon.'

'Think it over, Franz. You don't know where you will go, and here are most of the group!'

He looked at me with his blue eyes, and said: 'Bert, I can't take any more!'

'Then live well, old friend. Get well and come back soon!' I shook his hand, having the feeling that I would never see him again in this world.

Our marching group was already drawn up so I have to hurry as I do not want to get separated from the strong ones. I wave to Franz once more, one last look, and then I go after the others at the double.

FROM BEKETOVKA TO KISSNER

We have reached the railway line and there stands our train already. We are not the first to be loaded. Most of the wagons are already packed full of people coming from the transit camps around Beketovka. After some standing around we are loaded aboard. Those of the same rank are put together. In our wagon are the remaining staff officers, majors, captains and a few lieutenants. It is a small 20-ton wagon into which forty-five prisoners have been thrust. In the other wagons are also so many prisoners, we are told, and already the wagon door has been secured. The staff officers have tried to set up their places on one side, on the other side are the captains. The remainder – some lieutenants – are trying out the middle of the wagon. It is crowded, the wagon is too small for everyone, and by the door it is bitterly cold. The train has long since set off for an unknown destination.

There is a stove in the middle of the wagon. Wood is available, but how can one cut down these thick planks? We have long had no knives. They were prized items for the Red Army soldiers and forbidden to us as prisoners of war. A flat piece of iron is fastened to one plank. If we can get it off we can use it to chop the wood. Following some exhausting work we are able to get the piece of iron loose. With it we can now reduce the size of the wood and get some heat. Although it is an exhausting task with only wet wood to heat the stove, it works! If one stands close enough to the oven door one can warm oneself a little.

My place must be the worst in the wagon. It is directly by the door to the toilet. The toilet consists of two right-angled planks that form a gutter, and this gutter sticks through a hole in the wagon door directly above the floor, the other end leading outside. It is unpleasant all day, day and night in fact, lying there right next to it. But what can I do? There is no free space! I am also not warm, as the stove burns so weakly that I cannot warm myself up. The tablecloth that someone gave me a few days ago at the Beketovka Club is practically useless at keeping me warm. I really must see about getting myself another place or I will catch my death of cold. My belly has already become cold, and I have to pass water much more often than before. My comrades are also not well. Many have diarrhoea. One problem is thirst. Only seldom, far too seldom, do we get something to drink. And straight after eating the dry bread we get such a thirst! With my mess tin, which is fastened to me with various straps and cords, the person sitting on the upper plank bed tries to collect snow during the journey. No one looks to see if the snow is clean, as how can it be clean right next to the railway line with oil, rust and various rubbish? Everyone yearns for water! Even bread is being offered in return for snow water. When the Russians hand in a bucket of water no one asks where the water came from, we are so desperate to quench our thirst. Moss or mud is of no consequence.

After the thirst that torments us most of all, there are two other factors of about the same priority: lice and hunger. As we lack water to drink, we cannot think about washing, and shaving is also impossible. I feel more ill than ever before, sticky with dirt and disgusted with myself. In my dreams – even with open eyes – I concern myself most with the sumptuous meals that we had been offered in the past, especially one dish of sauerkraut with pigs' knuckles and mashed potatoes accompanied by a large glass of beer that pleased me. But these sweet hallucinations failed to satisfy one so long hungry. It was the same with my comrades. I noticed it in the conversations that often followed this theme for hours.

Our state of health became more doubtful from day to day. If I had not been so dulled, I would have been disgusted with the pictures that I had to see. Now and then some blocks of wood were thrown into the wagon and some stalwart would split them up with the piece of iron. The burning material is insufficient to keep the stove alight constantly, so it remains mainly cold. We get food very irregularly, but once a day there is something warm. If we are unlucky we are forgotten and have to wait until the next day. Where we are exactly, and in what direction we are going, I cannot say. The people up at the window are of the opinion that we have crossed the Pensa and already have the Volga behind us. But where would our destination be? The Urals? Siberia? The route we are taking leads there!

The train has been stopped for a considerable time when suddenly the wagon door is opened. The light from a lamp shines in. Several people can be seen outside, including women. They are wearing fur coats and felt boots. An interpreter asks: 'Are there any seriously ill in the wagon?' No one responds as we are all mistrustful. 'You needn't worry. The sick ones will go a hospital that is quite near.' Three men step forward, then a fourth. 'Now you go too, quietly, Herr Nudin, you squat on the toilet all day.' The man spoken to, a captain about 45 years old, who is fully run down and whose eyes show his insanity, bristles. He is already the sickest man here in the wagon. I too want to get out, to go with a woman in a dark coat, but a man who has just arrived says something to her and I am sent back. I have had diarrhoea for days, my teeth are chattering with the cold and I feel that I have a high fever. A wild despair comes over me: 'Will people let me perish here?' Did I shout it or think it? I do not know.

No, it cannot be! I must fight for my life to the end. Then it will be easier. I had hardly expected captivity at first, rather ignored the consequences. I lie on my space and ponder until, despite the cold, sleep catches up with me and leads me out of the present into another country.

A THIRD MARCH OF DEATH

Where are we now? On the station I can see some letters that I am unable to read. An interpreter, who had brought us something to eat, says that we are standing at Kissner station and that we will be unloaded here as this is the terminus. But how much longer are we going to wait? Today is the 11th of March 1943. We have already been here more than a day. There is talk that we still have to make a four-day march to reach the so-called base camp. When I think of my physical state and consider my comrades, all seems hopeless. The distance from here to Jelabuga, as the place is called, is 80 kilometres. No one can make it! If only it had already been done!

The 12th of March has broken. It is a winter day, like all the others, grey, cloudy, misty. The doors are suddenly opened. After nearly two weeks we are able to get out of this cattle wagon again. Most of us stumble the first steps like drunks, partly from weakness, partly from lying in the wagon. The familiar exercise begins again: 'Fall in and count off!'

We are ready, and the long mixed column of prisoners of war gets moving. The ranks are already strongly reduced. I now discover that on the way from Beketovka to here about two hundred prisoners have died. They were unloaded at the railway stations on the way. The very sick were taken off in Arak, the last big station from here. We are all sick. I too have a constant fever and am happy that my diarrhoea is not as bad as others'. In the overwhelming cold – it is about 25 to 30 degrees below freezing – there is no pleasure in dropping one's pants and pulling them up again. In no time at all one's hands are stiff and unable to fasten the buttons properly, and only with the help of others can one stand up properly again. The expenditure of strength in this borders on extravagance.

We have long since left Kissner station behind us. It is already midday. The sky has cleared. We go forward only slowly. There is no longer a recognisable marching column. How can it be otherwise with such a debilitated group? The road is mostly so narrow that we can only proceed in pairs. The last ones find it particularly difficult. They are the furthest back and are constantly being driven on by the guards with their sticks and rifle butts. Among them a Jewish prisoner of war called Grünpeter is very actively involved. Grünpeter is from Upper Silesia. At the outbreak of war he was in Russian service but was captured by the Wehrmacht and employed as an interpreter, and has now become a so-called German soldier in Russian captivity. He is frequently used by the Red Army soldiers and by us Germans as an interpreter.

If the guards are no longer shooting, the blows that they dish out are no less effective. With the column spread out over several kilometres, in late evening we reach our first objective more dead than alive. It is a small dilapidated village. We spend the night in the narrowest room of a cottage. Time seems to fly, and in no time the night is over. I am still numb when we march off again. The way through the villages is especially difficult for us. Here the wind has blown together metre-high snowdrifts around cottages and fences, which we now have to go around in truly sinuous lines. Anyone who tries to take a shortcut over such a snowdrift finds himself up to his stomach in snow and has to make his way back and take a longer route.

For a long time now most of the men have abandoned anywhere along the track their back packs, which had become pointless ballast. Our physical strength is simply insufficient to take them along. The land here looks as if it is dead. Very seldom do we see people or a sledge coming towards us. And even where the way takes us through a widely spread-out community, there is no one to be seen. Most of the way the route runs endlessly between wooden posts standing to the left and right of the road. It is just as well that such a still frost reigns! It would be a real catastrophe for us if the wind was blowing to worsen everyone's misery over the open ground.

For hours now the guards have given up beating us with their sticks. They are content that we are still moving forward. One guard leads the front and shows the way, another brings up the rear. The guards commander has obtained some skis for himself and travels back and forth between the head and the tail. The column, so hard hit by fate, is widely spread out. Several men fall unconscious along the way. Friends try to help these unfortunate ones. I crawl on, having enough to do looking after myself, and I do not know what will happen to these men. Only when nothing else will do, do I take a few steps to the side.

The whole thing seems to me like a feverish hallucination. My head is fit to burst. And yet I have to go on, not daring to give up. I maintain a connection with the fellow sufferers who have been with me since the first days. They are marching somewhere in the middle of this column of misery. We have already put about 25 kilometres behind us. How many of my comrades remain on the roadside, I cannot say. As I enter the village that is to accommodate us tonight, they are still not all there. It is already getting dark. All that matters is getting a place, no matter where, to sleep. Even hunger is of lesser significance than the constant thirst.

I have already lain down, for the night will soon be over. Only reluctantly can I convince myself that it is so. My feet are burning, my body hurts as if it were exhausted, my head is feverish. The guards and some personnel from the Russian camp directorate have come from the main camp to try to console us. The journey today will be quite short, only 13 kilometres! The first stretch goes all right, but soon we have the same picture as yesterday, only many more men have collapsed, simply unable to continue. The Russians now make arrangements to pick up the worst cases from the road and take them to the nearest destination with small panje sledges. As I hear, a large number have died in the last three days.

A tall, gaunt Russian appears. He is said to be a lieutenant-colonel and commandant of the camp that we are going to. Accompanying him are two persons, one of whom is a doctor. They go through the rooms to which we were brought after some standing around and look at the misery. The doctor has the worst cases laid apart from the rest. In the morning the weakest will be sorted out and those who want to rest here for another day can report themselves. The remainder will continue the march. We are told that this is the last stage of about 22 kilometres. Everything is prepared for our arrival at the camp. It will be better there and we will be able to live like human beings again.

I stay with those marching on. The goal is in sight and I will not waste a minute to delay reaching it. Once more it is a case of mustering all our strength not to weaken too soon. Everyone marching on today makes better progress, but despite everything the way today seems absolutely endless. When we climb a hill, another one comes into sight in the distance. Otherwise there is hardly any change in the landscape, only the glittering snow.

The weakly penetrating disc of the sun shows that midday has long since passed and we are still unable to see a town. An old motherly person comes out towards us, stops on the roadside and hands out sunflower seeds. She gives ten or twelve with an outstretched hand to those passing. Her face tells us without a word how she feels for us.

As soon as she had given me some seeds she was chased away by the guards with loud complaints. The old woman remains on my mind. So there are good people here too – the old woman has made that clear to me.

THE MONASTERY CAMP AT JELABUGA

The saving call comes from up ahead. Jelabuga is in sight! We breathe out! Now we too can see it. Nevertheless our road goes on for about 4 kilometres more, gradually dropping down to the town. But at least we have our goal in sight! We can take our last break with the town at our feet. Everyone tries to spot the camp, but it is impossible. Is it there by the church? Close together stand three large old churches built in the Byzantine style. Or is it the large, dark red stone building that looks like a castle? Then there are some long white buildings to be seen right forward on the edge of the town. We will soon make it now. Hopefully, it is not too far!

Some of us have reached the first wooden houses on the edge of the town. The roads here are wider that those outside the town. The leaders turn left. After a few hundred metres we are standing in front of a long four-metre-high wall. Along the wall is a strip of ground five metres wide encircled with barbed wire. Wooden watch towers occupied by guards stand at the corners of the wall. We wander along the wall until we come to a great wooden door on the southern side.

Meanwhile some have already discovered that the camp is a former nunnery and that the buildings inside are of stone. I still cannot take all this in. The walls and door conceal from our eyes what is beyond them.

Finally we are paraded and counted into the camp. It is full of heaps of snow that have been shovelled together over the course of the winter. My gaze wanders around. The buildings are really of stone. I count four of them grouped around a large square. What else the camp consists of I cannot see as we are directly led into the building opposite the gate. We are told that we will all be accommodated here temporarily until we have been deloused. I don't care, I just want to lie down and sleep.

The entrance to the building is very low. Tall men have to duck when entering. Then comes a dark passage, then another door that leads to a long, dark corridor. There are doors to the left and right giving access to individual rooms. It ends in a large room that one could almost call a hall. I walk straight past a door that has a glass pane in it. There must have been Germans here once as behind the glass hangs a notice in German script: 'Repairs only on Tuesdays and Thursdays'! I wonder if the notice stems from the First World War?

God be praised, we have our place right in front of the hall, which is already full of people, so we are taken to a small room that is now accommodating sixteen persons. We all lie down there with our heads to the wall, feet together, lifeless bundles!

In due course all our lice come to life. As long as we were marching outside in the cold winter air they hardly moved themselves, but now they become an unbearable plague again and do not let us rest like in the railway wagon or the other accommodation. Soon we are all sitting there searching for the damned things! The woollen items are especially full of nits and there is hardly a stitch in our clothing where their small pin-sized eggs cannot be seen. The so long yearned-for sleep cannot come as long as these animals torment us! We strip down to our shirts and then there is not one man who is not bitten and scratched all over his body. We have to scratch ourselves again and again even though we do not want to. It is enough to make one despair. Our only comfort is the coming delousing. It has already been started. Unfortunately the *banja*, as the Russians call it, is very small and each delousing takes 45 minutes. Nevertheless, it will be our turn in due course, but the sooner the better. We will certainly not get through it today, as they started with the hall and it will be a long while before all its occupants have been dealt with.

The night passes seemingly endlessly with groans and swearing, scratching and hunting for lice. I am now as shattered as on the previous day but, and this is the main thing, I don't need to march any further, I will be deloused today and will be able to shave and take a bath. When I consider the state of my comrades and myself, I could be disgusted. We are all covered in dirt and can hardly recognise each other under our long beards. We have been unable to shave for an average of two to three weeks.

The day crawls along and ever more men are called forward for delousing. But not us. We soon discover the reason. The second marching column has arrived with the seriously ill, who were immediately taken to start the delousing treatment so that they do not have to go into temporary accommodation. Obviously it is a bitter pill for us. We arrived yesterday, on the 16th of March and will not be deloused until tomorrow.

However, the Russians apparently have something else lined up for us, as unexpectedly we are taken out into the yard. There we are subjected to yet another thorough search, in which medicines, identity discs and pay books are all taken from us. Finally everyone who has been searched is given a haircut. It was a shameful feeling for me to have my head shaved by a woman, but I am too ill to protest.

All over the yard there are heaps of shit that show diarrhoea already has a wide grip. 20, 50 and 100 Mark notes have been used for wiping clean, even individual pages from pay books have been used. The state of my health is not improved by the sight. I have had a temperature for days. My diarrhoea has not diminished, and I feel weak and miserable. It is fortunate that everything in this world comes to an end. This is also the moment when we are queuing up for delousing. We are led through the camp that I had only had a brief glimpse of until now. My route keeps taking me to the toilet and back again into the warm accommodation. Next we are brought some soup. We can lay aside those things that we do not need under the assumption that we will get them back later. I only give up my second bread bag as I have nothing else. Finally we are taken to the bath. It is in a shallow shed leaning against the nunnery wall.

Pressed close together, we stand in a small room and freeze. Our clothing is hung up on iron rings and put in the delousing oven. Every time the outside door opens cold air forces its way into our room and the great difference in temperature becomes visible as a white cloud. In the room immediately next to the furnace a badly dressed woman is operating as a barber. One could describe her clothing as a rag bag. Her face shows reluctance and disdain. Horrified, I realise that this woman shaves off the hair from my comrades from under the armpits, the chest and the genitals.

Some refuse to be shaved in such parts by a woman, but in vain. I had never gone through such a procedure before. Anger and shame overcame me but my protests made no difference. As I later discovered, the woman was a prisoner from the town gaol. Finally the head, armpits and all formerly hairy parts of the body are smeared with an evil-smelling paste against the lice, as we were told! Now we were in the bathroom, a small room with seven benches. There are wooden grids on the floor and the washtubs are also of wood. The floor is slippery and we can only move carefully. The room is almost invisible because of the hot steam. The damp lies heavily on our lungs. Everyone gets a bucket with warm water and a small piece of soap that is not quite sufficient for a full body wash. Shame that there is so little soap! If only there was not such a long wait for our clothing. We had finished washing for quite a while but our clothing was still hanging in the delousing oven. I am freezing. How gaunt we are already. Will the food be any better in this camp? We can only wait and see!

At last our clothing is ready. There is some confusion until everyone has found his own clothing. How comfortably warm it is, only the smell is not so good. It comes from the sweat, the burnt nits and the lice. The eggs have become quite brown. I press down with my thumbnails. Yes, the bugs have been destroyed. Were all the lice burnt too?

A Russian is waiting outside to take us to our new accommodation. We now go to another building, called No. 1 Block. After some coming and going I am at last lying in a room. We are divided up by rank. The hunger hardly bothers me. I wander about as if in a dream, racked by a high fever.

How did the night go? I do not know but my state of health has not improved. A Russian appears and speaks to a comrade who knows Russian; the latter tells us that we have to go through delousing again. Some lice have been found, and delousing will continue until the last louse has been destroyed. People are already saying that some prisoners have been taken to the town hospital with typhus.

We have to parade in front of our building with all our belongings. A Red Army soldier who speaks a bit of German, and gives the impression of being an officer, leads us out of the camp. As a Russian woman comes towards us he says, 'There Russian madam, you officer, not good', and an interpreter says something which translates as: 'Comrades, you must pull together and not ridicule the Russian women!' And here, tottering through the streets, are forty sick men, enough to make one weep, but these men are warned to behave!

We stop in front of a large building that is surrounded by a high wooden fence with a barbed wire fence around it. Everything is closed and at the corners stand high wooden towers manned by armed guards. The windows are covered from the exterior with wooden blinds that look like air shafts. A little wooden flap in the door is opened and a face looks out. Our escort speaks with the guard and shortly afterwards the door opens for us. It is immediately shut again once we have passed through. Now a second door is opened. Going through the second door I notice another sentry standing to the right. We are immediately led to the bathroom and go through the same delousing procedure. The personnel here have also had their heads shaved and from questioning I discover that we are in a prison. Now I understand the security.

Again follows an hour of washing, shaving and waiting for our deloused clothing. Many of us are lacking items of clothing. I do not get back my armless fur waistcoat that I wear next to my skin. My purse has also been robbed. We are too weak and miserable to protest strongly about it. We are driven out to the entrance with swearing and abuse. It is obvious to me that the prisoners did this on the guards' orders.

Stretched out in our room, I lie down on my bed with all my limbs shaking. It was too much. I simply cannot take any more. Towards evening a small, dark-haired woman comes into our room and asks something. I do not really know what happened. As if at a foggy distance I see the woman say something to my comrade, who leads me out of the room somewhere. I follow him like a sleepwalker.

TYPHUS
Where am I? Why is my head so hot, my throat so dry? What stinks so much here? I open my eyes and look slowly around me, not fully

conscious. I am lying in a small room with some others. I count seven men lying like me on the floor in the small room. We are all still in our uniforms. The only thing to be heard from outside is the hoarse sound of crows and rooks flying around. There must be a lot of them. I feel very listless, try to get up and collapse. What stinks so much? A penetrating smell is rising and makes me realise that it is coming from me. With difficulty I manage to unbutton my trousers. I realise that they are full of shit that has run down my legs. I am overcome with indescribable disgust. How long have I been lying here? Are there no orderlies that could help us? My eyes wander around, but the pitiful figures lying on the floor are incapable of helping me. My eyes widen with shock. They are all dead! The man next to me is no longer living! His open eyes show this quite clearly. A feeling of unspeakable abandonment overcomes me. Should I remain lying on the floor here like my comrades and die? Tears roll unstoppably down my sunken cheeks. No, that cannot be! I am not going to die here!

I force myself up, clenching my teeth. My clothing has to come off! My body has to be cleaned of this shit! I am able to do this using an old razor blade that I find in my bread bag. Using all my strength I get my uniform trousers off, cutting away the underpants with my razor blade, pulling the trouser legs off one by one so I can roughly clean the still unsoiled parts of my body.

Whether it takes an eternity, I am unable to say. My stomach is grumbling, for I have not eaten anything for days. How long have I not eaten anything? Have I actually eaten something? My eyes look around and find some properly sliced bread lying around. So someone must have come here from time to time. There is a knock at the window. Through the thick, dirty glass I recognise Captain Crainer. I wave to him. Soon he is in the room with my divisional comrade Captain Michaelis. They ask me how I am. I tell them what is wrong with me, the tears coming to my eyes. Crainer asks if there is anything he can do for me, and I ask for some hot tea. He promises to prepare some for me.

'What is the date today?' I look at both of them questioningly.

'It is the 25th of March.'

'Then I have already been lying here for five days and only woke up an hour ago!'

'It is obvious that you had a fever. We must go now, typhus is contagious!'

When my comrades leave I feel more confident. I give them my bread as I am unable to eat it myself. Shortly after the two of them have gone a Russian woman comes into the room. She examines all those lying on the floor and vanishes again. A little later two soldiers appear with a stretcher. They put the dead men on it and take them out. The Russian woman took the dead men's possessions with her.

What is going to happen now? Must I keep on lying on the bare floor? The pressure in my stomach indicates that something is about to happen. I raise myself up with difficulty and crawl to the bucket standing by the door. It is dirty but, nevertheless, I have to sit on it. What happens now I have no idea, but blood comes out all the same! So on top of the fever I now have typhus! But I am not going to die! I will not!

Completely exhausted, I lay myself down again in my place on the floor. A small woman enters the room. It is the same one who came to me when I had the high fever. She seems to be a doctor. I can now see her clearly and realise that she is a Jewess. She examines every sick person without any change of expression. In poor German she asks anyone that can speak how they feel, goes to them and listens. She feels the pulses of the sleeping ones. On her instructions I get from the sister, the same one who had the dead removed, two powders wrapped in papers. One I have to take immediately, the other one later. To the question how much longer I must remain lying on the floor she replies: 'Everything will be better tomorrow!'

Thoughtfully I look at the door through which she has disappeared. She was a representative of the race that we fight in Germany.

The next days bring considerable improvement. Wooden beds are set up, straw mats laid and blankets distributed. Before we can get into the beds we have to take everything off. Our clothing is bundled up and removed. Two comrades who still have some strength take us on stretchers to the *banja*. A whole lot of people must have been carried in on the stretchers as the floor is very wet. The cold assaults me in the yard, taking my breath away. My teeth are chattering when I am placed in the bath. How comforting the warm water is, though. If only I was not so dizzy. I can only move slowly and with extreme care over the slippery floor. Ever more comrades as sick as ourselves are brought in. We all look like ghosts. I examine my arms, which are as thin as a child's. My skin is wrinkled like that of an old man. It reminds me of parchment. Then the stretcher bearers bring in a sick man who can no longer stand. He had hardly sat down on the bench when he lay down. Another one prods him: 'You have to wash yourself!' He looks more closely at him and says: 'He is dead!' He lies there motionless with his limbs stretched out, a little bag of skin and bones. Two minutes ago he was still able to sit and lie down, but now his heart has given up beating. We are all so deadly sick that we cannot assess the current tragedy. We look on indifferently as the dead man is taken out on the same stretcher that we were brought in on and finally return to our sick bays on. When was I last able to put on clean clothing? I am unable to give myself an answer. I have been here so long. But what short shirts are they giving us now? They only reach to the navel! They are something for infants and not for grown men. The linen laundry that we now get into is narrow and cold on our bodies. Pressed close together, we crowd round the stove which exudes only a little heat. Then we are taken back to our wards one at a time. We learn from the stretcher bearers that already a third of the camp prisoners have died from the fever or typhus, and that the whole camp is like a hospital. When I look at my body I am not surprised. How can this emaciated, run-down body resist after starving for weeks? I have already been lying a long time in my bed and am still frightfully cold.

Days have already passed. Together with Captains von Reibnitz and Pfeiffer, I have been taken out of the little rooms that were only intended for hopeless cases. We are lying with the less serious cases in a large room that I saw during my first days here. My place is right forward on the stage, where there are five beds together side by side, mine being in the middle. I am pleased to be here. I tenderly caress my water bottle. It is my life saver. When I wake up the morning after my bath the chap in the bed on my right has died. On the window sill stands a water bottle and a small coffee spoon. I must take them before the sister comes round and confirms that he is dead. One grasp and the water bottle and spoon have vanished under the blanket. Shortly afterwards the sister comes and has the dead man removed. The water bottle is now in my possession, and when hot water is brought in I fill the bottle with it and lay it as hot as it is against my stomach. I am now doing this mornings or evenings whenever hot tea or water is available. I noticed an improvement after a few days. The fever subsided and my stomach also improved. My bowels gradually became normal, but the water bottle still lies on my belly.

The little Jewish lady doctor comes again. She goes to every bed and listens to what the sick have to say. I wonder about her. The means available to her have been reduced and are no longer sufficient by far, but she is constantly on her feet. A small woman with thin arms and equally thin legs, dark eyes and a small dark mole on her nose, we address her as 'Frau Doctor'. Now she is standing beside my bed, feeling my pulse, giving me powder wrapped in old propaganda leaflets about Goebbels and Göring. I feel that my crisis is over, but I still have a fever. If I sleep or lie semi-conscious on my bed then it seems to me that I am flying. I have not really flown, but now it seems as if I am sitting in a Ju [*Junkers*]. At times we are thousands of metres up and the earth is far below us and only vaguely to be seen, then we roar close to the earth's surface and I fear that the aircraft will hit the tree tops. Oddly we always fly westwards!

We rarely see the sister; apparently she comes only when food is being handed out, when she stays for a short time, or when the dead have to be removed. Two cases interest me in particular: one a lieutenant wearing a black tanker's uniform, the other a specialist. The specialist even still has a watch. He speaks with a Hessian accent and some people address him as 'Herr Becker', while the lieutenant is apparently a Berliner called Lohmann.

As far as my condition allows, I help when I can. The misery around me is considerable, most men being weak. Many drink themselves almost to death, forgetting the warnings. Finally they crawl to the buckets standing right at the entrance to the room and a disgusting smell emerges.

Five men have died immediately next to me in the past days. Most of them lacked the necessary energy to live, no longer taking any food, lying in a high fever until their hearts stopped beating.

The Russian sister often comes by when a victim is dying, never missing the moment when she can take their property. She is especially there when items of jewellery are involved and there is no one else in the vicinity.

My immediate neighbour but one on the right has given up. I try with difficulty to make him eat, speaking to him like a mother, or with a commanding military voice, reminding him of his family, but all in vain. He eats too little. He is removed the next morning. Many go this way. Every day the stretcher bearers carry out their sad burdens. As I have discovered, the dead are loaded on the carts at night and then taken out of the prison and the camp. Where are they taken?

Right next to me lies a young second-lieutenant, a big, blue-eyed blond boy. He talks lovingly of his home and his parents.

The lady doctor was here again just now. The first convalescents are to be discharged today, making their beds free for others. I am one of them. This evening I will be lying in a bedroom. In the late afternoon the sister brings some things in and throws them at us. My uniform is not there. I protest and refuse to take the scraps of clothing. I am put off with the hopes that they will give me my things next day, but the stores are now closed. Reluctantly I draw on the clothing which is far too big for me. I look like a clown in uniform. After our evening soup we leave the hall. There are four of us and we have been allocated to Block III, Room 31, for accommodation. In the darkness of the night we feel our way forward carefully and uncertainly through the long corridors out into the yard. We stagger like drunks. I feel weak. A comrade with a long coat cannot see and staggers here and there holding firmly onto me. I am happy that I am now in a position to be able to help him.

A figure comes towards us out of the darkness. We ask for Room 31 and are told where to go. Feeling our way carefully, not knowing where we are walking, we go up a small wooden staircase. Coming to a corridor, we go at random into the next room and ask for Room 31 again – and find ourselves in it. Here too everything is dark. I can only make out that there is a long row of double bunks in front of us, without mattresses, only covered in wooden planks that have wide joints. From somewhere a voice comes out of the darkness that we should lie down and cover ourselves with whatever we have, for there are no blankets or mattresses. My night-blinded comrade, who meanwhile has introduced himself as Technical Inspector Heinz Lutter, lies down with us on a bottom plank bed and we cover ourselves with his blanket. Soon fatigue wins and we sleep until the cold wakes us up again.

Where am I? I look around. The beds and comrades lying near me bring me back to the present. It must now be early in the morning. Most are lying down curled up under their tunic or coat. Lutter has also woken up. We get up, one supporting the other. The way to the toilet is too far so we go into the corner of the building. The crows are flying in swarms, cawing loudly to announce the coming spring.

'What is the date today?' I ask Lutter.

'I believe today is the 12th of April!' comes the reply.

Chapter 2

The Emigrants and the National Committee *Freies Deutschland*

It is a sultry August day. The sun sends its pitiless hot rays over the dried out, fissured earth. Storm clouds stand on the other side of the banks of the Kam. The wide river acts like a weather shield. It holds back the black rainclouds and forces them to give up their life-bringing moisture before it reaches the town and its surroundings. I sit on a bench in front of the outpatients department, the shade of the birches protecting me from the sun's rays. It is now too threateningly oppressive to bear. Here in the open air one can at least muse along with one's thoughts a little. One can hardly take a step without stumbling over a prisoner of war. I am happy to be somewhat undisturbed here. Today is the 16th of August, so we have been here in this camp for five months. How the camp has changed in this time! The atmosphere has become oppressive and unedifying, just like a storm cloud over the prisoners of war. How did that come about?

After the vast mass deaths that had gone on until May, those who recovered were laid down in the rooms, where the rows of prisoners had already been considerably reduced. Of the two thousand or so officers who boarded the train in Beketovka only 835 had survived. Except for up to 132 men needed for essential duties, like chopping wood, doing the washing for baths, kitchen, hospital and sanitary installations, all the convalescents were incapable of working. Nevertheless the Russians were prepared to set some of them to clearing the ruins of the former convent chapel. Josef Kayser, the Catholic priest of the 76th Infantry Division, after he had returned from the founding celebrations of the National Committee *Freies Deutschland* in Moscow, said of this place a few weeks later: 'Here in the ruins of the former convent chapel I have seen the light!' The pathos in his voice still rings in my ears and I can clearly see the scorn in the face of the Guards major watching. At that time none of us had any idea of what still awaited us. When I saw the Communist emigrant Knippschild and spoke to him for the first time, I thought he was a Russian. A little later I discovered that he was actually a German who had emigrated to Russia in 1933. The emigrants Steiner and Wolf, who had fought in the German Legion on the Red Spanish side, appeared among us, along with the writer Dr Friedrich Wold and the wife of the Austrian Communist Party leader Peter Fischer, but as yet we did not realise what significance their visits would have for us.

At the request of my regimental commander, Colonel Reinisch, I had taken over the responsibility for a so-called company consisting of 152 soldiers, NCOs and officers. But I soon realised that my position as leader of the company was untenable. I came into conflict with the emigrants who were looking for people that they could manipulate for their political machinations. As a soldier, I naturally reject all political collaboration, especially as we were prisoners here. I did not want to be a traitor. I soon found a successor in Captain Hilweg, who came from Breslau, and I was relieved of my post on health grounds.

What a circus they had tried to make of us when a photographer appeared to take pictures for propaganda purposes. They sat the staff officers outside in the yard at white-covered tables laden with food that was expressly only intended for the photographs. Finally the prisoners from individual rooms were summoned to the meal and snapped. The finale was formed by the company. I still recall the greedy eyes of the men, who could hardly wait to be able to start eating. But it was so windy that the tablecloths almost blew away, so that after the photographs of the company were taken they ate in the normal dining room. Some of them had the bread taken from them that evening because at lunchtime they had taken more than their share. Some of the prisoners even had to converse loudly although there was no electricity during the day and at night they produced such terrible sounds that one could not understand them and nobody listened. Who would believe that Potemkin was dead?

I can see now Weiss-Wolf sitting opposite me as he tried to enlist me for the Communists. I was to go with him to Moscow to be baptised as a traitor. I had even withdrawn from the cultural group that wanted to use me to present our best and greatest poet for the 'progress'. And then the most monstrous thing that the German officers did was founding the National Committee *Freies Deutschland* on the 14th of July 1943. As their colours they chose those of the Second Reich: black, white and red. The president was the emigrant Erich Weinert, with vice-presidents Heinrich Graf von Einsiedel and Engineer Major Karl Hetz, whom we called 'Karlchen' because of the whining tone that he had developed after the marches and the spotted fever. Further leading roles in the foundation ceremonies were played in our camp by Major Heinrich Hohmann, Captain Karl-Heinz Stolz, Lieutenant Dr Heinrich Abel and a few others.

Lieutenant Raier I saw standing on the podium delivering wild hymns of hate against the Third Reich in a tone that would have done credit to an ordinary pimp. Raier had been captured on the first or second day of the war. Herr Heinrich Graf von Einsiedel, 22 years old, and a great-grandson of the Iron Chancellor, also stood at the tribune and, as a worthy representative of his great predecessors, spoke about the mistakes made in the 1918 revolution. But as one could tell from his speech, it galled him greatly that he had not been awarded the Knights' Cross by 'the Corporal'.

Mistrust and unrest had arisen among the prisoners. Our grievances – bugs, poor accommodation, insufficient food, etc. – now retreated into the background. Those who yesterday had been irreproachable were already seen as traitors in the enemy camp. Even my fellow countryman Hund, the headmaster of a primary school, was among them. His behaviour had already earned him, the nickname 'Pig Dog'! One could no longer trust one's closest friends. Only if two stood alone were their thoughts valid; informers were everywhere! Especially relevant for me was a talk I had with Captain Lützelberger, a headmaster from Lippstadt. Three of his sons were still fighting in the grey tunic. The eldest was a captain, like himself. Old Lützelberger wanted to join the National Committee. There were tears in his eyes when I reproached him with what his eldest son would say, but the next day he gave in to the pressure from the emigrants and likewise joined the traitors.

At the moment my divisional comrade Second-Lieutenant Karl Proschinsky is shaky. He was a dashing lad, though he has used little of this gift here. The enemy works with lies and intrigues, using the most common means.

In April we were allowed to send letters home. A few weeks later it was said that the post had been rejected by the German government, but a few days ago comrades found this 'rejected' post in a building in the Kama. The rooms had previously belonged to the church and were now being made into a new camp. The Russians had only wanted to read what we had to report back home!

My heart is full of uneasy concern. What will this lead to? Even my comrades Imig and Peter, with whom I was going to flee shortly before being taken prisoner, have joined the traitors. Has Jim Fürstenburger also taken this step? I don't believe it! He has been lying for a few months now in the woodland cemetery north of the town. The good cavalry Captain Rapp has also not returned from the hospital, nor Second-Lieutenant Haferkamp. They have found their eternal home and now lie undisturbed by the turmoil of these days.

ARRESTED AS LEADER OF A BAND OF CONSPIRATORS
I sit up. Has someone called my name? Yes, again: 'Captain Holl!' It is coming from the entrance to Block II. 'Here!' I answer, shaken out of my gloomy dreams. Already as I approach I see by the gate sentry the former camp officer of the day. He is a tall, pockmarked Russian now working as a runner for the NKVD. We call him 'the Tout'. I feel uneasy.

'Captain Holl?' he asked, in a high, unmanly voice that sounds repulsive to my ears. I acknowledge. He orders me to follow him. Without pulling a face, I obey. Questioning glances from comrades meet me as we go towards the club building. I enter the building with my body taut and without looking to right or left. Although I am not aware of committing any offences, I instinctively scent trouble. Inside, we go up to the first floor. The Tout stops in the corridor in front of the last door on the left and opens it.

Inside I see a lieutenant whom I know well by sight, and a young Jewish woman. The lieutenant has propped an elbow on the table and is holding his angular head, which is polished bare, in his hand.

The Tout reports. My name is given. The lieutenant asks

something, but I cannot understand what is being said. The Tout asks me in bad German where I am quartered. We go to my room, where I have to pack my things. Now it is clear to me that I will not be coming back here. As I go out, I am able to pass my pay book, which I have been able to conceal until now, along with some photos and a map of Russia, to Captain Spannagel.

Again I stand before the NKVD bully. He says something, which the Jewish girl translates as: 'Captain Holl, you are under arrest!' I had expected something like this but was nevertheless a little pale. 'May I ask on what grounds I am being arrested?' The interpreter translates. The reply banishes my original depression: 'You are the leader of a band of conspirators and have been spreading Pro-Fascist propaganda!' So it was only this, nothing concrete. 'May I then see the band whose leader I have the honour to be?' My smile did not seem to please him and he said something in a cynical tone. The interpreter translated: 'Smiling will not help you!' So that was a threat.

The Tout then receives some instructions from the bullying lieutenant, after which we leave the room. My few things are taken to the room next door, which was the Tout's accommodation. Then we go down the stairs again and he leads me over the yard towards the bathroom. He stops shortly before it, takes a key from his pocket, opens some double doors and orders me to enter.

I was now standing in an anteroom. In entering I had seen that there was a door straight ahead. The double doors are closed behind me. I stand in the dark and feel my way forward to the door that I had seen. I open it but the room beyond is also dark. Now I try on my right. Ah, there is light. I am able to open a door and enter a bright room. It is vaulted like a cellar with two barred windows from where one can see across to the camp bakery. Moss hangs from the ceiling, so it must rain inside. I sit down on one of the three wooden racks in the room, then lie down on it in my thin Wehrmacht overcoat that I have been able to bring with me – and think. What do the Russians want from me? Wait! One thing I already know for certain: I would never become a traitor! I would rather die! I then go round the room looking at the walls. One victim had tried to draw Africa with a pencil. In the corner is the name Corporal Shäfer. I can take twelve paces straight ahead and eight paces from side to side.

FURTHER AS 'CONSPIRACY LEADER'

At the double doors outside I hear the noise of the lock as the door is opened and immediately closed again. There is a short silence, then a groping forward and the door to my room opens. I get up reluctantly from my bed and give a greeting in a taut manner. In front of me stands the Ia of the 71st Infantry Division, Lieutenant-Colonel von Below, who is surprised to see me here. His face shows amazement at the encounter.

'What brings the lieutenant-colonel here?' I ask. Still standing at the door, he replies: 'I have been arrested as leader of a conspiracy!' I have to smile and say: 'I too, Colonel.' 'But what do the Russians want from us?' He looks at me questioningly. 'They want us to become traitors, and that we will never be, Colonel, even if they line us up against the wall!' We look at each other and shake hands.

We have already been six days in the cell and today we have had reinforcement. It is Colonel Crome, who, as a former corps commander, is highly regarded. Meanwhile the interrogations that we have already undergone clearly indicate what the intention is. They want to force us, at whatever the cost, into joining the National Committee. They hope that a number of resisting officers will follow our example. The growth of the traitor movement is going too slowly for the Russians.

Until now all interrogations have proved negative. On the first occasion a young Jewish second-lieutenant interrogated me. The next day it was the Guards major himself. With the face of a GPU executioner – he seemed to have had some experience as such – he ordered me to sit down. Sitting opposite him, I looked him straight in the eye. He apparently could not take this, as he kept looking away. Then came question and answer. I had nothing to keep silent about. My replies were clear and I did not lie. Questions I could not answer as a soldier, I refused.

Kudriatschov saw that he was not achieving his aim and became abusive. He threatened me: 'You will never see your homeland again! We will destroy you physically and emotionally! Siberia is vast and has many silver and lead mines!'

The threatening aroused my obstinacy. Did this proletarian believe that his gorilla behaviour could intimidate me? Turning to the interpreter, I said: 'The Guards major thinks that he can weaken me with his threats, but he will only achieve the opposite!'

The interpreter translated this. What a comical effect it had! Kudriatschov jumped up from his chair and shouted out: 'Who is doing the threatening here? Even if we had two Captain Holls here, each armed with a machine-pistol, and I with just my Browning, I will finish both of them!' I could only smile.

The same process took place with Lieutenant-Colonel von Below and Colonel Crome, both without success. Long hours of questioning, always to the same end: join the National Committee! And always the same reply was given. The Russians now tried other means on us. I would never have thought it possible, but it was. Every two or three days we were taken to the NKVD and there wrote a report on our performance and work, as well as the talks that Crome, von Below and myself had had.

If this cellar could talk, why would it not report everything? This is where our dead comrades had been put after they had been snatched away by the spotted fever. At night the female Russian dentist we called 'Sauminna' would appear and use her pliers to pull the gold teeth of the dead out of their mouths. Among the informers was one Böven, from Unterrath near Düsseldorf, who had been brought up strongly religious and whose studies had been paid for by the Catholic Church. As Judas gold for his work, he was given special dishes from the kitchen. They were carried right past our window. Working as prison supervisor was the leader of the Anti-fascists, Senior Paymaster Hohmann from the Bückerberger area, who was responsible for ensuring that our comrades could not communicate with us. This Hohmann, as well as Captain Hilwig, Lieutenant Baltin, Lieutenant Frey from Saxony, and four other officers had given the Russians reports about me that led to my arrest. Immediately afterwards I had no contact with these gentlemen as I was avoided as a traitor. I was so surprised when I was able to even read their signatures in an unguarded moment. I would never have believed it.

They also tried to soften us up with hunger. Instead of the usual daily ration we received 400 grams of bread daily and precisely measured out warm broth that was issued in the presence of a guard. It was water with stinging nettles. If one was lucky, one also found a cooked pea pod. If we had potatoes in their jackets, often two or three out of four would be rotten. There was never any butter or sugar. We discussed among ourselves anything that would help pass the time, recited poetry, went over German history, played chess, sang. We omitted only the one thing the Russians wanted: we never discussed politics.

A new guest, Lieutenant Breining, a Swabian, was also brought to join us from time to time by the NKVD. It seemed to me that he took things too much to heart.

In front of the whole camp, even the cooks and other employed personnel had to parade, the interpreter issues an order from Guards Major Kudriatschov whereby Crome, von Below and I were to go before the war crimes tribunal in Kasan. With this manoeuvre the Russians expected that even the most fickle and anxious of those interrogated would become more flexible, ready for admittance to the National Committee. Wonderful! The former courts-martial adviser Klein was one of the first members of the National Committee, so was now a traitor. His batman, a German Wehrmacht corporal, was sentenced to death in his absence. A few weeks ago Klein himself had been sentencing such persons, but now they sit together at a table and let themselves be served by them.

Gradually our beards were becoming even longer as nobody shaved us. A special pleasure for us was when some stalwarts came to the doors under cover of night and brought us bread. They had spared it from their own mouths. We also got the latest camp news from them. As this took place in the anteroom, Böven was unable to establish who the visitors were. The bread was shared fairly, with even Böven getting a share so that he did not notice that we were reporting about him.

We have now been in the lock-up for over a month but I have not been called for interrogation for about a week. The Russians seem to have realised that I am a hopeless case. The files pile up from interrogation to interrogation and the result is the same: nothing.

Our lock-up company has meanwhile increased after our camp senior, my last regimental commander, Colonel Reinisch, who came from Kärnten, was sent for punishment during an inspection of the camp by the Minister of the Interior of the Tartar Republic. The reason given was that as the Minister was leaving a room he said it was dirty. The true reason was actually Colonel Reinisch's aversion to politics. As the camp senior, he therefore had to go. His successor is Major Friedel, a Swabian, who better meets the expectations of the Russians.

A change has occurred in the daily monotony. Crome, von Below and I were taken to the bathroom, shaved and given clean clothing. The guard tells us to get ready to leave, as we will be moving on shortly. Where will we be going? Dressed, and with our few belongings ready on our beds – The Tout brought them to us a short while ago – we say farewell to the inhabitants of the lock-up. It is evening and already quite dark in the lock-up. Böven does not feel comfortable in his skin. As I go to him to say goodbye, I see sweat on his brow and even his hands are damp. With the words: 'I will never be a traitor!', I say goodbye to him looking him straight in the eye.

FROM NUNNERY CAMP TO KAMA CAMP
Nunnery Camp lies behind us. We three are marching one behind the other. In front of us is a guard with a rifle and fixed bayonet, and behind us two more guards, one with a submachine-gun, the other with a rifle and fixed bayonet. One guard for each of us: we must be bad boys! Today is the 21st of September, so we spent almost five weeks in the oppressive lock-up. We converse in whispers about where we might be going. There are three possibilities: Jelabuga Prison, the Courts-Martial Tribunal in Kasan, or the newly established Kama Camp, which lies in the church town of Jelabuga directly on the bank of the Kama. The prison comes in sight, but we go past. Now only two possibilities are left: the way to the harbour in order to be taken to Kasan, or the way to Kama Camp.

The Russians and Tartars passing us look at us curiously. Now we are on the street leading directly to Kama Camp, but it also leads right to the harbour. I know the place here well, having seen it for the first time in May, when I and my men had had to unload a barge in the harbour that had brought a load of flour. My mind held on to the unusual memory of an old woman in a fur coat with a hunting rifle standing sentry in front of the bread depot.

Now we have gone past the crossing so there can only be one goal for us: Kama Camp. We halt right in front of the newly erected camp and are handed over to the officer on duty.

We are curious about what is going to happen to us. Before we enter the camp the duty officer, Brijanzev, warns us not to speak. The few inhabitants of the camp have been sent to their rooms. We are quickly led through the camp to a large block that greatly exceeds the other buildings in size. Soon we find ourselves in a large room on the first floor. A Red Army soldier stands guard in front of the door.

To our great surprise we find the room occupied. Three men dressed in tattered rags, their heads shaven and as white as death, are already there. The little Jewish woman has already examined them.

'They are putting us in with serious Russian criminals now!' I whispered to Lieutenant-Colonel von Below. We went to the opposite corner of the room and laid our things down on the boards of the iron bedframes. We waited curiously to see what would happen next. Would these Russians leave? Would be searched again?

One of the three figures came up to us. He had a smooth skull, clear blue eyes and a sharp, slightly bent nose. His skin had the pallor of a corpse. He said with a slight bow: 'May I introduce myself, Lieutenant Herfurth.'

We looked at each other in surprise. 'What, you are Germans! We thought you were Russians!'

With a slightly sad smile Herfurth replied: 'You are right, gentlemen, we no longer look like Germans, but when one has sat in prison for two years one's clothing gets no better.'

'How is it possible that you have been in prison for two years?' we asked, full of curiosity, for standing here in front of us was a long-term prisoner, who had been overtaken by the heavy fate of imprisonment shortly after the outbreak of war.

Once the female doctor had left, and we had introduced ourselves to the other prisoners, we heard their story. All three, Lieutenant Herfurth, Sergeant Eibel and Senior Corporal van Alst, had become prisoners of war of the Russians in 1941, Herfurth as a fighter pilot, Eibel as a signaller and van Alst as a motorcyclist in a reconnaissance battalion. They were brought to Jelabuga, where they lived with a few other prisoners. There was little to eat. Soon afterwards attempts were made by the Russians to undermine the morale of prisoners of war. Herfurth was the camp senior and in contrast to Lieutenant Raier he did not succumb to traitorous dealings. His clean behaviour was an example for some of his comrades. So it came about that in December 1941 the Russians brought sixteen men to the Jelabuga Prison with Herfurth at their head. Some were released again after a short time, but eight of them, including these three, were sentenced to death by a so-called war tribunal that consisted of a lieutenant, a sergeant-major and a sergeant. The prosecution read out the sentences. They waited eighty-seven days in the death cell, expecting every night to be taken out and hanged, but always it was someone else who was taken out. So they slowly languished. They told of the last hours of a robber and murderer who walked up and down the cell like a caged tiger, of the neighbouring cell in which a condemned woman brought a child into the world, and of the time in which they were taken to a normal cell that was full of convicted people of all nationalities. Half of those condemned with them had long since died. One day Lieutenant Vierk was released. They waited in vain as month after month went by. They had almost given up all hopes of release. One day the Minister of the Interior of the Tartar Republic visited the prison and appeared in our condemned men's cell. By chance he noted that they were German prisoners of war and gave the order to have them removed to the prisoner of war camp. Days of uncertainty followed until they had been brought here today. They could hardly hold back their joy, after such mental stress and uncertainty. Hastily spoken words mixed with Russian poured out of them. We tried to hide the pity that their appearance aroused in us. Van Alst was paralysed up to the hips and could only move forward with difficulty, while the sight of the two others recalled memories of the spotted fever. The details that they recounted of their prison cells were to us Middle Europeans improbable and barely believable.

A few days after our transfer to Kama Camp we had to go to Nunnery Camp for delousing. There, in order to influence the waverers, the rumour had already been spread that Crome, von Below and I were to be brought before a war tribunal in Kasan. Despite the darkness we were recognised in the camp and these Russian lies were refuted. Such lies have really quite short legs!

We had already spent weeks in Kama Camp. German officers were brought here from Susdal and Krasnigorsk. Our company had meanwhile been moved into a smaller room at the opposite end of the corridor and been increased by three: Colonels Reinisch and Kratsch, as well as the Romanian Major Nikolai, were also obstacles to the National Committee and thus had to go into isolation. It was an isolation that we had meanwhile got to know well. For one hour in the morning we could get some fresh air in the yard under the supervision of a Russian guard. The rest of the time we spent in our small room – number 21 – and played chess or dice or chatted. No unauthorised person could approach our room, which lay at the furthest end of the corridor. Next to our room was the lock-up, a dark cell in which officers who tried to escape were locked up.

The Russians had finally given up trying to recruit us for the National Committee. A last interrogation, during which we were informed of the founding of the League of German Officers on the 12th of September 1943, under the leadership of General of Artillery von Seydlitz, had shown them that we could not be persuaded to become traitors, even with the news that Field Marshal Paulus would shortly join the League.

I will never forget one small episode. Our fellow prisoners were taken for questioning, and Crome, von Below and I found ourselves alone in the room. Suddenly the door was unlocked and a Russian captain entered the room. He limped and walked with a stick. His expression clearly displayed hatred for us Germans. He said a few words that I did not understand. I looked at him quietly and firmly. This did not seem to please him as he suddenly raised his stick and made a move as if to hit me on the head. Perhaps he believed that I would react. I showed no reaction. He stopped his stick about five centimetres from my skull. Finally he turned to von Below and hit him with his stick on the red stripe of the General Staff on his trousers. But von Below and Crome also failed to react to this proletarian behaviour. After he had spat at us several times he left the room complaining loudly.

There has been an increase in the numbers accommodated in the neighbouring room. There are far more of them than us, about thirty altogether, of whom Colonel von Hanstein is particularly striking. They too have been isolated for taking up a clear position against the League of German Officers and the National Committee. It is pleasing to see the good mood and behaviour of these comrades.

BLOCK II

13th November 1943. There is a big move today as there are too many isolated persons now. Because of this the Russians have arranged the erection of a whole isolation block: Block II. With about sixty other prisoners of war, we enter the upper room of the block, which is surrounded by barbed wire and separated from the rest of the camp. A gate that is only unlocked when we are taken for our meals ensures that no unauthorised person can get near us.

Until now I had had no experience of Germans denouncing, ridiculing and dishonouring their countrymen, but here I can watch Mangold do all these things in his capacity as block senior, with his watchdogs, Second-Lieutenants Kahlbaum, Richter and Kaiser, as our guards. Their job is to ensure that our connections with the outside world – i.e. the other prisoners of war – are forestalled. Mangold has lost all respect from his old comrades and is a worthy representative of the League of German Officers. As a reward for his good work as block senior of the isolation block, he soon became camp senior and his role as block senior was passed to Major Hartberger, an Austrian who had long been a loyal servant of the Russians.

Before Mangold handed over Block II to the Austrian he provided me with five days in the lock-up through Colonel Nikiforov in response to my reproaching him one morning at roll call for getting at an old gentleman in a nasty way.

We occupied the upper rooms for two days before being assigned to our individual rooms. Room 7 had been set up for the particularly black sheep and right next to it was a little room for Colonels Crome, Wolff and Erler. We were called by name from the individual rooms in which we were lying, and so the room association was formed in which I now felt so well. Along with the room senior, Lieutenant-Colonel Burmann, I shared with Parson Roth, Major Blume, Major Lubbe, Courts-Martial Adviser Mewes, Lieutenant-Colonel von Below and another four gentlemen; we formed a congenial community.

Hardly a day passed in which we did not have a comrade in the lock-up. As it was inside the building, we were able to support our arrestee through the broken pane of glass or the cracks in the door. It was all so well organised that the person under punishment suffered no hardship.

Once, when Colonel von Hanstein was sitting in the lock-up with two others, a man from the kitchen brought food for five persons by mistake: 200 grams of bread each and five pieces of fish. The Russian duty officer, a second-lieutenant, who unlocked the door, told the man to leave all the food there. The Russian himself then took a portion of bread and fish. Minutes later I saw him standing in an empty room greedily gulping both down. When he noticed me he tucked the remains of the fish in his coat pocket.

Every day the arrestees had to look after one room. Even when Mangold had me locked up for five days, everything went like clockwork. Second-Lieutenant Helms, a fighter pilot, accompanied me. Of course, we shared the contributions passed on to us. Helms told me his story. The Russians wanted to persuade him to return to his unit and then fly an ME 109 over to them. In the same building in which he was held prisoner on the Murmansk front there was also a captured German lieutenant from Hamburg, with whom Helms once spoke to briefly. As Helms said, he was a large, handsome man with an upright figure and a straight walk. Later on, he was able to observe him through a keyhole when the lieutenant was taken for interrogation. He could see that he was being mishandled. One day he was lacking an eye. Helms, shortly before he came away, was called for questioning again, and his route took him past the room where the lieutenant was held. From inside came the chatter of a lunatic. Helms had been unable to learn anything more about the lieutenant since then. Had the Russians treated many prisoners of war to make them traitors like this lieutenant, torturing them to death?

What is happening? Lieutenant-Colonel von Below has instructions to pack his things and go to the guardroom. Will he too go for special treatment? When he had packed his things and said farewell to his comrades, I accompanied him to the gate. We looked at each other once more as we shook hands and knew that whatever happened to us we would never be traitors! A last farewell and the gate was shut. A dear old comrade, who during the days of our joint examinations had been very valuable, has gone off into the unknown. When would I see him again?

Christmas is coming and in Room 7 we are mentally preparing ourselves. When Christmas Eve comes we lie on our iron bunks and sing Christmas songs. We begin the day with a chat. Our thoughts are very much back home.

Yesterday and today our comrades who had been in Oranki Camp arrived here. My regimental comrades Schüler and Krell are among thcm. God be praised! – at least some are still living. So many remained on the road who simply could not take any more.

Yesterday evening, unnoticed in the darkness, I was able to slip out of Room 7 and visit my friend Krell. Full of the horror of it, he told me about the time they had to bury 35,000 men in Beketovka who had died from spotted fever, stomach typhus or under-nourishment. But it had been no different in Oranki Camp than in Jelabuga. By far the greatest number of dead there had fallen victim to epidemics. Among the Italians on the transport there were even victims of cannibalism. Krell had thought me dead and was very happy to see me again.

Today my friend Hans-Joachim Schüler slipped into the room. He was our battalion adjutant and we last saw each other almost a year ago. How happy one is to see an old trusted face after such a long time and discover that the person has not changed. I was also able to greet Second-Lieutenant Augst again, whose appearance also remains unchanged.

24th December 1944. The men of Block II sit in their rooms. Their hearts are certainly festive, their thoughts back at home. In simple, brief ways we celebrate the biggest festival of the year far from home, true sons of our people, undisturbed by the dirt of treason that goes on around us. We had succeeded in persuading the Russians to provide a little tree that has been adorned with home-made Christmas decorations. Some of us saved a little from our rations to have at least something for Christmas Eve. I too have put aside 300 grams of bread and sliced it with prayers, as one does at home with Christmas stollen. My thoughts are of home and my loved ones there. How and where are they celebrating Christmas?

1st January 1944. A new year has begun. Will it bring us the longed-for victory? We hope and yearn for it. What the year will also bring is no change in my behaviour and beliefs. In the individual rooms many others likewise use the simple memorial hour to renew their faith.

I spend the long day refreshing my English. Then I write poetry and learn it by heart. I have to smile when I think of the possibilities I previously had for learning and compare them with the means that I now have. But how much more precious are these small home-made booklets in which I copy the poems of Goethe, Schiller, Arndt,

Binding and Rilke. No, this time in captivity cannot be for nothing. In overcoming the results of spotted fever with disciplined learning, I must force myself to concentrate.

The former Generals Lattmann and Schlömer, escorted by von Einsiedel and the former Major Hühnermörder, have gathered in the camp for a publicity campaign. We too are obliged to listen to a speech by Lattmann. The Russians are very tense about the effects of this speech. It is only a defensive speech that the traitorous general has for us. An icy silence reigns among us from beginning to end. We form an immovable wall. The two traitor generals are also given the cold shoulder in their attempts to resume personal contacts with old acquaintances.

BLOCK VI

Today is the 13th of February and again there is a move. Two days before my birthday the whole of Block II was moved to Block VI. Now the Russians have achieved what they had already long intended, but had been unable to until now. Block VI is hermetically cut off from the outside world. Every contact with our friends is interrupted. The entrance to Block VI is through a small guardroom in which sits a Russian sentry who does not allow any unauthorised persons into the block. The exercise area set aside for us – now more than 150 men – is the inner yard, which is about twenty metres long and six metres wide. The food is carried in from the kitchen in canisters, which we collect once the porters have left the guardroom.

Our new accommodation is cold during the first days and very unfriendly, as the block had long been standing empty. Some doors and windows are broken or missing, and the wind drives snow into the rooms. After the first night several of us showed positive evidence of frostbite. We turned to self-help. Once the stair railings had been burnt, we turned to the roof timberwork, in accordance with our plan. It had been professionally built, so the roof had not collapsed under the weight of the snow. As a saw we use a straightened barrel hoop. It was just as well that the roof was built in the time of the Tsar with double the expenditure than would be the case today. The wood is divided up equally among the rooms. Had we only had what the Russians gave us for heating, it would have been bitterly cold. We did not ask what tomorrow would bring; it is bitterly cold today and we do not want to freeze any more than we must.

The days are becoming longer, and now and then the sun comes through. The cranes and jackdaws play over the buildings, their loud cawing announcing the approach of spring. Life in the isolation block has its own stamp to it. From an NCO to an old colonel, who really should be a general, all ranks are represented. There are lawyers and priests, and teachers of all professional groups. Some followed their inclinations and used their time as they liked. The doctors, lawyers and farmers had their own clubs, while others refreshed their knowledge of history or conducted professional language studies. The choir formed the crown and consisted of about forty-five prisoners of war. Great difficulties were encountered with every undertaking and always had to be overcome again and again. It might only be the shortage of writing paper, which was sometimes partly replaced with small slivers of wood or wall tiles, or pencils, which could be made out of lead taken from the so-called executions wall. The latter derived its name from the revolutionary period, when White Guards had been executed here. But where there's a will, there's a way.

Next to my historical and language studies, the choir gives me the most pleasure. Even if I cannot sing particularly well, I am still wholeheartedly involved. Under the conducting of our 'Maestro', as we called Lieutenant Fromlowitz, our choir leader, we sang the 'Ave verum' and other hymns.

20th April 1944. After the morning roll call by the duty officer, we assembled in the right wing of the block. Second-Lieutenant Oberhofer read a poem. Finally the choir sang the 'Ave verum'. Then the block senior, Colonel Crome, spoke. He said that as soldiers we only knew our fatherland and served it and were no politicians. The national anthem concluded our impressive celebration.

THE FIRST HUNGER STRIKE

The 21st of April was a day like most days. We made our morning toilet with the half cup of tea that we had saved from the previous evening, as otherwise there was no water. We used this fluid liberally as it was brown in colour, although its true substance was unascertainable. Shortly after the morning count we discovered that

Klement, the Russian camp coffin-maker, with some Anti-fascist men, had brought in ladders and special wooden structures. We soon discovered that these were being fastened to the windows of the rooms overlooking the road. They were exactly the same as those that hung in front of the prison windows in Jelabuga. The rooms were made constantly half-dark by these shutters.

We were completely enraged. We could not, and would not, accept this. If we did not react to this, the terror measures taken against us would only increase.

Our reaction took the form of thirty-two prisoners from the affected rooms refusing their food. In our room, which had six men in it, there were three hunger-strikers: Surgeon-Major Dr Weber, Lieutenant von Putkamer and the Hungarian Senior Doctor Dr Bajor. We were anxious to see how the Russians reacted! We knew that every hunger strike had to be reported after 24 hours to the Prisoner of War Department at the Ministry of the Interior in Moscow. An investigatory commission then appeared very quickly. These commissions were very unpopular with the Russians, because if they uncovered some reason for it, all means and promises were employed to force the strikers to give up.

During the first three days none of the Russians, apart from the duty officer, took any notice of the hunger strike. However, as our men continued to resolutely refuse food, it soon became more noticeable. The female doctor appeared and tried with requests and soothing words to persuade the strikers to eat. When this also proved unsuccessful, the Guards major appeared in person. At first he tried with harshly spoken commands, then with threats, but had no success and finally vanished.

Our mood had almost reached boiling point. Our comrades had been on hunger strike already for five days. Weak and pale they lay on their beds, no one leaving their place. Their pulses beat only weakly. I expressed the intention of also joining the hunger strike, and others want to follow suit, but we were advised to wait another day. The sight of the striking comrades impressed me. I would have liked to take these Russians by the throat if I could.

The sixth day begins and there is still no stronger reaction to be seen from the Russians. Our demand is: 'Down with the blinds!' Towards noon there is a sudden: 'Watch out! The Guards proletarian is on the march!' We now sit in our rooms fully tense and wait for what is to come. First of all he vanishes into the staff officers' room. Next he enters Room 12, which is next to ours, and then our door opens and Kudriatschov comes in, accompanied by his whole administrative staff. Since the time he interrogated me, he has put on weight and looks repulsive. When I see him he always makes me think of a bulldog. Colonel Crome is following him, with the other Russians behind.

With a furious face, as if he could eat up every one of us, the Guards major goes through Room 10 and the adjacent Room 11. He looks grimly at the strikers, the weak and apathetic men lying there. Apart from 'Attention!', which was given as he entered, not a word is said. The semi-darkness resulting from the blinds gives the already stressed situation an additional frisson. A Serb who speaks fluent Russian and German is acting as interpreter. As he is about to leave the room my voice resounds: 'I have a question for the Guards major.' He stops in mid-stride and turns around, tensed to meet whatever was coming and says something. The interpreter translates: 'Ask!'

I begin: 'I know that if the Guards major had the possibility of having me shot, he would do so. Is that right?' He confirmed. 'But I also know that he cannot do this, that he has his orders from Moscow according to which he has to hold back. I am convinced that Moscow knows nothing about the blinds that hang from our windows here. We have done our duty as soldiers and demand treatment commiserate with our rank as officers! On these grounds these comrades have refused all nourishment. It is inhuman to treat us like criminals. A few months ago you said to me that I would be destroyed physically and mentally; apparently you are now making that true. From today I also refuse all food until the blinds have been removed!' The interpreter translated sentence for sentence. The face of the Guards major became increasingly poisonous. He left the room without replying.

Some of my comrades thought that I should not have spoken to him like that and it would only make the situation worse, but others approved my efforts. Our block senior, Colonel Crome, followed the Guards major silently. He returned after half an hour and announced: 'Gentlemen, please cease the hunger strike and resume taking food.

This evening the blinds will be made shorter by half. I know this is a compromise, but we cannot force the issue as the Guards major does not want to see any nakedness from outside. The doctor will come in a few minutes and take the comrades who have been on strike to the hospital.'

I was not so happy with the result. If we had stood our ground firmly enough and demanded that the blinds had to go immediately, it would have happened. Nevertheless, Colonel Crome is our block senior, and consequently we must leave to him to do what is best for the community. This incident has shown that the hunger strike is the sharpest weapon we have, but it is one that we only dare use in the most extreme cases if it is not to be blunted. But the remaining half of the blinds must go at the next opportunity.

The days go by in their usual way. The strikers have meanwhile all reappeared back in the block. They had also been isolated from the others in the hospital and anxiously watched lest they make contact with the other camp inmates. Nevertheless some had been able to establish contact with friends in the general camp and to report what had happened.

A SPY IS EXPOSED

We enlivened Whitsun with the choir, as we sang when the whole camp was paraded for roll call. Invisible to the camp, but still audible, we sang the second verse particularly loudly: 'The Reich that our fathers' swords won will let you stand.'

Now and then emigrants visited us. Mostly it was the emigrant Maurer, a small, insignificant little man with an apparently high voice and a wrinkled face. He tried to lecture us but came to grief especially in Rooms 1 and 2. They let him talk in other rooms without reacting. Special Leader Heinrich, a fifty-year-old who had been born near the Baltic and spoke fluent Russian, made little Maurer so upset that he fled with tears in his eyes. Finally they gave up trying to give us political instruction.

The news that came to us regularly about the conduct of the fighting on all fronts gave rise to long, concerned discussions, especially among the older comrades. I took little part in these as I thought it was all enemy propaganda to soften us up. And if the news really should be true, we could do nothing about it from captivity.

Despite all the bad news, I believed in the victory of our people! I had fulfilled my duty to the very last and was ready to set out my behaviour before any court. What comes next is not going to be influenced by me.

My daily routine is firmly linked to my study timetable, so there is no chance of being bored. The dialogues I have with Dr Manitz, in which we exchange recitations from Faust, extracts of which we have learned by heart, are always pleasant. If one engages oneself intensively with spirited matters, one forgets the constant feeling of hunger for a few hours.

Organised by a colonel from Moscow who has been inspecting the camp for a few days, we are obliged to watch a film on the Charkov show trials. It shows the condemnation and hanging of several SS and Wehrmacht members who had conducted inhuman crimes in Charkov.

It is a glorious, threateningly hot summer's day. Only a few stalwarts do their daily circuits in the blazing midday sun. The front yard is once more, as so often, closed as a repressive measure against us. I am busy learning English vocabulary by heart when the gate is opened and two persons enter the inner yard. One of those entering is a Romanian officer, the other a lieutenant with the Knight's Cross. Suddenly Captain Sacha's eyes widen: 'What is this then? I know him! He is not a lieutenant and certainly not with a Knight's Cross! He is a corporal!'

'Do you know this man then?' I ask him.

'Certainly, he is a corporal and called Nissen, already long working for the NKVD.'

Now it is clear to me that this man has been sent here as a spy. To make him look more trustworthy he has been given a Knight's Cross. However, the Russians had not reckoned on this lad being recognised in our block.

A few minutes after 'Lieutenant Nissen' had reported to the block senior, he appeared completely stripped in the yard. He was to perform now as the dirty dog who had to keep the toilets clean.

This was the second attempt by the Russians to put a spy in Block VI. The first occasion was with the NKVD spy Lohoff, a flight lieutenant from Oberhausen, who did not succeed in getting a foot in with us. We made him understand quite clearly that if he loved life he should clear the field. A complaint was made about him to his bread suppliers and he was never seen in the block again.

A SUMMER IN ISOLATION

An event has occurred. Suddenly, yesterday morning, the Guards major appeared and informed us in a cheerful speech that there was now a Second Front in France again. The earth was soaked in blood, covered in iron and the skies constantly full of thousands of Allied aircraft.

The colonel from Moscow has also appeared among us. He is listening to the wishes of the prisoners of war. Colonel Crome told him in short sentences of our complaints about the window blinds and the demand for their immediate removal. The colonel agreed to this, so now the bedrooms on the roadside have normal daylight again.

The duty officer entered the yard. He had a note with him and read out the names Crome, Wolff, Spiegelberg, von Hanstein, von Güldenfeld, Mewes, Lübbe, Webere, Middeldorf and Holl. We were ordered to get dressed and follow him. We went through the guardroom and out of the camp into the administrative building, to the office of the major-general. We were led into Kudriatschov's room, where he waited with the interpreter. We formed up in a line and waited for him to speak. The Guards major was nervous. Under my gaze, which was constantly directed at him, he became even more nervous. I knew from my interrogation here that he could not bear this. Suddenly he shouted out, demanding to know why was I staring at him. Did I look like that at my Führer? I replied that I was used to looking people in the eye. A jab in the ribs from Colonel Crome, who was standing on my right, warned me to keep quiet.

The door behind the Guards major opened a little. For a brief moment we saw and recognised the face of the colonel from Moscow. Kudriatschov now told us that he was letting the blinds be removed. He had ordered us to come to him to say that we were exclusively responsible for quiet and order in Block VI. If there were disturbances, we could expect severe punishment. We were the hostages he was holding. A wave of the hand and we were dismissed.

We went back to the block aware that we had got off lightly. In the yard the one-legged Second-Lieutenant Stöhr was making another attempt to walk with the artificial leg that Dr Feller had contrived for him out of the most primitive means. Even the blinded Wissebach was in Block VI for a short while because he was in the SS.

It is already high summer. When one looks back, the past time does not seem to have been so long. When the sky announces a storm, old and young alike stand up so as not to miss the little drops of precious moisture. As the roofs and their gutters are defective, the water accumulates and the lovely showers give us an opportunity for a full wash. This is also absolutely necessary, as in our midnight bathing hours – every two to three weeks – we are given only a half-basin of lukewarm water. If one wants to wash out one's hand towel for drying one's self, its diverse shreds and patches leave little to 'bathe' with. The bathroom staff are strongly forbidden to converse with us. The person in charge of bathing is a strong Anti-fascist and will react strongly.

The summer has long since been pushed aside by autumn. One might almost say that it has become winter already. According to reports, the Allied invasion has not been driven back, but rather has been able to push further forward. With it has come retreat in the east, with the collapse of the central sector and the dropping-off of Romania after the collapse of the front there. The increasing worsening of the political and military situation also weighs on the mood of some of my comrades. They have learnt to think factually and level-headedly, and show themselves to be full of concern for the future. Nevertheless they know that it is fully absurd to draw the consequences that the Russians and their satellites would like to see. The question 'Traitor or not?' is a matter of character and has absolutely nothing to do with the political situation! This is pressed even more often at the interrogations. Many duels have meanwhile been fought. Comrades are constantly being put in the cells, but little can be got out of them, either by dirty tricks or by terror.

With regret we saw Senior Veterinary Surgeon Hülsmann, a German-born southwest African, leave the block after he had been interrogated once and join the League of German Officers. As a reward he was given a job in the kitchen. The Anti-fascists rejoiced, seeing this as a success, while we shrugged our shoulders regretfully.

Some comrades had meanwhile been taken away to unknown destinations, including Lieutenant-Colonels von Sass and Dr

Westerburg. For von Sass the outlook seemed bleak as he had been the defender of Veliki-Luki. The Russians there had suffered heavy losses against a reinforced German regiment and were now endeavouring to bring a case against them. As the Guards major had earlier told von Sass, the punishment was already prepared. I believe all that the Russians say!

There is no lack of latrine rumours of all kinds. They were known to come from the Russians and were meant to keep the prisoners of war in constant mental turmoil. I was as aware of them as all the others. My daily prayers are and remain for Germany and victory. I believe in it firmly! Behind walls six metres high and barbed wire one can hardly get a true picture of the situation. That it is very serious we all know. But even if we remain denied a victory, do we have to become traitors? Who could then trust us in later life? How do the teachers, theologians and jurists who subscribe to Bolshevism explain this? Do they then have the right to teach and judge about loyalty and honour? I would always so deal with such things that I could be accountable to my people at any time!

A great general amusement broke out in the whole block as a result of the following story. It happened that all prisoners of Jewish origin were to be sent away from the camp to an unknown destination. These men had held various key positions in the camp. The Hungarian Jew Birn, who had been head cook for a long time, was carefully searched by the guard. As some gold was found on him, he had to hand over all his clothing and was given only a pair of old Russian trousers to wear. In the following thorough search a quantity of melted gold was found in the high heels of his boots. In the rest of his clothing were found gold rings, and several thousand roubles had been sewn in. As head cook Birn had been bartering with the camp inhabitants, taking rings and gold from individual prisoners of war who were all suffering from hunger. As appropriate punishment the cheat received several weeks or months on bread and warm gruel. The NKVD spies had done well.

The cold weather that had arrived overnight again gave us the problem of procuring wood. Full of irony, I thought back to the moment when Kudriatschov, now promoted to Guards lieutenant-colonel, wanted to arrange for us to collect wood. It was about three weeks ago that we had to parade in the front yard and Kudriatschov appeared with a colonel from the Kasan Ministry of the Interior. He set us the challenge of getting the wood to heat our block ourselves. None of us made any move to take up this offer. Thereupon he said to Colonel Wolff, who had become the block senior after the transfer of Colonel Crome to Moscow, 'Give the order for this!' Wolff replied: 'I have no right to do so, as we are all prisoners of war!' At this, Kudriatschov, who wanted to demonstrate his authority before his Kasan guest, himself went through the ranks, looking at our boots and shoes, or what was left of them, and decided from this who would go to collect the wood. Most of us had already shown ourselves ready to start. When Kudriatschov and his entourage were almost ready, a loud, clear voice said unmistakably: 'Colonel, I am not going to collect wood as I am not obliged to by the Geneva Convention!' The already separated ones answered almost as one: 'I am also not going to collect wood!' Kudriatschov threatened the men, and ordered them to move, but nothing helped. After some hard discussion, in which Lieutenant-Colonel Burmann clearly emphasised that he did not think he should be forced into reinforcing the Russian front and weakening the German front, we were driven into the inner yard. An increased reign of terror had started but it would remain unsuccessful.

Until now, only a little wood had been delivered and yet our rooms were quite warm, much to the amazement of the duty officer. Our old system of self-help, developed the previous winter, worked excellently. Over time we established a routine for hiding the files and choppers with which we reduced the size of the looted wood. I would not previously have believed it possible that with a saw made from a simple iron barrel hoop one could cut through planks forty centimetres thick in the shortest possible time. Naturally this required a well implemented organisation: it started with the sentries set to warn of surprise visits, and ran via the timber removers to end with the men sawing. It was often said about the handover of tasks that it often came down to the minute, often seconds. It had failed twice already. The duty officer took the saw and the wood away, and Colonel Wolff, as the block senior, was put in the lock-up and relieved of his duties. During the next mornings, when the duty officer appeared for the tally, the yard was empty. Only individual prisoners of war made their morning circuits. When the commandant said something, it was not understood. Even the interpreter was unable to move us. There was an unholy confusion. No one obeyed the orders.

'We only take orders from our block senior!'

'Where is Colonel Wolff?'

'Let him out!' So it went on, with the angry crowd of men shouting down the duty officer to get at the commandant. The duty officer left the block and made his report. But even the appearance of the 'Guards bully' or 'Guards proletarian', as we called him, did not alter the situation. Each of the block inhabitants newly tasked with taking charge of the block rejected it. 'I cannot keep order properly in the block and I do not want Colonel Wolff to be locked up when he is innocent!' came the responses. The Russians left the block swearing, and that evening Colonel Wolff reappeared, to be greeted with great delight. He was re-established as our block senior with all honours by the Guards lieutenant-colonel. A written agreement had been made over the reciprocal duties and rights of the senior officers on both sides. They even invited him to a conciliatory meal consisting of roast potatoes with cutlets and vodka. The only camp cutlery – a knife and spoon – was brought for him. He declined with thanks, but could not help drinking a slug of vodka, as otherwise the whole contract would have been under threat. Finally he watched as Kravierz and Kudriatschov attacked the cutlets and potatoes. As true sons of their country, they used their hands extensively as 'cultural implements'. Colonel Wolff became doubtful whether the Darwin Theory was based on the truth.

Despite the loss of our home-made saw, which we had nicknamed Laura, we were not discouraged from making another one. The frost was strong and we did not want to freeze.

THE DISPUTE IN THE CHURCH

8th December 1944. It is evening, 20.00 hours. Our water soup was consumed two hours ago. It has no lasting effect. With a lot of care we have removed a thick plank from the coach house that immediately borders the sickbay and lies very close to the guardroom. Almost all the prisoners in Room 10 were involved, as a check could have taken place at any minute.

Now the plank lies in our room. The light is off, as it so often is, and the room, like the whole camp, lies in complete darkness. We have already sawn off two blocks and the third is half done. The room is full of sawdust. The ready pieces are already firmly nailed under the beds, as they must not be found. Early tomorrow morning we must heat up the stove so that no smoke is seen in daylight. Not all the rooms can be heated with the paltry amount of wood the Russians bring us every day for the whole block. Apart from that, the wood delivered is also wet. Now, with our careful planning, we can survive a third winter without having to freeze. It is just as well that Ivan has not yet discovered our wood depot.

Suddenly one of our sentries bursts into the room: 'Hide the wood quickly, the Guards bully is on the way!' He is quite out of breath. We react like lightning. One grabs the saw and hides it; two others conceal the sawn-off pieces; a third scatters the sawdust a bit.

I have grabbed the remains of the plank and put it in a corner. It is now about two metres long. A long driving coat gives it rough cover. This is hardly done when four figures come into the room. I cannot understand what they are saying. Kudriatschov strides forward, lighting the floor with a long pocket torch. He appears not to hear a loudly called 'Achtung!' Without concerning themselves with us, they go into the adjacent Room 11, then turn round and leave the room the way they came. That went well! But they have not yet left the block so we have to get the pieces and the plank out of the room immediately. Where? The toilet! We quickly carry the plank to the required destination. I sit down in there so that no one would think of looking in. Should someone come in, I can always call out 'Occupied!' There is noise on the stairs again. The Russians are coming back. They quickly run into the rooms, and drag some wood out of the staff officers' room. I leave the toilet and go to see what the situation is. The wood has been found as a result of some suspicious signs drawing their attention. If only the Russians had turned round again and looked for wood in other rooms! Meanwhile all traces have been disposed of. One certainly needs luck!

Today is Saturday, the 9th December. We parade outside for counting. It is a damned cold day. The cold has been persisting for days. I guess it is 30 to 35 degrees below zero. Immediately after the head count comes breakfast, and after that we have a last rehearsal for tomorrow's Advent celebrations with our double quartet. The prelude has already been given, last Sunday, on the first day of

Advent. We had an appreciative audience. We wanted to polish our performance and the crown will be the celebration on Christmas Eve.

Why is the duty officer so late? If we have to wait for much longer we will go away, not wanting to freeze. Ah, here comes a second-lieutenant, who looks to be either Kazach or Usbech judging from his appearance. He is relatively large, with black hair and equally dark unfathomable eyes. Colonel Wolff reports the strength. Once the Russian is convinced that the whole block is on parade in the yard, he pulls out a whistle and blows hard into it. Immediately the wooden door opens and six soldiers burst into the yard, occupying the entrances to the block like lightning. None of us is allowed back into the block, and we are told that a general search is taking place.

This is a right mess! Now we have to stand out in the cold until these sub-humans have rummaged through everything. Our anger becomes even greater, but we can do nothing about it.

Then the names are read out of those who have to pack their things and go to the guardroom. In our room the Russians have already made a thorough search and turned everything inside out. With our teeth gritted, we pack our few things together. There is another check before the guardroom and we can hear that a precise and thorough search is taking place there. The emigrant Knippschild is supervising it.

Now we too are inside. I go straight to the soldier on duty and open my bread bag. He looks at the things inside and retains all the written notes. But I am able to smuggle my photographs through, as well as my small knife, which I had concealed in my water bottle. A little water that is always kept in the bottle sees to it that shaking the bottle will not reveal the knife. Outside, in front of the guardroom, stands a guard waiting for us. He leads us through the camp which until now I had not entered without an escort. We are greeted by acquaintances from some distance away. They had been chased away by members of the League of German Officers.

We go past Block 1 towards the middle one of the three churches that lie directly behind the east side of the camp and are separated from the camp by a barbed wire fence. A small gate leads the way in. Now it is becoming clear to me that we are being taken inside the church. At the beginning of the cold period the church had been the quarantine quarters of some officer prisoners of war who had been captured by the Romanians. Right at the entrance to the church my attention is caught by two frescos that have been whitewashed, but without completely obscuring the colours. An attempt had apparently been made to protect the Virgin Mary, her eyes having been dug out. Sprayed chalk on the head showed that the cover had been applied by hand.

We were led into the church itself through a long passageway. Most of our comrades who had been taken out of the block ahead of us were already here. Some, however, were now in the administrative building for special investigation. Finally they also came to join us. Hindenlang recounted what happened to him while he was being interrogated by Major Kravietz, the head of the NKVD operational detachment, who, because of his steel teeth, we call 'Silvermine'.

A copy of *Mein Kampf* had been found in our block and Kravietz wanted to know whose it was. Naturally Hindenlang said that he had no idea that such a book existed among us. In fact, Hindenlang had it himself. It was strapped to the inside of his thigh. We burst out laughing at this trick.

It is terribly cold inside the church, almost as cold as outside. We stand together in the big church, our breath freezing in the air. We are wearing every item of our clothing but it hardly keeps us warm. There is only one old oil stove in the whole room, and several comrades are trying to warm themselves a little around it. Now and again one of the last emigrants appears and by evening we are all together. Little is said. The events of the day have to be thought through. The orderly officer appears again and looks at the group. He seems to be happy and soon vanishes again.

With my two room comrades, Staff Surgeon Dr Weber and Captain von Wenczowski, I settle down on the tiled floor. We appear to be lying in the middle of the church. Our exhausted and weakened bodies want to rest, but we cannot do this because it is so cold here. Even if several stoves were set up, one would only get a moderate warmth. And who would deliver the necessary fuel for a number of stoves?

All kinds of thoughts go through my head. I think about the Guards lieutenant-colonel's threat a year ago to destroy my physical and emotional strength. Will this slowly but surely prepare us for the 'cold journey'? It seems so to me. But then . . . No way will I allow these brutes to triumph! But what can I do? There is only one thing: hunger strike! I am determined to take this step even if I do it alone. However, I am convinced that others will think the same. The time passes between freezing and dark brooding. It seems usual for these unpleasant experiences to appear twice as long as they truly are.

And so the night passes leading to the second day of Advent 1944. My two neighbours, Dr Weber and von Wenczowski, have also found no rest. As we exchange the first words between us, we are agreed. We must get the whole of Block VI determined to start a hunger strike, but it must be so organised that our block senior is not involved and in no way can be liable. I have long been on my feet and trying to warm my body by walking to and fro. Padre Roth has also been on his feet for a long time. I speak to him:

'Now, Minister, how do you see the story here?'

'Yes, you know, Holl, it seems as if we are going to spend the winter here.'

'That is what it looks like to me, too. But I have no desire to let myself be prepared for that "cold journey".'

'And what are you thinking of doing?' He looks at me quietly and thoughtfully, as is his way. 'I will start a hunger strike!'

'Have you thought it over and do you believe that all the comrades will join you?' Again he looks at me with his clear eyes.

'Naturally, Padre, we have had the whole night to think about it. I do not think that anyone will not take part if it is properly approached.'

'That means, though, if it is a hunger strike, it is everyone!'

'Yes, Padre, but rather an end with horror than horror without end!'

Dr Weber and von Wenczowski were standing with some comrades. They too are agreed that our plan would go ahead without a fuss. We must get out of the church and go back to our old block!

Our rations distributor, Captain Krause, has already been instructed. He will first call Room 1, whose senior is Lieutenant Sochatzi, also known as 'Prince'. The comrades of Room 1 have shown decisive action against the Russians and are immediately ready to try to force a clear reaction from the Russians by means of a hunger strike. The other rooms follow in turn after the call for collecting food.

The old barrel with the morning soup and half of our daily bread ration are brought in. Krause goes with both his assistants to the barrel and calls Room 1 to get their food. No one gets up from the room or makes a move. After Krause has called three times, he calls the next room. The same scene. In the subsequent rooms no one makes a move to get the food, so that the whole block (192 men) refuse the food.

Towards 9 o'clock Schuck, the duty officer, whose name in German means beetle, summons the morning roll call. Nobody gets up. Colonel Wolff tells him that the prisoners of war will not comply with his orders any more and that we had also refused the morning meal. Schuck opens his eyes wide and begins to swear quietly. However, realising that the matter is serious, he disappears.

He comes back again in half an hour, accompanied by Inspector Brijanzev, who asks us not to do something so nonsensical and just accept the food. He says he will see to it that we get wood for heating. No one reacts to his promises, we have all had enough sad experiences not to believe the promises of a Russian any more.

Both men see that their endeavours are in vain and disappear once more. We have all lain down on the stone floor and covered ourselves with the blankets and coats available. Nevertheless it is bitterly cold.

At about 12 o'clock the word came: 'The Guards bully is coming!' Nobody pays any attention when he enters the church, escorted by his staff. Even the camp elder, Mangold, and several other traitors such as the former Colonel Hermann, and another two whose names I do not know, are brought to persuade us to be reasonable. Colonel Wolff makes a report. Kudriatschov asks why the prisoners of war have not stood up. Wolff replies that they are not responding to his orders any more. Now the Russians try to get us to stand up. But as soon as the Russians get one man up and turn to the next man, the first lies down again.

After a long time, however, they are able to drive the majority of us into the centre of the church, where Kudriatschov makes a speech. He is an old fox and tries with threats and orders to make us eat. But when he sees that this is unsuccessful he tries another means. Mangold, the pioneer Captain Germer – a teacher from the Saarland who had been captured on the Romanian front a few weeks previously – and the other traitors must now talk to us on his orders.

They too make promises to us, all without result. They are fighting against an icy wall of rejection. Our demand is simple: we will only take food upon our immediate release from the church!

I look at the traitors with contempt. There stands, for instance, Hermann, who was once called colonel. He has set himself against his comrades who are still fighting and his people, but is unashamed of wearing Third Reich decorations. Here he stands wearing his Knight's Cross. It is simply shameful for us!

Lieutenant Nowak, a son of Königsberg city, now steps forward and asks permission to speak. You can tell he is a lawyer as his quiet, well thought-out sentences are spoken clearly to the Guards lieutenant-colonel. 'Trusting in Stalin's order No. 55 of the 15th February 1943, I became a prisoner in Stalingrad. The order said that all prisoners of war would receive dignified treatment and be returned to their homeland six months after the end of the war.' He waited after every sentence until the interpreter had translated. 'The treatment that I am now experiencing here stands exactly in contradiction to this order. I have fought as a soldier and also demand that I be treated as one. If I am to be destroyed, then I should be granted a respectable death such as I have earned as a soldier. It is unfair to try to liquidate us here in this way and manner! I know that I am not the only one who thinks this way and I am convinced that many of my comrades here are of the same opinion.'

I threw back the blanket that had been covering me and advanced a few steps to support the last words of Lieutenant-Colonel Nowak. I now stood in the middle of the half circle and waited there for Nowak to finish his speech, firmly willing the 'Guards Bully' to recall the words he had said about physical and emotional destruction. My eyes were firmly fixed upon him. With my lips pressed tightly together, without distorting my face, I looked only at him. As he felt my staring gaze directed at him, he became uneasy and, trying to evade me, he stepped to one side. A right turn on my part brought him back into my view. His deputy, Captain Grusev, noticed that Kudriatschov was finding this unpleasant and tried to pull me back into the ranks, but I did not move from the spot.

When Nowak had finished, the Guards lieutenant-colonel told him that he did not want people to commit suicide, and that we all must eat, as Germany would need us again later. This came from the mouth of this man with scorn. Then he turned quickly to go. He knew that I intended to confront him and wanted to avoid being snubbed openly, as had already twice been the case. As Kudriatschov was leaving, Grusev asked me my name. 'The Guards lieutenant-colonel already knows me!' I said loudly, as Kudriatschov hastened away.

The situation had come to an extreme head. The camp commandant had withdrawn without success. The lunch was also not accepted. For some time it had stood outside the church and was not taken away. No unauthorised person dared come near us and we dared not stand outside. When some comrades did not immediately comply with a sentry's order to go into the church, he opened fire into the wall over the men's heads.

The emigrant Knippschild now had some beds brought into the church by reliable men of the Anti-fascists on the orders of the Guards lieutenant-colonel. He asked where they should be erected but got no answer. So these beds were dumped anywhere.

Late afternoon has come and still the Russians do not let us hear anything from them. We must be patient. We are 192 men and Moscow knows all about us. Famous officers with the highest decorations can be found among us. Tomorrow at the latest the commandant must report this incident to Moscow and a commission will result. Whether Kudriatschov will let it happen? Wait and see!

As nothing extraordinary is happening, our 'Maestro' Fromlowitch gathers together his double quartet for the planned Advent presentation. We still do not know what the next days will bring, but we want to make a stand for our beloved country. Eight of us singers stand in the middle of the church. I am the second tenor. All is quiet. We raise our voices with a quiet childlike simplicity. The tones are as if breathed, yet one can hear them crystal clear even in the far corners of the room. 'Lightly flutters down the snow, still and glassy rests the sea' we sing to the quiet audience. One can see from their faces that in spirit they are far away. Old bearded men and youngsters alike see themselves again as children in their parents' home at Christmas time or as parents singing with their children in the glow of the Advent candles. The fateful state of our camp gives this Advent celebration a special quality. There is not a word spoken, and one could have heard a pin drop in this large church. And then came our second song: 'A star stood over the woods that had a bright shine; the Christ child is coming soon into our village. The snow lies on the fields, the wind whistles behind the fence, the deer in the woods all look up at the star.' As it dies away comes the last song, 'Night of clear stars that stand like a wide bridge.' Yes, that is our bridge to our home so far away, to our mothers, who worry about us and are full of uncertainty as to whether we are still alive.

When the last note has been sung, nobody says a word. Only by the slamming of the door are we brought back to the present. Knippschild appears again with some satellites and brings bedsteads. Even he, who as a Communist is an atheist, had not dared to disturb our simple Advent celebration, but had waited listening at the door until we were finished. I wondered what impression our simple songs had made on him.

And again it is evening. The camp food carriers brought all the meals of the day, including the evening soup, into the church. In order to tempt our palates, they have brought an especially thick soup at the cost of the general camp. A turnip soup and goulash are included. Sugar, bread and butter are visibly featured in the display.

Schuck appears, accompanied by an NKVD second-lieutenant. Colonels Wolff, Weber and Hanstein, as well as the Senior Surgeon Dr Spiegelberg, are ordered to the Guards lieutenant-colonel. Schuck stays with us. He knows all the tricks as he was formerly a warder in Jelabuga Prison and believes that he can catch us out in his own way. On the assumption that we are like the Russians, he summons the spy Nissen, who has been completely exposed by us. Nissen, a lowly creature, had not taken any food until then out of fear. Now that he is ordered to eat by the duty officer, he grasps greedily at it. He can take whatever he wants from our food. Schuck plies him with ever more food. Goulash such as Nissen would never have expected in his wildest dreams is pressed upon him. But none of us react to this. We are not Russians and cannot be tricked into eating in this way.

I lay down to rest. However, this time I am not on the cold stone floor, as on the previous night, but on a bed. Suddenly I hear my name. The NKVD second-lieutenant is back again and looking for me. I get up and follow him.

Soon we are in the administrative building in which the camp commandant has his office. I know it well. The second-lieutenant leads me along the second floor to the far corner of the corridor, which is in complete darkness. I sit down on a stool. Soon Schuck appears. From his smile and some words, I gather that his trick with Nissen has pleased him greatly.

From the adjacent room I can hear the notes of Offenbach's 'Tales of Hofmann'. I can also make out voices. Apparently a ballerina is dancing. I often have to cough as a consequence of the night before. My mood is such that my greatest enemy could say the greatest untruths dispassionately and indifferently about me to no effect. Either I am dealt with as a human being or they will have to take drastic measures against me! Torture will not defeat me, and the moment I realise that my last hour has come, the Russians will experience another wonder!

I can hear the angry voice of the Guards bully from a nearby room. Apparently the colonel is there. Suddenly a door is slammed. Kudriatschov quickly disappears down the stairs wiping the sweat from his brow. He seems to hurry ahead. Some female creatures come from the dancing room. They have strongly painted faces and are wearing fur coats and dainty white felt boots on their feet. What a contrast in this country that alleges no class differences any more, when I think of the lumpy figures one can see going about the town. I have never seen such a big difference in the clothing as right here in Russia until now! But perhaps this goes with Communism, like the various rations that the Party and army have here.

I am shocked out of my thoughts. It had to do with a person I met, Special Leader Heinrich. We talked quietly together, watched by the NKVD second-lieutenant, who spits strongly and frequently on the floor. He orders me to follow him through the music room, in which some of the women are hopping around, although I do not watch them, then through a further room that was empty and then into the Guards lieutenant-colonel's room. Here, in addition to Kudriatschov, there is also a female interpreter, the head of the operational detachment and the political major. Bowing slightly, I remain standing at the door without acknowledging the occupants. My eyes are directed at a big map that shows the front lines with red flags.

The female interpreter addresses me: 'Captain Holl, you stepped forward in the church this morning. What did you want to say?' Without changing my expression, I answer in a quiet monotonous voice that their indifference could not deny: 'I have done my duty as a soldier. A year ago the Guards lieutenant-colonel told me that he would destroy me physically and mentally. I see now that he was in earnest. I am reckless and defenceless, but not dishonourable! I request that I be shot!' I directed my gaze at the map. A fit of coughing shook me and my nose ran. I blew my nose with an old rag. The Guards lieutenant-colonel then spoke urgently to the interpreter, who translated: 'It is wrong and not good for you to do away with yourself. Just think that Germany will need you after the war. You are still a young man and must live to support your people!'

With a scornful expression I looked at him slowly: 'The Guards lieutenant-colonel need have no fear that I would commit suicide. I leave it to him to destroy me! As long as I am in the church and my fate lies before my eyes, I reject all nourishment!'

Still sweating, and hardly able to hide his nervousness, Kudriatschov signals that I can go. I am led through the outer room in which the colonel was sitting, as I had rightly suspected. We exchange no words but look at each other earnestly and decisively. A few minutes later I am back in the church. I recount my experience to those comrades who want to know.

After about half an hour the colonels return. The camp commandant tries again to persuade people to eat with all kinds of expressions, but comes up against a block of granite. We do not make the least concession. Even Sonderführer Heinrich, who could converse with Kudriatschov without an interpreter, made this absolutely clear. Lieutenant Nowak this morning and I myself this afternoon have shown him that we are taking this seriously. Now comes the waiting.

We huddle in small groups around the stove that has meanwhile been brought in and the Russian camp carpenter Klement, who must have made the blinds for the windows of Block VI, is keen to hang long raffia mats over the vast windows of the church to keep out the cold. Large amounts of wood have been brought into the anteroom of the church during the day. As I have been feeling hungry for months, I do not find the hunger so bad.

Colonel Wolff has been taken off alone to speak with the Guards lieutenant-colonel. We suppose that this will be the last talk, as Kudriatschov must avoid sending a message to Moscow in any case.

Forty-five minutes drags by and midnight passes. Suddenly Colonel Wolff is back again.

Quietly and clearly, with an earnest tone, he speaks. 'Gentlemen, I ask you please not to break out in happy howling, or make any stupid remarks. Please pack your things, we are going back to Block VI. Krause, please ensure that the food comes with us. Those of you who can carry wood, take it with you. Everyone back to Block VI.'

His instructions were carried out quickly and quietly. Schuck is already standing there with some soldiers to take us back to Block VI. We are full of joy over this victory, as well as over the reverse we had inflicted on our country's traitors. How they will gawp when they find the church empty in the morning!

Within an hour the status quo has been restored. Everyone is back in their old room and has already had something to eat. Once the stoves have warmed up properly we all lie down for a well earned night's sleep. The NKVD spy Nissen has not been sent back to the block, on grounds of expediency, but has gone to the Work Battalion instead.

BACK IN BLOCK VI
The final preparations for our Christmas celebrations to begin on Christmas Eve are complete. Every member of the room has thought how he can prepare a small Christmas gift for his friends. Especially keen is Luftwaffe Captain Freimann.

The main ornament in our room is the Christmas Crown, which took weeks of work to make and even survived the strike in the church. The base of it is formed by the Advent Cross. As we could not get any pine branches, it was carved out of wood. An octagon shape, it has candles on four corners made out of matching water cylinders filled with kerosene. On each of the remaining four corners stands a pine tree carved out of wood. Between them have been inserted fairytale figures such as the Rat Catcher, Tom Thumb, Little Red Riding Hood, and Snow White, but the Christ Child and St Nicholas are also there. About thirty centimetres above the octagon hangs a hexagon decorated with the divisional emblems of all the members in the room, and above that is a square bearing allegorical wooden figures of the seasons, spring, summer, autumn and winter. All the remains of the coloured crayons to be found have been used, but also medicines and even painted bricks have been used to establish colours. The individual garlands are fastened together with thin wire so that the Christmas Crown resembles a pyramid.

Also everyone has saved, according to their needs and ability, a slice of bread and a little sugar, as well as fat. It is not easy to do, as with constant hunger the urge to eat up all the scraps is very great. Several men who are unable to trust themselves give their saved bread to a comrade to keep.

Rooms 3 and 4 have as their centrepiece a carved Christmas crib, of the sort which is also to be seen under every Christmas tree at home. The artists are Second-Lieutenants Mohr and Hofmann. The room associations each have their private celebrations, but the whole block is also celebrating this great German festival, in which the choir with its Christmas carols forms the focus. All of us turn our thoughts on this day particularly to our own homes, and this most German of old festivals reminds us not to disown our German heritage. Our prayer to our Lord is: Give our people their peace again!

The fateful turn of the year 1944/1945. We sit together in a festive mood in Room 10. We have cleaned up our already frightfully tattered uniforms as well as we can. Captain Dr Hollunder conducts a review of the past year, 1944. Factually and clearly he presents his account, and the time already passed once more runs through our minds' eyes. Captain Schmidt, Mayor of Brieg, also gives an outlook on the past year. He is especially knowledgeable about the seriousness of the situation, and shows us the storm clouds gathering over our people: today it is more necessary than ever to remain true to our people.

15th February 1945, my third birthday in captivity. Our choir wakes me from my sleep singing a local song from the Rhine. Captain Knauff also has his birthday with me, his third in captivity, having become a prisoner in Veliki-Luki. He too had a song for his birthday.

As we return to our room after roll call, we remain transfixed in happy surprise. A whole table full of gifts for the birthday boys is standing there. My eyes fall on a little wooden figure of the 'Manneken Pis'! I consider with amusement the image of the little fountain figure that I have passed in my home town so many times. My countryman and friend Hans Mohr carved it for me as a greeting from our home town. It even has the town's arms carved in wood. Almost every one of my comrades and fellow sufferers has given me special pleasure today on my birthday. Those who have never known real hunger can hardly understand what it means to give half a day's bread ration to a friend so that for one day in the year he can have a full meal. 300 grams of moist bread baked in clay! At this time when other men are throwing away their honour from hunger, this is beyond price!

The day ends with a good-natured celebratory hour, to which close friends from the other rooms have been invited. The arrangements have been taken over by some comrades from the room, and also our master narrators Dr Mewes and Gerischer come for a chat.

The news penetrating the block by both legal and illegal means is getting ever worse. Long debates start among some comrades. Others have heavy thoughts about the fate of our people. I am also depressed by this news, but I simply cannot believe that the most difficult fight by our people can end in such a sad way! I have confidence as before in our leadership. The enemy news service seems to me deliberately directed at undermining our morale and depressing us! In individual cases I can see that the news is having an effect on their behaviour. Sacha and Pfeiffer, for example, have recently spoken in such a way that one has the impression that they regret having backed the wrong horse. I once spoke with them about it but have since held myself back in such situations.

When we look out of our window, the administrative area, which is outside the camp, lies before us. Next to it is the Russians' shop. How well the people live here is shown to me by observing them from our room. A middle-aged Russian woman in the usual poor clothing has got some butter in a container and is sitting on a step right opposite our block licking this expensive item of food, which was obviously not intended for her. Furtively she looks to right and left, anxiously hoping that no one has seen her. After she has refreshed herself for a good quarter of an hour, she gets up and goes off without noticing us.

On Heroes' Memorial Day we remember our fallen comrades with heart and soul. More than ever it is clear to me that we cannot betray the German people. The deaths of so many of our best men awakes in us a powerful sense of obligation. My best friends remain on the battlefield and many a comrade under my orders fell to enemy hands. How could I ever look a German mother in the eye if I should betray the living and the dead?

For several days the food has been getting progressively worse, even worse than it was before. We have the impression that we are being cheated by the German kitchen staff. However, the Russians appear to have a hand in this. As in the previous year, there has been no sugar or bread for several days. Allegedly this has to do with transportation difficulties. The Kama is frozen over, halting the winter supplies of vital products, and now we have to wait until the Kama is navigable again.

The anger of the block's occupants grows from day to day. It reaches its climax on the 6th of April when the whole block goes on hunger strike with the demand that we want whatever is available in our own hands so that we can feed ourselves. After long negotiations between Colonel Wolff and Kudriatschov, the latter agrees to Colonel Wolff setting up our own kitchen for the block. We now believe that our situation will improve.

The next morning, however, Schuck appears and informs us that we must pack our things as Block VI is to be cleared. So this is the Russians' retaliation. It has become obvious to them that such a strongly united group as the men of Block VI will inevitably become less manageable. The demands that we made yesterday had shown our understanding of the weakness of the Russians and were detrimental to the Anti-fascists. Kudriatschov now intended to divide us between the two Jelabuga camps. My group was marched off to Cloister Camp after a detailed baggage search.

With sack and pack, like the departure of the children of Israel from Egypt, we wandered through the melting snow of Jelabuga's streets. The Anti-fascists had already prepared well. As we arrived in darkness, the room seniors were already ready to call us to their rooms. After one and a half years I was back in the camp from where I was supposed to go before the war tribunal.

The camp senior here is Lieutenant-Colonel Wölfel, who had had to clear the field in Kama Camp as the Russians had taken his Knight's Cross for a theatrical play. Because of his monocle and his high-pitched voice, we called him 'Broken Willy'.

Lieutenant Hein and I were taken to Room 21 in Block II by a prisoner of war whom I did not recognise in the darkness. We were shown to a place in the corner. Without being able to discern much in the darkness, and not knowing with whom we had to share, we laid ourselves down. We did not accept the invitation to go to supper. Nor did we go to breakfast in the morning but we did attend the muster parade. We could see that most of those in the camp no longer wore army insignia on their uniforms but rather the colours of the National Committee and the League of German Officers.

I was happy to see a few old faces here in the camp, including my former regimental adjutant, Lieutenant-Colonel Brendgen. He told me that most of the occupants of the camp in the summer of 1944 were at the middle point of their captivity and were being schooled by old League of German Officers, in which the *Kashport*, as the porridge bowl was called here, had played a prominent role. Now the majority of these prisoners were members of the League. Only a few had stood up to the pressure and the interrogations, and they now quickly made contact with us. They had only heard rumours of the stalwarts isolated in Block VI. We were represented to them as abnormal and criminals who were unwilling to understand the signs of the times and accept the League of German Officers. So much greater was the surprise, then, as the new prisoners saw these 'Criminals' and 'Abnormals' with their own eyes. On the afternoon of the 7th of April the hunger strike was re-established when the head of Convent Camp, Captain Grusev, assured us that work in the camp was voluntary.

UNDER THE TERROR OF THE LEAGUE OF GERMAN OFFICERS

Several days later I realised that this assurance was just more lies when I was assigned to wood sawing with some comrades. Although the wood cutters were firmly assigned people, they wanted to mislead us by doing this. With my comrades I flatly declined to comply. In reprisal the duty officer, a second-lieutenant, known to us as 'Jumbo' because of his bulky appearance, made us stay standing at attention outside the camp until the evening under the supervision of a sentry. Jumbo hit Captain Schmelzer with a stick, which made him resist and ended with him taken to the lock-up.

It had already gone 2000 hours when we were allowed back into the camp, but the matter did not end there. In order to set the whole camp against us, our lunch would not be served until 1400 hours instead of the usual 1200 hours. The grounds for this were given to the camp as our refusing to work. With an amused smile, however, I noticed that the camp commandant Wölfel and his staff had the lunch 'that was not yet ready' at the usual 1200 hours. The camp inhabitants had to wait for another two full hours.

In the room I met an icy silence that I inwardly enjoyed. Even at suppertime the food carriers refused to bring us our food, finally showing themselves as true Anti-fascists. Smiling, we fetched our own soup.

As we were leaving, someone whispered to me: 'Watch out! You're going to be beaten up tonight!' That too! I had to laugh out loud. So the camp staff in combination with the Anti-fascists want to soften us up with all sorts of nasty tricks. The Russians sit in the background with the emigrants and grin at us.

It is very sad that former German officers should be misused for such tomfoolery! Just let them come! Before lying down I take my two wooden slippers and tuck them under the head end of my bed so that they are readily accessible. My neighbour, Lieutenant Theo Brach, a twelve-year man, says to me: 'Captain, let them come!' In a facetious tone I ask the two men on my left: 'Do you two also want to arrange a free stay in the hospital?' They seem uncertain, but it does not matter, they will wake me up!

Then the room political organiser, Second-Lieutenant Schulze, raises his voice: 'Comrades, in our room are elements set against the general order of the camp. They refuse to work, which means that we should have to work for them! That is not acceptable! Today our food was held up for two hours later than usual because of this. In future these gentlemen will conform to the general will!' I keep quiet. The lad knows quite well that every voluntary worker here takes the place of a Russian who can return to the front against our brothers who are still fighting. Above all, I sometimes doubt that I am among normal people. Almost daily I observe now, in the fast advance of the Allies, how these officers mutually congratulate themselves that their homeland will be freed by Soviet or other troops.

The month of May has begun. Until now I and my comrades have been able to avoid so-called camp work. With regret I discover that some old acquaintances who had been firm until now have begun to waver. At present the situation for our country grows worse every day. I myself no longer care to think over the situation but rather live from day to day, concentrating on my study of English. But is this situation sufficient grounds for breaking one's oath of allegiance?

Yesterday, at the 1st of May celebration, the most active of the Anti-fascists, Hartmann, particularly distinguished himself in a celebratory pro-Communism speech. And this man had been a teacher and was allegedly an official in the Hitler Youth movement. But names such as Pickel, Lettau, Janeba and Seidel sound well in the camp activities of the League of German Officers!

My room senior brings me a request to come to the camp gate. I think that somebody wants something from me. Correct. At the camp gate stands the camp senior Wölfel, his monocle shining in the sun. I go up to him. 'Herr' Esch, former colonel and regimental commander, now Anti-fascist and commander of the Work Battalion, is standing beside him. 'What do you want?' I ask of Wölfel, standing in front of me. 'You are to go to the Work Battalion in the garrison. Go through that gate!' I laugh mockingly. 'I do not think I will work, as I am not obliged to.' 'Crackpot!' he replies in his nasal voice. 'We will soon see! Go through!' The deputy camp commandant, a major of Asiatic appearance, now steps forward and asks what the matter is. Someone translates something for him that I do not understand. I am the last one to step forward.

Next to me stand a Hungarian and a German. Once the leading man has marched off, we too should follow, but I remain standing still. The men alongside me get the order to bring me through by force. My look stops them. The Russian major then gives an order and two guards standing by the camp gate drag me with fists and kicks out of the camp. The gate closes immediately behind me. The guard commander draws his pistol and shouts: 'March!' I comply with his order as I know that his pistol has been used in other cases. Only a few days ago a prisoner of war was shot while working in the fields. The man hit was sitting with his comrades on the staked-out boundary having a rest. For no reason at all the guard fired at him as he sat on the ground. No one went to the help of the man writhing on the ground in his death throes. The soldiers saw nothing. When the news of this outrage reached the camp, Wölfel and the camp commandant Grusev were at the sports ground behind Block II watching a football game played by the camp experts, who were the only ones in the camp to play at sport. The game was not broken off, but something else occurred. Wölfel received the news of the incident like Grusev: he laughed.

I am assigned to cleaning the barrack yard, the Russian sergeant standing with a drawn pistol next to me, forcing me to work.

That evening the room senior brought me the news that I was to get up early in the morning to gather straw. The morning was rainy, the sky cloudy. When we were called, I stayed behind in the room. After a short time my company commander, 'Herr' Kehrhahn arrived and ordered me to go to the guardroom. I declined. Kehrhahn disappeared and returned a few minutes later with the commander of the Work Battalion, 'Herr' Esch. But Esch was also unsuccessful. Finally they fetched a Russian guard. The guard, an elderly man nicknamed 'Hindenburg' because he had a Wilhelmish moustache like the dead Reich's President, said that I should get dressed. I had ignored Esch and Kehrhahn because they meant nothing to me, but I complied peaceably with the Russian's orders.

Tearing off my old tunic, I pulled on my old, holey pullover before putting my tunic back on. Then I got my boots, grabbed my overcoat and pulled it on roughly, put my cap on and said 'Ready' to 'Hindenburg'.

The old man set off with me following, and Esch and Kehrhahn behind me. The whole of the camp had already paraded in the back yard for the morning muster. Apparently they were waiting for me. 'Hindenburg' now went to a lock-up, unlocked it and then I was inside, standing in the dark. There was another person in the lock-up but I was not able to recognise him and I did not answer his curious questions.

Perhaps half an hour passed. Suddenly the lock-up was opened and a guard took me to the guardroom. There to receive me was Inspector Anissimov, whom I had known during my time in command of the Work Battalion. He asked me quietly why I had refused to work. Equally quietly I told him.

Through the gate leading to the town came the Asiatic-looking major. He recognised me immediately and asked the reason for my being there. When he heard the reason he told me, via the interpreter:

'If you refuse, you will be forced to work at gunpoint!' I answered: 'If you are going to repeat the same scene as yesterday, then I will go, but I insist that I only go under pressure!' In reply the interpreter stated: 'You can think what you like.' The guard took me to the others, who had already been waiting for me for over an hour. I said to Lieutenant Götz in a jovial manner: 'They want to force me at gunpoint, but as I no longer let myself be in a position like yesterday, I will go under duress.' The furious reply I got from the League of German Officers was: 'Quite right! It would be better if you were put up against a wall!' I gave him a contemptuous look and an ironic smile.

THE ANNOUNCEMENT OF GERMANY'S UNCONDITIONAL SURRENDER AT NUNNERY CAMP IN JELABUGA

9th May 1945. At about 0900 hours the political officer came into our room and announced: 'The whole camp is to parade! In a few minutes the Guards lieutenant-colonel will come and make an important announcement!'

What can this be? Here and there one hears rumours that the war has ended. The prisoners of war are pressed close together on the camp square in front of the home-made clay barrack that bears the proud name 'Deutschlandhalle'. A rostrum adorned with the colours of the National Committee stands in front of the hall against the base of the wall. Right and left behind this are standing the senior activists and emigrants. The duty officer of the day reports as the camp commandant and his entire staff, including a woman in uniform, make their entrance.

Then the camp commandant occupies the speaker's rostrum. In a manner we have experienced on numerous occasions, he begins with '*Voina konshili!*' The interpreter translates. 'The war is over! From tonight the weapons on all the fronts will fall silent. The Fascist conquerors and their criminal system have been smashed. The main role was that played by the Red Army under the leadership of the great Stalin.'

I did not believe my ears as I heard Kudriatschov's words, followed by loud applause from the Anti-fascist side. What an insult! Here, former officers once thought of as the elite of the German people, are applauding the downfall of their own country! I wanted to sink into the ground for shame. Such a lack of dignity I would never have thought possible. Now began a new road of suffering for us. Our Wehrmacht beaten, our people lying helpless on the ground – being celebrated here with applause!

I looked around me and saw my comrades from Block VI were standing among the listeners with earnest faces full of incomprehension at the conduct of these former officers.

The Guards lieutenant-colonel had finished. Now the former Major Cranz took the rostrum. How could things have sunk so low! Cranz thanked the Red Army and the great Stalin for our liberation from Hitler's yoke. His colleagues applauded again. This same Cranz had previously been a ministerial head of department in the Propaganda Ministry! If only I had had a pistol, this creature would not have lived another minute!

I went away, not listening to the end of this victory celebration. My thoughts flew back home to my people who had held out to the last minute and then had been denied victory. Now our enemies would trample on us and ensure that we got an even worse deal than we had with the Versailles peace treaty. Today I will avoid if possible all company and ensure that some of my comrades do the same. It is over for us now. Bolshevism, which until now always knew that we had the backing of the Wehrmacht to protect us, will show its true face.

The general situation runs through my head. To set myself against the Russians now would be absurd. If I continue to refuse to work, the Russians will have good reason to render me harmless. The Wehrmacht no longer exists, which means that my brothers are no longer fighting, so I can no longer be ashamed – except of myself. It now means that I can adopt the same tactics that the Communists did in Germany after 1933: stay silent and swim with the current, without giving anything away. I will not participate in rallies and such events any more. As always, politics means nothing to me. I was made a prisoner as a soldier and I will go back home again as a soldier, if God wills it! I will never return home any other way!

Chapter 3

A White Slave of the Twentieth Century

The unconditional surrender brought little change to the monotonous daily routine at the prison camp. The only sign of it was an increase in work activity. A few days ago most of Nunnery Camp prisoners were transferred to Kama Camp in order to make room for fresh prisoners of war from the Königsberg cauldron. Only a few proven activists remained to deal with their arrival at Nunnery Camp.

We went out daily from Kama Camp in great columns to the endless steppe lying west of the town. On our way to the workplace we had to pass the former Jelabuga cemetery. The graves had collapsed and the memorial stones fallen down, but trucks and farm carts drove over them through a scene that would have been regarded as holy by other people.

Our task is to dig up 100 square metres of the steppe every day. The intention was for 2,000 hectares to be dug up and planted with potatoes. Using the prisoners in shifts the area would be cultivated more quickly – or was that the view of the Russian camp administration? Every day fourteen men were yoked to a plough. As I was pulling it, along with my team neighbour, Lieutenant Francois, we discussed the advantages that slaves had in the Middle Ages and in Nero's time in contrast to us. In ploughing, we had it better. We pulled the plough with only ten men, as it was lighter; apart from that, if our German supervisors were not watching closely, we could steal a few potatoes, which were then consumed raw. They tasted wonderful with salt, almost like an apple in the old days. Not every stomach was suited to this, several of us getting diarrhoea from eating a potato. My stomach is agreeable to this unusual taste and I have managed up to twenty potatoes in a morning!

In the first days a certain number of potatoes were pulled up and we could not go back to the camp until all the potatoes were in place. In order to establish our 'norm', several baskets were emptied in an unobserved moment and the potatoes buried in a heap. However, the Russians got wind of this and became infernally alert!

THE WOODLAND CAMP OF XILTAU (KOSILTAU)

Yesterday there was a search of the Ambulatorium and today we are to march to Xiltau Woodland Camp with eighty men. I am pleased that it is not Hilwig Woodland Camp, with whose 'gentlemen' I had come into conflict, apart from which the former Captain Rothe, the politician, and Büdenbinder, Minister of Labour, are there. There were unpleasant scenes.

The journey took place in the afternoon. It was 32 kilometres. As we went past Hilwig Camp we had to pick up a delousing wagon and a thick rope.

At first we went forward quite energetically, but with time our strength faded. Everyone had to carry a sack of straw as well as his pack, apart from those pulling the wagon. As we approached the first camp it was already nearly dark, but we went on. At midnight we came to a village in the woods. The guards themselves did not know the way. Finally it was agreed that we could sleep until dawn. Our supplies had long since run out and our stomachs were demanding food. God be thanked it was not cold, the June nights being mild.

The chill woke me up in the morning. My clothing was soaked with dew. I tried to warm myself by moving around. Finally we went on. After several hours of wandering around we came to the ferry. The Kama is about 600 metres wide here, flowing quietly and stolidly along. Wherever one looks, there are woods, nothing but woods. The near side bank is very steep. We have to wait a long time here. Klecha, a very young second-lieutenant who had his birthday two days ago, offers me a piece of bread, which I will have to return in kind. I take it thankfully as I have a powerful hunger.

Finally there is room for us on the small boat and we reach our destination. This will be our new working area. We have heard conflicting news about the place. Now we will soon be able to judge for ourselves. Behind the camp gate stands a man wearing the rank badges of a major. So that is Hermann! He is about 1.76 metres tall, with blond hair and a pale face with prominent cheekbones and blue eyes. His attitude is dismissive. No word comes from his lips. Even when we are in the camp he does not think it necessary to present himself.

Of my comrades from Block VI, I meet Knackstaedt, Keller, Sache and Pfeiffer. What one describes as accommodation here is fully occupied. There is a small wooden hut and a tent. All that is left for us is the hut attic and the yard. We are literally lying in the dirt. Even the bracken that we collected on our first tour of the woodlands cannot quite cover the dirt. The area is too small for the camp occupants. The kitchen stands in the middle of the yard and consists of two field kitchen kettles positioned in a square hole about one and half metres deep. The latrines are not six paces away. When it rains, the kitchen hands are fully occupied keeping the rainwater and dirt from falling into the kitchen.

Specialist Becker is the most active of the Anti-fascists. Becker was the sick attendant in Nunnery Camp during my episode of spotted fever, though I only saw him when food was being issued. So he has remained faithful to his line and may be called a true-blue 'Kaschist'. People of his kind are dangerous for their deviousness. We had not possessed eating utensils for a long time – they were, and still are, valued items among the Russians, which is why the Russian camp staff in Jelabuga very soon slipped them out into the town – and eating implements were lacking at mealtimes at first. A few lucky ones still have their mess tins, but we newcomers own virtually nothing. Our mess tins had been taken from us months before in Jelabuga. As I got close someone said 'Mess tins here!' We could relax if someone we knew offered the use of his tin once he had eaten. Some food tins were completely rusted, yet the owner was still happy to have one at all. The dirt does not matter. Other tins have been laboriously cut, with inadequate tools, out of beech wood or husks. There are even not enough spoons to go around.

And what do they give us to eat? In the morning we get our square tablets baked in clay and containing more water than flour, together with a piece of ham and our allocated 40 grams of sugar with a soup cooked on a tripod. We have to collect items for the soup on our daily expeditions, and it depends on the benevolence of the guard commander whether we can collect enough. Should we return to the camp at midday after an eight-hour journey, we get three-quarters of a litre of pea soup or barley broth, in which the whole of the pulses that we get per day is contained. Finally, in the evenings we get another tripod soup.

If there is no work to do, we can survive on this amount of food if necessary. But what work we are obliged to do! Immediately after the meals comes the order 'Get ready!' and the teams, each of ten men, assemble at their vehicles, small four-wheeled carts or two-wheelers with long shafts. They only have a wooden hub and some wooden axles. Eight men then go to the towropes left and right at the front. There are slings on them that go over the right or left shoulder, so that there are eight prisoners of war pulling on either side. With time, however, another way of pulling the wagons develops in which there are two wooden rails with two men pulling them, holding the rail either in front of their stomachs or behind their backs.

Many prisoners of war know this kind of work from the main camp, having had to haul wood in the same kind of carts from the woods 23 kilometres away. Once the guard commander has counted us, he gives the order to fall in. The leading cart sets off and soon we reach the village where the exiles live; these former Tsarist officers and officials do forestry work here on the Kama. The wood loading place is 10 to 12 kilometres distant and the journey takes two or three hours. Fortunately the carts are empty on the outward journey as the road steadily climbs; this makes it easier on the return, but the generally poor state of the road impedes us considerably. Between sixteen and twenty-two carts daily make their way one behind the other in a long train, which is visible at many points along the route.

When we arrive at the loading point, the wagon supervisor is ready to instruct the teams. A wood-cutting team is there every day to cut the necessary wood. Often it is not easy to work in this undergrowth, and we have to fight our way through to the tree trunks to be loaded. Once we have loaded the tree trunks, with great difficulty, 1.2 to 3 cubic metres being the norm per cart, then it becomes even more difficult to get out of the woods and back to the track. We have learned that these difficulties can only be overcome by working together as a team. The more we build ourselves up bodily, the more touchy we become. It is very important to work together with similarly tempered comrades.

The Anti-fascists are opposed to our requests as they regard all our group bearing the number 24 as black sheep. We are at least open among ourselves and no longer have to deal with troublemakers or informers. Our group leader is the army captain Bruno Schäfer from Kassel, who, as a Romanian prisoner of war, belongs to the few who have remained unpolitical and has not broken his oath of allegiance. The remaining members, apart from me, are Captain Wassmann, Lieutenant Haber, Second-Lieutenant Dr Meier, Second-Lieutenant Kommescher, Lieutenant Hax, Pharmacist Wendt, and Senior Paymasters Becker and Neun.

On our work trips I often think about a book that was left in Block VI. It had the title *We Surinam Slaves* and concerned the fate of the natives of the Dutch colony of Guyana. How I envy those slaves in comparison to our fate in 'the most socialist country on earth!'

Work has begun in the camp on the construction of two wooden barracks that are being built into the earth. We have to haul the necessary wood for them once we have returned from our grand tour, from the afternoon to late evening.

I have fallen out with my former comrades Sacha and Pfeiffer, who have both joined the Restoration Proposition, the wording of which was composed by the teacher and former flak captain Röckmann. After some hesitation they eventually signed the Restoration List. As I had noticed from their discussions in the last days at Block VI, they regretted having backed the wrong horse and they are now concerned with eradicating this error. They have been moved by Hartmann, the activity leader of Nunnery Camp, to Jelabuga and there joined the League of German Officers. As a reward Pfeiffer is able to work as a laundryman, and Sacha as the leader of the harbour workers. Knackstaedt and Keeler have already been taken back to the main camp because of illness and there are now only Götz and myself from Block VI here. We have become close and are good friends.

Second-Lieutenant Hax, a naval officer from Berlin, died in the camp from dysentery. The camp doctor, Dr Schulz, the former detachment doctor with Hermann, had not thought it necessary to send him to hospital. In order to imprint his death firmly in my mind,

I asked the ambulance nurse to strip the dead man. Shattered and with clenched teeth, I stood before the corpse. Hax too was a Stalingrad prisoner. A few weeks ago we had worked together as 'white slaves of the twentieth century' as we ironically described ourselves in the pulling of the cart. He had fortunately survived the spotted fever period, which soon after we were taken prisoner had done away with tens of thousands of our comrades. Now, due to the inhumanity of a German doctor clinging to his post, he has perished miserably! Our indignation is great, even among the members of the League of German Officers, and we want to punish Senior Surgeon Dr Schulz. It is said that he comes from Glogau. The Russians also seem to want Schulz removed from his post. His successor, Staff Surgeon Dr Kunde, appeals to us twice as much because of his humane nature.

The first 'Königsbergers', as we call those captured at Königsberg, have arrived in the camp as reinforcements. This is the first time that we have been able to speak personally to men who were captured shortly before Germany's collapse. They reported how the Red Army soldiers in East Prussia had played havoc as 'defenders of culture', and of the cruelties committed against women and children. Truly worthy Soviet men! Finally we warned these men, who were telling us such unbelievable things: 'Don't talk about it, always think about it!' And this Red Army was praised and cheered on the 9th of May by the traitors as liberators from Hitler's yoke!

From one Königsberger prisoner I also discovered that my former platoon leader, Second-Lieutenant Peter, with whom I had wanted to flee shortly before being taken prisoner, had appeared in the Königsberg cauldron as a German lieutenant with the Knight's Cross under special orders from the Red Army.

Soon the camp senior, Hermann, will have to go. His position in the camp has become untenable after the death of poor Hax. In addition, a large proportion of the camp inmates are undernourished and have to be brought completely exhausted to Jelabuga. Hermann was even ready to chase the prisoners of war tasked with building rafts stark naked into the Kama in the cold days of October. When finally, trembling all over, they pleaded to return to the camp, he refused them, saying: 'You must fulfil your norm!' The craziest incident, however, was that Second-Lieutenant Nöther, a district court lawyer from East Prussia, was shot by the Russians one night. He had crawled through the forbidden area to get some potatoes from the field immediately bordering the camp. Nöther was the father of three children. As my new group leader Hereus said, he unwillingly opened his mouth too wide. Hermann had been warned two days previously by the Russians who had found tracks in the forbidden area, but he did not think it necessary to pass on this warning to the camp inmates. In our eyes he is equally responsible for Nöther's death because he did not speak up.

Hermann's successor is Captain Korff, a Hamburger, who brought a normal human tone back to the camp. The company commanders Hardt and Weiler, who have long been members of the League of German Officers, were angry that Korff had been appointed camp senior, although he was a new prisoner with no political merit. Korff might not have been able to do much for us with the Russians, but by his behaviour he saw to it that the general atmosphere in the camp, especially the tone, was raised. It was agreeable to see that he was sober in every way. For our new political advisers, Ridder and Konsorten, he was naturally an obstacle, but they could not touch him.

Other elements had also arrived with the Königsbergers. Above all there was Captain Hereus, a lawyer from Bonn, with his divisional comrade. Lutz, as they call him, is a typical opportunist. As he said to me in our first discussion, to which he had invited me one evening, he had been sent here by Hartmann in order to clarify the true situation in Germany. I laughed inwardly as he tried to explain the true events in Germany, as he was too young to have correctly understood the political situation in Germany during the period 1920 to 1933. I was tempted to say: 'Yes, grandpa, you are right!'

Meanwhile he has already made progress. As a platoon commander, he goes behind the vehicles with a measuring stick. He has attained his goal. He does not need to do physical work. He likes to politically assess other prisoners and take these written assessments via the Anti-fascists to the Russians. It is disgusting when one hears of such people. God be thanked not all are like Hereus!

There is Gerhard Schinnerling, a senior naval officer cadet and a son of Chemnitz city. With his poems, which are inspired by the wood trips, he prepares many a happy hour for us. Through our joint love of words we become very close and enjoy talks that enable us to forget the bitter reality for hours. Rilke, Binding, Uhland, Möricke, Eichendorff and others are our companions. We have not forgotten our views of the beauty of nature, despite the difficulties of our existence, and every day there is a new wonder of godly creation to astound us. Although our stomachs are empty, we also take the mushrooms that grow along the way. These are then cooked in the evening and provide a little supplement to our sparse nourishment. This way we also eat all kinds of mushrooms that are not considered poisonous but are known to be inedible. Hunger drives everything in!

Today the emigrant Maurer came and left a Russian order. We have to remove our badges of rank and decorations. Through Ridder, Weiler and Hardt those prisoners of war who had burnt their decorations were denounced and sent to the punishment company in the main camp, including the veterinary surgeon Dr Güldenhaupt, who was in the punishment company for three months.

THE FLOUR AND BRICK TRIP

The frost has still not won: the sun is still coming through in the daytime. Daily, however, we expect the snowfall to start. Slates are being prepared for our camp bakery that is to be built so that we don't have to bring the bread from Jelabuga. The brickworks are only a short distance beyond Jelnie.

Four wagons set off, the crews taking two days' rations with them. Flour for baking will also be brought back. We have to collect it in Jelnie. I am happy that my sledge crew is with the flour collecting party.

We set off early in the morning. As the Russian responsible for the expedition, the deputy camp commandant comes, together with the supply administrator Grotthoff and a sergeant, and another Asian, whose face is strongly pockmarked.

As the Kama is not yet frozen over, we have to use the land route, which is several kilometres longer. It is 18 or 20 kilometres to Jelnie. About halfway along the stretch lies a brook that we have to cross. The journey there goes relatively quickly as the wagons are empty and the track looks good. When we reach our destination we have to wait an inexplicably long time until we get the flour. As we start the return journey it is already long after midday. On the way we catch up with the brick carriers, who had set off straight after lunch. The roads are deteriorating as the sun shines strongly after midday, and the weight of the carts, each carrying four two-hundredweight sacks, is very great. It is not easy either for the wagon drivers; because of the way the carts are made, the loads have to be well forward so that the carts are not broken. It has already happened to one cart. As the wagon driver I take particular care, not wanting to attract the scorn of the whole team, apart from which the strain on my comrades is great enough.

It is already beginning to become dusk and we are first at the brook. Grotthoff makes a mistake again and lets us stop here. What stupidity! Full of concern, I think of the marshy section ahead of us. I had already considered the return journey and what it would look like now. The little wooden bridge with the steep slope is going to be particularly dangerous.

The night sinks down around us. We have advanced several hundred metres, but now it is quite impossible to make progress. Again and again a cart sinks fast in a hole. The next cannot overtake as the track is too narrow, and we are obliged to help or to let others help us. Our strength is running out. In order not to run into danger and have the cart overturn – which could have serious consequences for me – I clamp the shaft fast under the axle so that I am lying more on the ground in the mud and dirt as I go along. It is a relief when I swear. I complain about the whole system and the idiot Grotthoff. It is a shame that I cannot speak Russian! But if Grotthoff and his Asian have noticed what is wrong, they remain very quiet – which means that Grotthoff has gone on ahead and is now waiting until we have made our way through the marsh. It is a marvel that none of the carts has fallen from the narrow wooden bridges and landed in the stream, which is four metres deep. It must already be midnight before the last of the carts is finally through. Another short rest and then we drive on. With failing strength we manage the last few hundred metres to our goal. Some prisoners are standing ready to unload the carts in the camp. Incapable of doing anything more, we stumble into our shelters.

The next day brings us yet another woodland tour. We are not here to recover but to work! There is no plan of action. Care for the people is here a foreign notion, and quite openly misused by the camp commandant for his shady dealings, without us being able to do anything about it. The Germans provide him with odd job services. Korff is also powerless against this. Should he not stay, another will come in his place and our situation will be even worse.

The men who went to the brickworks are now also back, arriving a day later than us. As the prisoners of war had already eaten their rations – which had been estimated to last two days – on the first day, they have been starving for fifty hours. With the inadequate food, the high expenditure of energy, and another long night in which they were locked in a stable and had no sleep because of the cold, several were so run down that they had to be taken to the sickbay. What we experience here is criminally nonsensical and yet we must remain silent. Germany has capitulated unconditionally and the Russians keep us permanently aware of it. For me, it seems pointless doing anything against it. With all my energy I have to get through this time and drift along with the mass without losing my way. I often discuss the situation with my comrade Otto Götz. We have become good friends during this time. With gritted teeth and fists clenched in our pockets, we look disdainfully upon the events of this 'Pigs' Fiddle', as we call it.

Schinnerling is ill. Apparently he also took part in the brick trip. The symptoms of his illness are quite unusual. When he moves, he cries out with pain. The doctor thinks it is rheumatism. Hereus is of the opinion that Schinnerling wants to avoid working and convinces the doctor of this too. I am angry that Hereus found it necessary to say such a thing, when his every effort is made in order to get a cushy job. Dr Kunde says that Schinnerling needs to go to hospital. I too should go back to the camp to recuperate and the camp commandant, 'Jumbo', agrees.

WINTER IN XILTAU WOODLAND CAMP, 1945/6

Now winter has finally won the victory. Wherever one looks there is snow and ice. The Kama is frozen over and it is no longer necessary to bring supplies across the river by barge. But other routes too are closed off by the Kama ice road. Our trips to Jelnie for flour go along the river. Orlovka, too, which is about 10 kilometres downstream on the same side of the Kama bank, becomes ever more frequently our regular destination. Because of the snow, in place of the carts we get sledges that work well for carrying wood and our team is reduced from ten to eight men.

We now have two regular treks: the woodland route and the Kama route. First we carry to the camp the tree trunks that have been felled in the wood. On other days we go by river back to Orlovka, where the wood for the prisoners of war in Hilweg Woodland Camp is taken over and transported further.

In the woods we also have to shovel snow by the cubic metre to reach the tree trunks that were felled in the summer, but at least there is no wind here in the woods. The extensive woodlands do not allow through the strong winds that flourish in the river valley. Once we have left the wood and are approaching the river valley, the icy wind picks up, penetrating through all our items of clothing. So that our noses and the other parts of our faces do not freeze, we have prepared nose and face protectors. If a normal central European saw us now he would think that we have come from a masquerade. Felt boots, which we have received in place of our bad footwear, some of it no more than cloth, quickly become useless. Especially when we go along the Kama they often get wet, as there is water in certain places where there is a gap in the ice covered by the snow and the water is unable to freeze. From the sledge driver is demanded a high degree of concentration when we are obliged to go along the embankment by the mass of ice. The sledges are often then crossing a slope of up to 35 degrees and it often happens that they overturn. Fortunately accidents of this kind almost always occur without inflicting injury.

When we have a trip along the Kama ahead of us, our first task in the morning is to look at the wind. There is relief when it is coming from behind or at least from the side, a feeling of trepidation if it is blowing icily in one's face. On those days we haul the sledges with our heads bent right forward, our caps pulled down hard over our faces, nose and cheeks covered so that only the eyes are to be seen. It is even more unpleasant for the driver, whose face is more exposed to the wind and who needs his hands in the open, his poor-quality gloves providing little protection. Frequent freezing is the consequence. We keep looking to one side in order to prevent the bare parts of the face from freezing. Water runs down the nose and freezes in the nostrils. If we wipe off the drops from the nose with a glove, it soon becomes sore from the rubbing. Nobody says a word, the icy wind forcing us to keep our mouths shut.

There is a certain place on the return journey where we regularly stop. Here, with our backs to the wind, we talk about all sorts of things with our pulling partners. As we rummage in the memory box, time passes more quickly and the current misery is forgotten for a few minutes. Hardly anyone dares to think about the future for fear of going crazy. No spark of hope is discernible. Even the news that the captain brought us a few weeks ago – that we could send post back home – has proved untrue until now. Even if it were so, I have remained sceptical since my experience in 1943. We can only wait with gritted teeth and ask God that he will make it possible.

Japan has also capitulated a few weeks ago. There are whispers that the Americans have dropped atomic bombs, which made the Japanese stop resisting immediately. On the last trip to Jelnie we saw a banner on which could be read – as our interpreter translated – 'After the victory, fasten your helmets tighter! Now the Japanese have been beaten we must arm ourselves against the western capitalists and their bourgeoisie!' That is the true story of this country! Although the Comintern has been disbanded, we follow as before the goal of world revolution by the proletariat. I believe that the western democracies will wonder again about this Asiatic sphinx.

The constant sledging work drains the last strength from our bones. New prisoners from the main camp are constantly replacing our sick. Until now about a thousand men have gone through the camp, which has a strength of about four hundred.

We also have to bring from Bonjuga, some 16 kilometres distant, our food supplies, principally potatoes and white cabbage. The potatoes are so inexpertly stored that we conduct a serious discussion about whether any schnaps factory in Germany would take such muck. Farmers in Germany would not have given these potatoes to the pigs! But we eat them as we have nothing else. Ottel and I are certain that we rejected this rubbish in Block VI, but there is nothing we can do about it here. The informers are too numerous to discuss this subject. We complain a lot, especially about those who find their way to the League of German Officers, but that is as far as it goes.

Christmas is over and the New Year has begun. The holidays were really days of rest for us. What the cooks prepared as additional dishes was consumed with our normal food weeks ago with our consent. Despite the general depression there were some men who took on additional work after the day's labours in order to get the whole camp community out of their lethargy and forget their misery for a few minutes.

The unhappy brick trip has claimed a victim. Schinnerling died in hospital as a result of the consequences of this trip. That which had originally been diagnosed as rheumatism was in fact blood poisoning caused by a foot wound that Schinnerling had suffered on the brick trip. By the time it was recognised, it was already too late.

I am very sad and still cannot accept that this big youngster with a noble heart is no longer alive. Above all, I think of his mother, a widow now waiting vainly for the return of her only son. I am filled with bitterness but nevertheless we must keep our emotions firmly in check, or we would go crazy. Not only not thinking, but not brooding! We concern ourselves with optimistic things and in this way try to forget our pitiful existence! Rilke gave me much strength at this time, as did Goethe's *Faust*.

Today our group is back on duty again to fetch potatoes from Bonjuga. It is going to be a long day. The sky is grey and the trip would be bearable if there were no wind to freeze our nostrils. After half an hour we reach the next village, where some try to exchange their monthly soap ration for a piece of bread. The population are already standing in wait as we march in. We are greedy for that rare item soap, which we need more urgently than unwanted bread. And even if it is only a little piece of several hundred grams, the stomach also cooperates somewhat.

Now we have a lovely stretch ahead of us to the stream from Xiltau to the town on the opposite bank of the Kama. Finally the river bank is reached and once we have crossed the river there are still several hundred metres up the apparently steep hill until we are in the town to collect our goods from the shop concerned. It is just as well that this slope has to be climbed with empty sledges.

Our leader, a cunning old Russian whom we call 'Egghead', leads us this way and that through the poor streets. Drawn up at the first collecting point, we wait almost two hours, but in vain. Our morale is already very poor, and dawdling about until dark makes matters worse. We go back with empty sledges after endlessly tramping here and there through the streets of this Tartar town.

Outside the town we stop at a collective farm. At last we can start loading the sledges. What is here exaggeratedly described as 'potatoes' is again little more than a frozen-together clump, indefinable and disgusting. Have they not got anything else? But it is no wonder when one sees how the 'agronomists' here protect the potatoes against frost.

There is a heap of hips lying in a corner. If we are careful, we can pinch a few, but the manager soon notices and we are obliged to stop.

At last we can set off back. Were we the first to get loaded? The way back down to the bank of the Kama is a problem in itself. First, we have to stop. The rope is taken to the rear so that the sledge is not hauled but slowed as it runs down the hill. Carefully we let the sledge begin to slip down the hill. Soon the speed increases and the sledge driver has his hands full keeping the sledge from racing down the slope. Our crew cannot hold it back. The sledge has a will of its own and races on. Only with difficulty is the sledge team ahead of us able to jump aside. Already the sledge has turned over and the sacks of potatoes have fallen out in the snow.

Only with great exertion can most crews get down this hill in one piece. The loading of the overturned sledges imposes a new delay.

As we start off again, it is already becoming dark. A light snowfall begins and in no time at all it is dark and the track hardly identifiable. Unfortunately it is also a new moon. One man must now go several steps ahead to make out the route. The pulling is even harder and the atmosphere even more irritable. But the complaining makes it bearable. We keep coming off the track, simply not seeing where to go, despite the scout. Constantly the sledges get stuck in the snow and can only be got going again with the help of two or three other teams.

We become stuck in the middle of the wasteland of snow. 'Egghead' has already gone ahead in his horse-drawn sledge to the next village to warm himself. He knows that none of us will try to run off. We are much too weak to get up to such tricks, but anyway – Where would we go? We had our last meal this morning at 6 o'clock. Now it is about midnight and we have already been eighteen hours on the way without any food. On top of this we all have cold noses as a result of the snowfall.

At last the last sledge has reached the village and we can set out on the last stage to the camp. At last there are some weak lights visible in the distance that must be Xiltau. But the route is still long enough. As we stagger through the camp gate, the camp senior waiting for us at the gate says that the time is 3.15.

An unaccustomed event has occurred: the whole camp can send home a postcard. They are double postcards with writing in the Russian and French languages. Only the upper half of the card can be written on. With the scepticism I have acquired from experience over the previous years, I write the following: 'My dear Ilse, after long years of scary uncertainty about you and our loved ones, you can put aside those things about my fate. I am healthy and hope to return home soon. Please greet my loved ones, especially my dear parents. I wish you all the best and am with hearty greetings and heartfelt kisses ever your Adelbert.'

This was the only opportunity I had of playing fast and loose with my name. Should a card really arrive in Germany, then fine; if not then it could not be misused for propaganda purposes. Now we would see what would happen. Today is the 15th of January 1946.

My birthday has already passed – it is the fourth that I have endured as a prisoner of war. By general decision every birthday boy in the camp gets a whole loaf and a small portion of sugar, as well as a double helping of warm food. In some camps there was even a work-free day for the birthday boy. For every prisoner the greatest wish is at least once a year to have a whole loaf and to be able to eat more than the few hundred grams we get daily. I dreamt of this weeks ago. It is a similar feeling to what a little child gets before Christmas.

From newly arrived prisoners we discover that Nunnery Camp has been cleared of Germans apart from a few exceptions, and that Japanese, our former allies, are being accommodated there. There has been a rumour going round for several days that we are going back to Kama Camp and that the Japanese will replace us here. It would be so good to get out of this bone-crusher that few of us dare believe it.

The arrival of spring has already passed, according to the calendar, though 'General Winter' still holds the sceptre. But on the 1st of April 1946 quite suddenly it has become warmer. The warmth starts a general melting of the snow and driving with sledges along the Kama is no pleasure any more. If it goes on we will soon see the ice melting and the river running again.

BACK TO THE MAIN CAMP

This morning the order comes quite suddenly for the whole camp to march off. It is the 7th of April 1946. Only a few will remain here to advise on and hand over the equipment. It is mainly members of the League of German Officers who now, in the haste of the break-up, cheat us of the items we have been saving for Easter. But that is our least concern. We are lucky that we can now take the sledges over to the other bank. If the Japanese come in the morning they will have the problem of very cracked ice.

We reached Kama Camp in Jelabuga after a very strenuous march. As we went past Nunnery Camp we could see for ourselves that the Japanese prisoners had arrived.

Once we have gone through the obligatory delousing, which is conducted for every arriving group, we go to Block 8 as preliminary accommodation. God be thanked, now we can rest for a little. Full of pleasure, I see again trusted faces in a row of comrades and establish that they are the same old crowd.

To my great regret I discover that the defender of Veliki-Luki, Lieutenant-Colonel von Sass, who was taken to Moscow several weeks before the closing down of Block VI, has been hanged by the Russians. Captain Knauff, who was in the lieutenant-colonel's regiment as a company commander, was sentenced to fifteen years' hard labour. A show trial demanded its victims yet conceals the fact that a single reinforced German regiment was able to resist several Russian divisions for several weeks and inflict heavy losses on them.

I have even met a person from back home: Captain Karl Kriebel, who was captured at Königsberg. As children we lived on the same street and now we meet here like this, far from our homeland, thousands of kilometres from our loved ones. Despite everything, the world is so small. A year ago I met Senior Corporal Karl Meier here, whom I also knew from my childhood. He brought me indirect news of my wife, whom he had seen on his last leave. At the moment he is on a collective farm commando near Kasan.

Hereus has done it again! He is a doorkeeper at the kitchen. His glutted face shows that it brings him something.

The cultivation of the land has begun like last year, the only difference being that it is conducted on a still bigger scale. No wonder, as this year the main organisers are experienced League of German Officers members, who presented themselves as farmers and provide great assistance to the Russians. New spades have been produced by the hundred. But also the old valued pulling of ploughs and harrows has been brought out to humiliate us. This time they even call out the weakest, that is the men of Work Group III, who are harnessed to the plough in teams of twenty-five men and are referred to as the 'Emergency Standard'. And so one can see the unusual picture of an old colonel next to a young second-lieutenant, who from his under-nourishment already looks like an old man, sharing the work with the sling around the neck or the stick on a rope in front of them.

Dr Schuster, the long-trusted camp doctor for 'restoration', deals here in many different cases not in the interest of his fellow prisoners, but rather for the Russians, who could otherwise relieve him of his post.

For offences against the order – i.e. stealing food or the incorrect planting of seed potatoes – the punishment is the lock-up.

And how does it look for the Japanese? They too go to work in small columns to fields a bit further from us, but still within sight. They perform their work in a leisurely way. There is no urging them on by their own people. When a Russian once failed to hit a Japanese sentry, the team leader, a Japanese colonel, gave the order to do it, despite the offensive cursing and threatening by the sentry at the baffled Germans watching.

How the marches can change. In the mass quarters of Kama Camp, in which even the corridors serve as accommodation, and the beds in the hall are stacked three high, a bad atmosphere prevails overall. The cause of this atmosphere is the demoralising work of the activists.

The friendships that have been made here are doubly valuable, despite the hunger and the mental outrages that are repeatedly attempted. Many were already thieves because they miss the nicotine or because they can see pieces of bread lying about. Thus everyone knows that no comrade has more than he himself, with the exception of certain 'experts' of the League of German Officers who hoard resources and profit at the expense of the community.

IN SELONI-DOLSK CAMP

I have been waiting for two days now for the call for transport in the Kasan direction. The precise objective is not known by any of us. Our transport commander is Cavalry Captain Eichhorn, who has been an Anti-fascist for years. His need for admiration always gains him a good position. The Russians are naturally touched by the cooperation of such 'gentlemen'.

The former Second-Lieutenant Wild, an old prisoner who was given the name 'corpse-robber Wild' after meeting the Stalingrad prisoners, is also there. As an old member of the National Committee and as an activist he was naturally a brigadier. Actually one may no longer say 'National Committee' and 'League of German Officers', as several months after the capitulation both establishments were disbanded. Every camp now has an Anti-fascist committee with a senior activist or so-called propagandist. Naturally the radical leftist prisoners of war were preferred for these posts.

After a two-day journey on a Kama steamer we came to Kasan. In embarking at Jelabuga I saw the Guards lieutenant-colonel for the last time. However, I avoided being seen by him. From Kasan we had to go about another 30 kilometres to Seloni-Dolsk ('Green Valley'), which lay where the Trans-Siberian Railway crossed the Volga. We were accommodated in a newly erected camp standing in the grounds of a factory. The camp had formerly been occupied by Russian convicts, but for us, with our previous experience, it makes a passable impression.

Right at the start the Minister of the Interior of the Tartar Republic appeared and told us in quite clear words that we had to work. There would be no cases of refusing work and they would only make things worse for us if we tried. I had my own thoughts about this.

Eichhorn put his back into it. As I learned, as leader of the punishment company he put Lieutenant-Colonel Hilsheimer, an old Knight's Cross holder, to do the dirtiest work.

I tried to explain that the whole camp profit came in one pot, as did the so-called 'additional supplies', but he rejected this and sought to attack me openly, boasting of his 'years long service in the Russian administration'. Literally he said: 'As others were banging at the door I was already busy in the cause of reparation.' He remarked provocatively on my troubles in Nunnery Camp at the beginning of

May 1945 but I kept quiet and refused to be drawn on the subject.

As a member of the 'Helmerding Saw', also known as the 'Singing Saw', I was set to work in a group consisting of twelve men. Our work is not easy, as we are part of a continuous work process and a considerable part of the production depends upon our efforts. We move the timber from a conveyor belt to the saw and then cut it into previously marked lengths. Then it is moved on further on another conveyor belt and allowed to fall into a bath.

Until this point I had yet to come across a Russian civilian. The whole factory is guarded. As in the camp, high watchtowers stand at the outermost corners of the grounds with sentries on them. It is therefore not possible to bring something out of the factory without permission. Our guards roam everywhere in the factory and we too can move about freely within the factory. The workers are mainly Tartars, while the manager and leading personnel are Russians. The first are friendly towards us, but themselves are so poor that they are unable to bring us things to eat; nevertheless, the whole sense and purpose of the prisoners is directed at getting something extra to eat.

Our sawing group is very sensible. Some intriguers were cut out right from the beginning and so we are able to ensure that within our sawing group everything is thrown into one pot. Without difference, everything is shared out equally at the end of the month. Unfortunately there is very little and it comes to barely 30 to 35 roubles per month. The so-called 'normal bread' is also shared out equally.

The workers told us they had been paid no money for several months, but they receive vouchers for food in the canteen. The rest of their earnings go to compulsory state funds. This was already being done during the war. How the workers were made to take on this compulsory acceptance of obligations they demonstrated with obscene hand gestures.

For several days our group has been working in the bakery. We have to take the flour from the mill, which is about 300 metres away, carrying the 60 kilogram sacks on our shoulders. There were forty-five sacks on the first day for each one of us to carry. The evening found us crawling back to camp exhausted and weak at the knees. But we had been able to carry on for the whole day, and that was the main thing for us. If we only get dry, freshly baked bread, and in the afternoon a pastry made with flour, salt and bran, we get enough envy from those who would have liked to have been with us. But it was because we had achieved this through our commitment that the head of the bakery called for us again. I am happy now to be in a situation where I can support individual comrades. The most impossible hiding places have been devised for smuggling flour from the mill or the bakery into the camp. If we are the first to get through the searches at the mill or bakery, then we have as good as won, for the camp guard has become friendly towards us. It is actually the first time that a Russian duty officer has dealt with us kindly.

How has the work gone in the mill or bakery in which we have been working for more than ten days already? If a railway wagon comes, we have to unload it. The railway official opens the sealed door and we can begin unloading the grain. On the ramp stands a large decimal scale on which the grain that we shovel into sacks is weighed. The railway official stands as controller next to the scale and notes the weight on a list that finally ascertains any discrepancy that has occurred during the long journey. The mill people try to cheat the official in all sorts of ways. It could be that the wagon has been stopped so that the underweight is shown, or that they have carried away unweighed sacks when the controller was not looking. I would never have believed that it would really work but we have already taken up to 1.5 tons from an 18-ton wagon, making such a row about it that the controller was unable to get it right. The miller and his men put the surplus into the mill. As payment, he then saw to it that we filled our pockets and bags with corn.

In moving flour from the mill to the bakery, we become muddy if the Russian workers who work with us take their sacks to the private quarters instead of to the bakery. Thus a sack of flour goes for the small sum of 200 roubles. It they so wanted – we had not yet experienced it – there were Siberian roubles instead. As payment we got bread from our comrades that they smuggled out of the bakery under their clothes. In addition, they ignored it when we opened a sack of flour in the mill and filled our tiny sacks.

Now and again appears one of those female creatures. As Soviet citizens with equal rights, they look quite funny in their working clothes, but they come and fill their tightly secured knickers with corn. It is also funny when they bind a life belt around their breasts and, after filling it with corn, they turn to a prisoner and ask for help in fastening it. In this whole business I have to keep asking myself: 'Who is deceiving whom?'

The Russians have imposed only one condition regarding our smuggling, which we agreed: not to act as competitors. They are particularly surprised over the amount I get away with. The smuggling gives me pleasure and I view it as a sport. I also regard it as a point of honour to help my hungry comrades and to do harm to the Russian state. I do not take anything in return for the smuggled items. We cannot change the times. We come here for our work like vagabonds and hardly one of us can still recognise that the tatters we carry on our bodies were once uniforms. My trousers show over a hundred patches and hardly any of the original material is discernible. But they are complete. Every time they tear they are sewn back together. If the sun shines while we are working, we go about stripped to the waist and even the tatters that we have as footwear are left in a corner, as we can go to and fro in canvas or wooden shoes for the time being.

Today we had a special pleasure. A Russian woman went past us carrying a child wearing a dress that had been sewn together from the curtains of a German Reichsbahn railway coach. She walked proudly past us in her new clothing bearing the DR insignia.

A quite wonderful event has occurred: for the first time a considerable amount of post has been distributed. Already a few weeks earlier I had heard that some post had been received from the homeland, but had not believed it. Now I can see it with my own eyes. If there is none for me, I can still hope. Perhaps they already know back home that I am alive. Are my darlings all well? My feeling is yes, but feelings can be wrong.

Weeks have passed on the land, meanwhile. The majority of prisoners in the camp have received news from home. Several cards bring heartache with their bad news. Poverty rules everywhere. The news from the Soviet Zone is particularly discouraging and stands in crass contrast to what the newspapers and radio report. There is still nothing for me. I am becoming more desperate. I sent a third card that I was able to write to the parents of my fallen friend Rolf-Werner.

A Russian film was announced with a lot of propaganda, and we made our way to the camp square to watch it. It was a film about soldiers in which the Germans are made to look ridiculous. Such lack of taste! I go back to the accommodation full of anger. If they have nothing else to show us, then I will not look at any films any more. It was embarrassing that not everyone went back to their accommodation immediately. Many were afraid and believed they would shame themselves if they did.

God be thanked! Today there was a lucky post delivery. A reply arrived in response to both my first cards written on the 15th of January and the 23rd of March 1946 and the senior Anti-fascist activist, Gilbert, handed it to me on the 21st of August 1946. I am overjoyed. My loved ones are all alive. What does it matter that my parents' house was bombed, and that all the things that I had left there have been destroyed. It doesn't matter. Again and again I read the words of my little wife: 'Beloved! God be praised, you are alive! We too and are all well. Your parents are now living with us here. Darling I am always with you! With my deepest, pining kiss, your Ilse.' The card has been on its way since May, so it has taken a full four months to get here.

ON A COLLECTIVE FARM
6th September 1946. For several days almost 150 prisoners of war have been gathering the potato harvest at the farm of the main camp. We had to march 18 kilometres to the farm. To my surprise, the camp senior here is Captain Hindenlang, who had sat with me in isolation when Block VI was closed down. His interpreter is my fellow-countryman Hans Mohr. The work that the Russians demand from us is strenuous and the accommodation appalling, as at times it rains through the torn tents. In compensation we help ourselves to supplementary potatoes; the Russians do not permit this, but the practice is appropriately camouflaged by Hindenlang and the booty shared out equally. I also meet here people I have not seen for a long time, including two of my comrades from Block VI, von Folksen and Oberhofer. Both were fortunate enough to be repatriated as invalids. I said goodbye to them yesterday. Hopefully they will get through.

The weather is very bad for the harvest. It has been raining for days already without a break. Nevertheless we have to go out day after day to lift potatoes from the clayey fields. Our clothing will no longer dry out. We have now been here for fourteen days and have another eight days to go.

It is evening. Ill-humoured, we lie in our damp tent and wait until the cook is ready with the potato soup. Suddenly Heuser, the group leader and an old activist, appears and gives the order to get ready to move. We ask, what is happening? The reply comes: 'The inspector from the Fournier Factory has appeared to fetch us in person. We have to fall in immediately!' He gets called the choicest names. It does not bother me. It will soon be 2200 hours. It is completely dark outside and the rain is falling in torrents. It would be better marching by day but unfortunately we are not given the choice. Our complaining and swearing finally stops without us getting our potato soup. This march back to Fournier Camp could be marvellous!

In single file to right and left of the actual track, searching for routes that are less muddy or already under water, we work our way forwards at intervals – depending on the size of the puddles – through the night. As my 'Progressive' wood and canvas shoes are soaked through, as is often the case, I take them off and carry on in bare feet. Then I suddenly stumble into a deep puddle and fall down heavily, and with the fall go my last restraints. Now I plod on forwards and straight on only! I have already lost a shoe, but complaining is useless. One just has to grit one's teeth and carry on. It doesn't matter. If one gets angry, one only damages oneself and becomes a bundle of nerves.

About a kilometre from the camp, as we are going straight down a steep bit of the road, I unfortunately collide with a thick stone. My shoeless foot disagrees with this and is very painful. I enter the camp limping badly, but soon I am fast asleep.

There are times when we have a day off, mainly on Thursdays. On such days I seek the company of my old, faithful friends whom I knew in the worst days of captivity. With a beaker of coffee, which we have recently been able to purchase for a few roubles, we pass the time in conversation or in thinking about our loved ones, exchanging our latest postal news. We sometimes get ideas from the post. On other days we avoid getting together as the 'gentlemen' of the National Committee look at us suspiciously if our meetings are too frequent.

This camp distinguishes itself especially for theft from comrades. It is sad and shattering, when I think that these men were once officers. When a comrade was given two months for having stolen

68 roubles, I decide to lead a fight against this criminality. I was successful in several cases and the thieves were then excluded from the community. However, I was unable to stop this thieving by comrades.

The year 1946 gradually comes to an end. The Russians say that Marshal Zhukov has fled to the Americans. With him were further eight generals. The truth or otherwise of this cannot be verified. Either way, the Zhukov portraits in the factory and various public rooms have disappeared.

ON THE VOLGA ICE

With the commencement of the icy period, the worst time of the year for us has begun again. The fight against the cold is the most frightful that a prisoner has to endure. Even the relatively warm rooms of our accommodation cannot make up for the eight to ten hours in the open air. But it is better than nothing. Unfortunately the food we eat at work in the cold is completely insufficient and has even become worse – it wasn't nice to begin with. The Volga has long since frozen over. Two big wooden rafts going to the Fournier Factory have become frozen in and have to be hacked free from the ice, pulled ashore and loaded by us.

We hold our heads when we hear the propaganda speeches or read the articles in the prisoner of war newspapers, in which Russian progress is praised in the highest tones. But the naked reality is here, among our cold, hungry bodies, reminiscent of the darkest Middle Ages. We hack away at the ice with crowbars and axes. Then an iron chain is fastened to a tree trunk, often a fat one. Teams of fifteen to twenty men, although sometimes as few as ten, then pull each tree trunk ashore, where another group is already waiting to roll the long and thick tree trunks on to a rack from which the trucks will be loaded.

The work is the most exhausting one can imagine. Even fur coats do not always keep out the wind that blows along the Volga. I vividly recall the Kama trip to Xiltau. In this work we earned virtually nothing. The calculation for payment of the fulfilled task – measured according to the State form – varied from 3 to 4 per cent. What made it even more difficult was that the bread ration for prisoners of war was reduced from 600 to 400 grams. The reason given was a crop failure in the Ukraine. In order to get the prisoners of war to make the final effort, the camp commandant could give those who overfilled their norm 200 grams from the bread allocation that was taken from the others.

For several days 'Herr' Kehrhahn, who in May 1945 took me with 'Herr' Colonel Esch to the lock-up in our camp, has been in our camp. The one-time political instructor and company commander in the League of German Officers has been sacked. With Work Level III, he is trying to be 'quite harmless'. As the son of a big landowner, is he really in favour of land reform?

Today is again particularly cold. We look at the thermometer in the hall – 33 degrees below zero! Fine, then we don't have to work today, as with a temperature below 30 degrees of frost we do not have to work. On the Volga the wind is certainly even colder! What are they saying there? We have to go out to work? It cannot be! But it is really so! Eichhorn personally, on the Russians' instructions, drives us out to work. His explanation: 'The Russians have said that not at 30 degrees but at 33 degrees below freezing is it work-free. The thermometer in the camp, however, shows 32.5 degrees below.' We reproach him; we know it will be even colder out on the Volga and we should not have to work in this sickening cold. Our objections fall on deaf ears with both Eichhorn and the Russians, so swearing mightily we go out to the Volga bank. The wind attacks us like a hungry wolf as soon as we are outside the camp. It is even worse on the tributary. Although everyone picked up a nose protector or some sort of mask as we were being chased out of the camp, some cheeks were already turning white on the way to the river. We check each other for frostbite. My left cheek has already become white. The blood returns after some vigorous rubbing with my hand. Now it is my nose's turn. I cannot keep my nose shield in place as my nose is running, and as soon as moisture from my nose meets the outside air, it freezes.

We get our working equipment from the workplace hut. The coldness of the iron bores through the gloves and our hands are like lumps of ice. No one is in a fit state to work. Guards and factory overseers start to complain and to hit out at us. Determinedly, we keep on looking for those places sheltered from the wind. Our feet are like ice. After we have been standing around for about an hour the camp commandant appears. It is quite apparent that nothing is to be done with us today and he lets us turn back. We all begin to leave at once. Suddenly, as a result of the weight of the many prisoners, a freshly frozen layer of ice breaks and several men fall into the water. My work comrade von der Heiden is one of the unfortunate ones. We run back to the camp so that we do not get pneumonia. For us there is yet another painful half hour before we are back in camp. The men are extremely angry with Eichhorn. He has shown quite clearly how he supports the interests of the Russians, as the position of a camp senior is a well fed one and the man does not have to do any physical work.

CHRISTMAS 1946 AND ITS CONSEQUENCES

The Christmas of 1946 is approaching. For several weeks now, as always before, we have been saving things, despite our hunger, for Christmas Eve.

A change has occurred in our camp life today. Eichhorn has been sent off to Kasan and Captain Gröppler, whom I already knew from Jelabuga, has replaced him. Gröppler is also an old League of German Officers member but he has his merits. He especially drew my attention when I recalled seeing him standing by the kitchen in Jelabuga, where he was waiting for a second helping. He is a tall chap with a big chest, so his yearning for the cooking pot is therefore understandable. Consequently I expect a little more understanding from him than we got from Eichhorn. His deputy, who is also the link to the NKVD, held the rank of captain in the military police in the 24th Panzer Division. Stratmann is very dangerous and delivers unconditionally on a plate to the Russians. Apparently, as a former military policeman, he fears complications.

With loving work, four of us have set up a small box in honour of this most German of all festivals. Although there are more than one hundred persons in our room, we are completely isolated from the outside world. The other prisoners have also made their tributes in small groups. Our greatest pleasure this year comes from the wax candles that we are able to buy at 5 roubles each. Pictures of our loved ones stand under the candles and provide the charm of home. Quietly the old beloved songs ring out. Our hearts tremble with homesickness and longing, and everyone is careful not to notice the others' tears.

To join my friends Horster, Schüler and von der Heiden come later Gerischer and my namesake Gerd Holl. Gerischer talks about his Erzgeberger homeland and their customs. The hours pass in quiet thoughts of home.

Towards 1100 hours we are joined by our team interpreter, von Bismarck – a successor to the brother of the 'Iron Chancellor', whose example is followed by Einsiedel and the League of German Officers. He tells me to join the night shift. I look at him and decline in quiet, clear words. Never in my life have I worked on Christmas Eve, and here, in imprisonment, I will definitely not do it! Apart from this, I know the orders from Moscow are that we do not have to work on Christmas Eve, except for vital tasks. After me, a further seven men refuse to work, although the most nervous ones dutifully comply.

The first day of the holiday passes peacefully.

My team commander Heuser, the political agent Hahn, who comes from Altena, and 'Herr' Arndt – also a tested member of the League of German Officers with considerable experience in kitchen and canteen matters – have protested to Stratmann and Gröppler about our refusal to work. Von Bismarck has already told me that we are to do the night shift.

The last week of the year is over. Tonight on New Year's Eve I am sitting with my friend Karl-Heinz Hintermeyer in a small group in the bath. After a good cup of coffee with which Hintermeyer serves his guests, I read an extract from the birthday speech of E.M. Arndt concerning the birthday of his majesty King Gustav of Sweden in 1809. When one reads this speech one can draw a good comparison with today. Then too there must already have been the same kind of low creatures in Prussia conducting the same kinds of traitorous role and crawling on their stomachs in front of him. But at the end of that time came Waterloo!

Before I went to this celebration I was called by the duty officer, who asked me why I had not gone on night duty. I put a counter question to him: 'If I work tonight, will I have to work tomorrow too?' He replied in the negative. 'Then I will work today, but definitely not tomorrow!' For me the Russians have authority, but not 'Herr' Stratmann, who wants to force me to make up for the missed shift of Christmas Eve.

For a good hour I have been standing with my work comrades on the wagons loading tree trunks. Since the frost arrived, the wood is brought here on the railway. It is crystal clear and cold at night. The work progresses only slowly. From time to time we vanish into a small wooden shack, taking it in turns to take shelter.

When the moment comes, we stop our work and sing out 'Happy New Year!' into the crystal clear winter night. It is the first time in my life that I have had to work exactly on the change of year. High up on the tree trunks I send my thoughts to my loved ones so far away.

The first day of 1947 passes quietly. Our talks draw us to the future once more and the possibility of our returning home. Would this year finally bring us the yearned-for journey home? We all hope so, yet without having any expectation of it. Certainly the first men had gone home in November, but who had been sent home? Real invalids and the sick! Two of my friends, Hugo Bartscher and Dieter Baumann, were among the lucky ones. With pleasure I heard that they had already called on my family and given them precise details of my fate until now. Now everyone knows!

On the morning of the 2nd of January I was preparing to go to work with my team as usual when somebody told me that I had been transferred to another team and had a late shift. I now belonged to the Dahlbeck team, which worked in the mine. That was fine for me, as it is quite warm in the mine. Haber was also transferred to another team.

Towards noon Haber and I received instructions to go to the camp administration. We obeyed. In Stratmann and Gröppler's accommodation was sitting our camp's NKVD officer, a young lieutenant who has not been here long. Second-Lieutenant Adam, one of the oldest prisoners of war, having been captured on the second day of the war, translated for us. Stratmann and Gröppler are hostile, but for me they are just hot air. The Russian wants to know from us why we have not gone to work! In clear, unmistakable words I give him the reasons. These are moral slaps in the face for Stratmann and Gröppler, who sit at the table with sunken heads as if they had still a spark of shame in them. On the report that the Russian lays down in front of us I can clearly read the signatures of the two scoundrels. I am pleased that Adam has translated word for word, in contrast to many other interpreters. I have also quite clearly explained that on the Holy Evening we had even less wanted to go to work when this suggestion was put to us. After half an hour of interrogation we were able to leave. It was clear to me that something was about to happen. The Russians could hardly leave us in the camp after my previous experiences.

VIA THE MAIN CAMP FROM SELONI-DOLSK TO MUNI CAMP

Two days after our hearing came a final interrogation, and by the 4th of January Haber and I no longer had to go out to work. Instead, we were told to pack our bags. We were given leather shoes from a store and a day's rations, and told to wait at the guardroom. After yet another thorough search of our baggage, we were led out.

The direction we took indicated that we were heading towards the main camp. This meant the punishment company. Now Rudi and I were also to join it. In view of the previous events, we have dropped the conventional formality and use the familiar *Du* for each other. We had known each other well for a long time and each of us felt that we had drawn even closer together through the recent events. Rudi was also a Stalingrader.

If only we did not have this damned waiting! We have been standing at the camp gate for quite a time. Ah, at last something is happening. A Russian appears, accompanied by a tall, lean Hungarian. I already know him. He is the camp senior. The administration of this camp lies in the hands of this Hungarian. To our great astonishment, the Hungarian says that we should report to the company commander of the German Work Company. Rudi and I look wide-eyed at each other. This means that we are considered as quite normal camp inmates.

My pleasure is great when I meet old friends and comrades here, such as Captain Wegener, Second-Lieutenant Mohr, and others. From Wegener I learn that Lieutenant-Colonels von Güldenfeld and Noffke are in the neighbouring barracks, in contrast to the other staff officers held under guard. How nice it is when one meets men who have proved themselves beyond reproach in the very worst of times.

The next morning we have to go out to work. It is the same thing everywhere: even if you arrive in the middle of the night you must go along with the others to the workplace. In this way I come down to the shipyard again. I can hardly understand how our factory could be so disorganised.

Ewald Korn, whom I knew from Block VI, comes to grief when a heavy iron block crushes both his legs. Fortunately no bones were broken. One thing I know for certain: during the war women worked in armament factories in Germany but not on the same scale as the 'equal rights women' here, who work the same hours as the men in the foundry and smithy. They do not make a pleasing sight in their dirty clothing. But youngsters too run about here in considerable numbers. Their heads are full of nonsense and they steal like ravens. When I pointed out to one of my comrades that a small fourteen-year-old lout was trying to steal his home-made pipe out of his trouser pocket, this hopeful Soviet youth threw a stone at my face in an unwatched moment. He was close to me and I was lucky that the stone did not go straight into my eye, but rather hit my lower cheekbone, which now hurts. Full of impotent anger, I curbed myself. There was nothing else I could do. Firstly I was too weak on my legs to be able to catch him, as he was faster than I was, and secondly his comrades would have stood by him if I had done what I wanted and given him a thorough beating. It is just like with the rats – one cannot do away with them!

8th January 1947. Within four days Rudolf Haber and I have experienced three camps. Yesterday evening we came with a task force from the main camp to the newly established Muni Camp, so-named as its inhabitants have to work in an ammunition factory.

During the war the factory had made munitions but it has now returned to peacetime production, which was why we had been moved from Camp 119/6 via the Main Camp 119 to Camp 119/5. Here I met more old acquaintances and friends from Block VI. A special treat was prepared for my arrival by Second-Lieutenant Breske, who gave me a large fish wrapped up in newspaper. He had smuggled it into the camp while unloading a railway wagon. Also, after a separation lasting almost ten months, I am once again back with my dear friend Otto Götz.

I left some good friends behind in Fournier Camp, but I met equally good friends here. And I remain only with comrades I knew before. Every unknown person is treated with caution, although the shared yoke of work causes joint complaining about the Russians.

From Captain Lieb I discover that Lieutenant Vogt, who was with me in Block VI, lost his life in a tragic manner. He was sitting with Lieb on a truck loaded with tree trunks that the Russians had not secured properly. On the slippery, snowy track the thick and heavy tree trunks rolled from side to side until one side of the cart collapsed and Vogt, who failed to react in time, was killed when the tree trunks rolled off. Lieb was able to jump off in time and escaped with shock.

I have found a good place to sleep next to my fellow-countryman, Captain Kribel. Every evening, lying on our beds, we had long chats about our lives and our home towns.

It gave us much pleasure having to work in the grounds of the Fournier Factory. Six days previously Haber and I had worked here from Camp 119/6, and now we were working here from Camp 119/5. Smiling, I told my friends from Camp 119/6 how the political worker Stratmann had had us moved to the punishment company.

We had to work not only on the slag heaps from the ammunition factory's furnaces but also on the coal heap where we had to unload the coal and shovel it upwards stage by stage from platform to platform. We were given the most unlikely tools for this work. I saw lying in the factory grounds a large cable drum complete with cable from the Duisburg Cable Works – a greeting from home.

As the town of Seloni-Dolsk is cleared of snow again by the approach of spring, a team of ten prisoners of war has to report every morning to the town authorities. A guard from the town, armed with an old rifle, takes us from the camp. Now and then a Red Army soldier also escorts us. With crowbars, wooden snow shovels and spades, we have the honourable task of clearing the refuse pits and public toilets of their dirt and rubbish.

My team leader, who came from Jelabuga several days ago, is the NKVD informer Lobhoff, who had not survived two days in Block VI and was moved on at our recommendation. He appears to have fulfilled his task in Jelabuga. It makes me wonder whether he would not soon have a responsible position here. He has already had a chat with his old colleague Stratmann from Fournier Camp. At the moment he acts harmlessly and tries to do his share of work as a team leader.

We see some crazy things. The whole town lacks drainage and it is lucky that everything is frozen and in this condition can be easily carried off on the truck. I have my own outlook towards work and am not shy about it. It's the same at home: if this kind of work is necessary, I do it immediately. But under these circumstances I find it doubly hard and difficult that the Russians treat officers of the German Wehrmacht like this. Unfortunately, some of the prisoners of war have lost their instincts for outrage. Hunger has reduced them so much that they take the frozen potatoes out of the worst filth and dirt to cook back in camp.

The dispute over the acceptance of the work performed is never-ending. If we do not achieve the amount of work set by the overseer, then he does not credit us with 100 per cent of the norm achieved and then we do not get the supplementary bread to go with it. Fortunately the allocation of bread here is not as precise as in Fournier Camp. Another, smaller advantage with this job is that at the end of the working day we do not have to stand around for another hour or more for a body search, which in the overwhelming cold is very unpleasant. Everyone who works in the factory has to submit to this daily.

I heard an outrageous story, which seems hardly believable, when I met some men who had been with me in the team company at Jelabuga in the summer of 1943. Corporal Jessen from the Aachen area told me that he, with more than two hundred men, had gone from Jelabuga in the summer of 1945 to a camp situated north of Kasan on an island in the Volga. Working conditions there were very bad and the food left much to be desired. The camp senior was Corporal van Alst, who, although he had sat in the prison at Jelabuga for almost two years and had been sentenced to death, had sold himself to the Russians. He had driven the men out to work with sticks, and, together with the Russian commandant, had stolen their food in such quantities that, when the ice froze in the spring of 1946 and the island was cut off from the rest of the world, there were so few supplies left that for weeks on end the prisoners were given just a bowl of cabbage soup and hardly any bread. The work demands, however, remained the same and more than 120 men died from this inhuman handling and its results. That was in the winter of 1945/6. In my mind I saw again the amateur boxer from Emmerich as he staggered through our prison, lamed in both legs, then the faces of Sergeant Köhler and other acquaintances no longer alive.

The truth of this atrocity was confirmed by other comrades who had been in this camp with Jessen. The prisoners of war were unable to protect themselves from this inhuman treatment, while the Russians kept a protective hand over van Alst. Herefurth, who was here in the camp, also heard about it.

A glimpse of light in the misery is another birthday. With much love and care Karl Kriebel has arranged a birthday dish for me and I am deeply happy with the evidence of unity with my friends from Fournier Camp and from here. How they managed to get the packages from Fournier Camp to here is a puzzle. The greatest pleasure of the day for me was two poems by Kriebel and Schroeter. Kriebel's poem was called *Belief and Prayer*:

> I believe in Germany like a God,
> even when the Devil is all over the world
> preventing us from returning to our country.
> I believe primarily in the right of our people in their
> deepest distress that lightens the darkness with its light
> and lets us find freedom one day.
> I ask with my deeds, and still fight to win,
> my life remains my duty and my prayer;
> I serve!
>
> I believe in Germany like a God,
> because duty to and the love of my people in my
> blood are the highest and holiest requirements!

Schroeter dedicated the following lines to me:

> Time does not fly past! If the enemy also gnaws at you;
> your heart cannot forget!
> Your faith does not diminish! Even if the courage
> within you wavers; your strength is not presumptuous!
> The enemy gives the heart strength in your beliefs,
> creating the courage of the brave!

Lohoff has done it! After some time in the main camp with the NKVD, he became the senior activist of the Anti-fascists. Now he is a colleague of Stratmann's once more. His predecessor, an Austrian who had not felt comfortable in his role as senior activist and exceptionally is a decent person, was pleased with this change from his unpleasant task. We are less happy, as Lohoff has already prepared a list that he has given to the Russians for a Judas bribe.

FROM SELONI-DOLSK TO SAPOROSCHJE

A rumour is going around that a large transport for some four to six hundred men is coming from the south. The reason is unknown. Some suggest a move to Ukraine, the more optimistic suggest it is for the journey home. I would not be surprised at anything for the most improbable things are possible with the Russians. One prisoner of war once described this country as 'a land of boundless impossibilities!' Unfortunately this has only had a negative sense until now.

The transport is formed up from the various 119 camps. Those concerned are certainly connected through the NKVD with the Anti-fascists. Next to be released are the inconvenient elements. It is naturally quite clear that in our camp the former inhabitants of Block VI are to be included. So when we board the train I meet up with a whole number of old comrades, some even from the two Kasan camps. It is always a great pleasure to meet up again. After a protest we are again given greatcoats, for it is still very cold on this 15th day of April.

'Herr' Eichhorn has fallen on his feet again. Having done a short course in Kasan, he is now in charge of our transport. The Russians know already those who are particularly suitable for such things. To our surprise, however, we discover that the food is considerably better than that on previous transports. The day-long railway journey is a relief for us all and many express the wish that this journey would last until our release.

The train is heading in a south-westerly direction and until we reach Charkov all routes remain open for the journey home. Soon, however, those in the know realise that it can only go to Saporoschje.

We get there on the 28th of April. Once everything is unloaded, we are taken to Camp 7100/5. Already the catchword is: 'Work in the Soviet Union is an honourable task for the German people! Put in all your strength for an increase in performance!' This makes it quite clear what is expected of us. We will now join up with other teams and keep on working hard.

The camp band prepares for us a progressive reception. This recalls to mind the head count in Jelabuga in April 1946 as we had to go to our individual accommodation to the sound of German marches played by the camp band. Our tattered and ragged clothes, with matching footwear, are all that's left of the once-immaculate uniforms of the German army.

There is also an old acquaintance of mine in Camp 7100/5, who has already graduated from the school in Moscow. The former Senior Paymaster Schmidt-Achat plays first violin here on the political stage.

With a great fanfare a message is read out, explaining that at the ministerial conference of the 'Big Four' in Moscow, a treaty was signed under which all German prisoners of war would be returned to their homelands by the 31st of December 1948 at the latest. For us this seems a very long time – twenty more months! – but at least we now have a firm date to look forward to. Apart from that, they cannot send us all home in December 1948. According to Soviet Union statements, there are still more than 840,000 German prisoners of war here.

I am pleased that some of us, including me, go to Camp 7100/1, where the main administration is located. With the Russians having moved all the less amenable prisoners out of Kasan, there is a crowd of us here who are not prepared to be led by the nose. From the first glance we realise that the majority of prisoners here are leading a miserable existence, which now, two years after the end of the war, is quite shocking.

It is really true that there is starvation in Ukraine. The people of Europe's breadbasket are starving. We can therefore be happy to still get our daily ration of 600 grams of bread. Some of the civilians here do not get as much, as we can establish from our work. A loaf of bread costs more than 100 roubles and a bucket of potatoes 150 rubbles. Many of the workers have to sell their clothes and shoes to enable them to buy essential things to eat. They stand in long queues in the mornings and evenings outside the shops, and each receives only enough bread for himself.

I cannot comprehend family life in this country. If, for example, the husband is working on a machine harvester, the wife will be busy on the railway. So each has his or her own separate workplace and that is where they get their food. It is often the case that a husband and wife see each other only briefly when they are coming from or going to work because one has the day shift and the other the night shift. The children are mainly left to themselves – and it shows. The tone of the Ukrainians is mainly very friendly, however, quite in contrast to the propaganda.

Yesterday, the 29th of April, we arrived at Camp 7100/1 at noon and had no peace until late at night, and yet the Russian camp commandant ordered us to go to work next day. Unhappy voices complained, but it seemed all the same to me as I knew what I wanted to do. Therefore I was pleased when this morning none of us got up to go to work. Even the nervous ones dared not swim against the tide. An hour-long discussion with the camp commandant, Captain Kogan, failed to persuade us to go to work.

Eichhorn is not comfortable. However, he has to deal with the will of the majority, who prefer 'Herr' Bender, who likewise has gained some merit in his work with the League of German Officers, and has caught sight of an ambitious comrade craving recognition. Captain Krause of our group is also his rival, with all those standing behind him who have never signed a reconciliation resolution and see in him their suitable representative. Those of us who were removed from Kasan as so-called 'black sheep' are quite numerous here. Our aim is to be independent of the fulfilling of the norm for the food entitlement, especially bread. Until now, the Russians have been very careful to provide the precise amount. We even get our cigarettes punctually, fifteen per day, while the teams only get five. I do not like seeing and knowing that we – in contrast to previously – get other rations than the troops. Our supplies are already insufficient, but the troops get even less!

After we had been working for several days in the 'Bone mill' brickworks, our group was sent to the oil factory. It is a pity when one sees how the poor troops were brought to the brickworks. The Russians had a good eye for dependable team leaders who managed the job without regard for their men.

When we first heard the words 'oil factory', we immediately connected it with oil cake and such, but this illusion vanished on our first day as the machinery here was built from an oil mill in Stettin. Did this also come from demilitarisation?

A special position was taken by the so-called 'WK men', or 'Hiwi' for short. Their leader in this camp is old Kahlbaum, formerly a hunting dog for Mangold when he was block senior of Isolation Block II at Jelabuga in the winter of 1943/4; he subsequently attended the Anti-fascist school in Moscow and is now the well-settled WK chief. The WK's role is to replace the Red Army soldiers guarding us. There are still one or two Russians with them, acting as supervisors.

The head cook, Second-Lieutenant Rose, a depraved Russian servant, avoids with effort and difficulty (and through the intervention of an NKVD officer) getting a sound thrashing when he tries to discover the names of some comrades who had torn down a malicious poster from a tree and thrown it into the toilets.

IN THE PUNISHMENT SECTION OF CAMP 7100/2

Conditions have now reached such a low point that on the 9th of May there is to be a work strike followed by a hunger strike. The team leaders have been informed. I myself hold back completely passively as on principle I do not want to be a group leader or anything like that.

Today is the 8th of May. It is very windy and working at the conveyor belt is not very pleasant, as the sand keeps getting into our eyes. An engineer has already reprimanded us for not working exactly as he wants. He does not seem to realise that prisoners of war would naturally oppose him. He will report it to the camp administration. Again I hold back, as I know that spies are at work here.

With Rudi Haber I go over the possibilities of progress in the Soviet Union, a discussion that is conducted in an entirely cynical tone and is unrecognisable as irony. The reason for this discussion was a story told to us by a Nuremburger who visits Rudi in the barracks in the evening from time to time. This man reported that during the last days of April he experienced an incident only possible here in the motor factory right behind the main camp. A young pregnant Russian girl went down to the toilets. He had already seen the girl several days previously staggering through the area and pointed her out to his comrades. On the day of the girl's confinement he saw a large number of men standing around the toilets. A Panjewagon had already appeared in which the young mother was laid down and covered with some cement sacks. The newly born child was wrapped in cement paper and laid beside its mother. Finally the wagon got under way. The traces left behind were strewn with sand and the 'Land of Socialism' had a new citizen.

That evening my friend Ottel and I enjoyed a special treat; we were able to purchase an egg each and cook them. Tomorrow is Sunday, which I want to greet with a breakfast of bread. It is already dark and I think about 2200 hours. Then a messenger comes and tells me I must get ready and come with all my kit. Five other men apart from me have received a similar summons: Eichhorn, Hindenlang and Kreise, the last two having been in Block VI, plus Putfarken and Jenatschek. It is immediately obvious to me that this is the result of a denunciation by one of the spies. I suspect Beltmann, a Baltic German who often acts as an interpreter and is much employed by the Russians. It is rumoured that he works for the NKVD.

Without being told where we were going, we were taken by truck to another camp. The Russian camp commandant and the NKVD chief personally saw to it that we were securely guarded. The truck stopped after a journey of about ten minutes. The guards took us to a washhouse and we discovered that we were in Camp 7100/2. All six of us were taken into a special zone and we now belong to the Punishment Section of Camp 7100/2, Saporoschje. Our commander is the former concentration camp inmate and Communist Hannes Schuster. We were not the first to have been delivered here, for sixteen officers from Camp 7100/4 were already here. We were moved in together and lay down to rest for the night, but the fleas prevented us getting any much-needed sleep.

Next morning saw us already at work at the 'Gorodok' building site. It lay immediately next to the camp and had a special fence around it with watchtowers. Here we could restore things. Eichhorn's conduct gave cause for a special inner amusement. He is upset and disturbed by being now in isolation after his year-long work with the administration. 'I will no longer take or lead a blind Red Army soldier to the shithouse!' he growls in his deep voice, the tall, gaunt cavalry captain with the obsessive desire for attention.

Being on a ten-hour shift, we regime inmates do not return to the camp. When I look at the men here in the Punishment Section, most of them for theft, my heart sinks. And I am unable to help! Little more than skin and bones, they slink about like predators, constantly concerned with getting hold of something to eat or smoke. Only extreme hunger and inhuman treatment can reduce normal men to this state. Many will find it difficult to find the right way again upon their return to Germany. Beatings by the so-called supervisors are part of the daily routine for these men. Especially hateful scenes occur at the gate in the mornings if one of them is late. This results in the whole camp waiting half an hour before the columns arrive to join the escorts for the three-kilometre march to the combine harvester factory.

I think back over the first day in the Punishment Camp. How our fate alters from day to day! As long as we still bear the designation prisoners of war it cannot be otherwise and we will get no peace. I have become like a rabbit locked in a cage and I have to hop wherever those people knocking against the wire want.

I can hear the noise through the thin wall. There are voices I know there. I immediately recognise Second-Lieutenant Ostermann, who tells me that Hoffmann and Geisberg are also there.

There was a strike in the main camp today, followed by a hunger strike. Altogether thirty-two men regarded as ringleaders were taken out and brought here to the Punishment Camp. They are of the opinion that the strike will not be successful, as the Russians have already identified the elements that gave them a helping hand. It is always the same. Denunciation!

I am waiting for the camp commandant to appear so I can formally protest about my transfer to the Punishment Section. That it will be unsuccessful is clear to me from the start. Schuster is careful and correct towards us, but not so much towards the men.

With pleasure I learn that the camp experts are known by the name 'Specker'. Little liked is the camp doctor, Dr Heinrichs, who ruthlessly sends the prisoners of war back to work, not writing them down as sick even when they can barely crawl. Like a cruel joke, a sign reading 'Work liberates you!' hangs over the Punishment Section. Whenever Mindak, the senior activist of the Anti-fascists, appears at the workplace we might almost think we have a catwalk model in front of us – he cuts such a figure in the various suits that he has made to measure for him in the camp tailors' shop, in contrast to the rags of the prisoners. There is a canteen in the camp under the supervision of the Anti-fascists, from which it is obvious where 'Herr' Mindak gets the money to buy a watch, for watches are expensive and valuable objects in this paradise. The conditions in this camp seem to me to be a small and poor imitation of the Soviet Union as a whole.

Fortunately there are also some respectable people here. I get to know new comrades, such as Laschtowitz, Stepat and Schurawa, who have become good friends. As they have already been in this camp for a long time and hold good positions in the factory, they help me when they can. I got to know them through my friend Otto Götz, who soon followed us into the Punishment Section because he had expressed ideas for escape. Karl Schurawa was a typist in his signals company and now, after more than five years, we meet up again by chance. My connection was also quite close with Fritz Laschtowitz, a Silesian second-lieutenant, who was taken prisoner after the capitulation in Czechoslovakia. Fritz is the eldest so has the nickname 'Father', while Wolf Stepat, the youngest, is known as 'Son'.

The cobbler for whom Fritz works gets us out of the Punishment Section occasionally in the evening. In long and anxious conversations we talk about the fate of our so heavily tested fatherland. We do not know how things are back in the homeland, despite the postal service, for hardly anything gets past the censors. We have not lost faith in our people, even if there are sufficient signs available to keep us doubting! Even the Russian propaganda is unable to influence us in our position. It is obvious to us that in difficult times we must continue straight and unwavering on our way without turning either to left or right. We know only one party, and it is called Germany! Only through unselfish work for the whole German people can we recover from the wounds that this unfortunate war has caused!

Without my knowledge, Fritz was able to get me into the Lowag Plumbing section. I am now working as a driller, which gives me the advantage of being able to remain in the camp.

Directly next to the Punishment Section stand some summer tents stuffed full of prisoners of war. One of the tents is set up as the workshop. Here, with trained plumbers and locksmiths, we prepare items for the combine harvester. Every eight to ten days these items are taken away by truck. The pay is good. I am like Croesus when I get 150 roubles for my first month's work. With my friend Otto Götz, who had joined us somewhat earlier, Korff, who had been the camp senior in Xiltau, Fischer, Selmer, Günther and Franke we form a small society that works well together. But we also get on well with the other work comrades. The (for me) unusually high rate of pay enables me to recover my strength a little, as I can buy things to supplement the food. It is certainly effective, for as soon as my stomach ceases to be empty, the world looks quite different.

Part of my earnings I use to buy English learning material printed in Moscow. An issue of *Greetings from the Front*, translated by Bernhard Isaak, is worth noting. On page 171 it describes how a female tractor driver had torn up some German graves after the inhabitants had been expelled from a village. The bones of the dead were strewn in all directions by the population and even the dogs played with them. When the tractor driver ploughed the land, she did not follow the straight lines of the fields but instead ground up the bones lying around everywhere with the caterpillar tracks.

Dysentery has reigned in our camp for more than two weeks, spreading more and more, so that the female Russian doctor is obliged to set up an isolation block. When one thinks that we are already living in 1947, two years since the war ended, then one asks oneself instinctively how can this be! Having already been forced to live here for two years, it is not difficult to puzzle it out. The insufficient and poor-quality rations mean that the prisoners of war can, without exception, be described as undernourished and they suffer chronic feelings of hunger so that they are constantly searching for supplementary foodstuffs. They thus come to the most absurd ideas that only a sick body can produce. There, where others perform their necessary functions, they pick weeds and grass with which to thicken their soup, imagining that it will satisfy them. They try to barter for fish, which in the warm times of year are very difficult to catch and are full of salt, and gulp them down. Their ensuing thirst is quenched with the usual unboiled tap water, or if that is unavailable, they will drink from almost anywhere, even in the most unlikely places. The unhygienic conditions in the kitchen considerably increase the danger of infections. Then there are the eating vessels, mainly made of zinc from the 'Sawod Komunar', that the prisoners bring with them. Although a considerable number of dysentery cases have already died in the town hospital, the food for the sick has nevertheless still not improved. The female Russian doctor, trying hard to ensure that none of the sick die in the camp, gives the sickest an injection that stimulates the heart for a short time. This means they die in the vehicle taking them to the hospital, but not in the camp!

The number of those succumbing to the epidemic increases every day. The healthy men all have their hands full at night trying to prevent their sick comrades from being driven out to work by dragging them into camp. In the mornings one can see as many as seventy men standing by the ambulance. When the time comes to break off work, the tall chief of the Propaganda Section, Lieutenant Makarenko, who makes a brutal impression, drives the pitiful cases to the camp gate with kicks and blows from his fists so that they do not escape!

This epidemic lasted almost a quarter of a year, carrying off many prisoners of war, and was reminiscent of the episodes in 1944 and 1945 in which ten thousand German prisoners of war died in the Saparoschje camps. The survivors then lasted longer than those affected by this current epidemic, who, like old men, weak and fragile, are merely shadows of their former selves.

Every four weeks a so-called Medical Commission took place – or, as the prisoners expressed it, a flesh exhibition. Many think like me that they are to blame, these women who call themselves doctors; they must be completely devoid of evidence when writing the prisoners off to Work Group I although they are not at all fit. I still do not succeed in appearing before the commission, as I have to report progress in front of these female deputies. This slave market is just like in the Middle Ages, determining what the slave prisoner of war is still capable of doing. Any differences of opinion among the commissioners on the work capability of those standing before them is then discussed. Typical 'evidence' for this is the crease in one's bottom and thigh!

Except for those working on production, the prisoners receive a very poor wage. Those in reconstruction can be pleased if the foreman, with cunning and malice (and nothing is without fraud here), drives the whole group for a few roubles. At least the group earns something, and the foreman constantly allocates some men a higher role than they actually performed. The rest get less. At the end of the month, the foreman shares out the money at his discretion, whereby he naturally gets the lion's share. Only very few foremen share out the money earned evenly.

But even the prisoner gets his 200 grams of bread and a cooked lunch so that he records a better percentage. In this way we are already doing up to 500 per cent of our work quota!

A new building is being constructed in the camp itself. Here work all those men who are not allowed to leave the camp because they are thought likely to try to escape and those awaiting sentences from the war tribunal.

There are two informers in the camp working for the NKVD, who have already delivered several comrades to the Russians at knifepoint. Foremost is the laundry supervisor, who wants to be a sergeant. Suspects are allocated to him and by listening to their harmless conversations he gets to know who eventually to report to the authorities. Often prisoners of war from other camps are sent straight to the laundry to sound them out on specific matters. The pinnacle of this dirty work came when the supervisor brought his best friend Rudi, a Saxon from Dresden, before the war tribunal and gave witness against him. Rudi was sentenced to fifteen years' hard labour. Many went the same way as Rudi, but even in the Tribune newspaper that we got from the eastern sector of Berlin, and other sources, the dirty sentiments of the alleged journalist were obvious.

A similar role was played by 'Herr' Lukviel, who purported to be a machine engineer. Through crafty conversation he tried to learn something about his victims so as to inform on them to the Bolshevists. A prominent job in which he was not pressured was his reward, along with other advantages.

The men were involved with the construction of the new building until dark. Anyone who resisted was driven on with clubs and other implements. Even on Sundays the men working on the new building were told: 'Get out and regain your honour!' Not only there but also in the factory there was work for us, and they liked it when the prisoners of war came on Sundays to clean up. It often seemed that Moscow did not take four days off a month!

Since I have been in the Lowag my health has improved a lot. It makes a considerable difference when one can buy supplementary items. The other members of the brigade also do not look bad. It is years since I had a feeling of gratification. I cannot say 'satisfaction', for which I must concentrate and eat fancy food.

The time flies for me as a drill operator. That I have to do this work standing up for hours without a break does not hinder me, for I get through it with a splash of water in my face and on my legs.

The conversations I have with the comrades of my brigade are interesting. There is hardly one that speaks well of the Russians. They care little for the 'Kanacken', as they call the Russians, but they can still adjust and feign interest if one of the Anti-fascists appears. I have to smile when Karl, a railwayman from Görlitz, recounts what he imagined about Russia. He says that he was formerly a Communist but had now had enough of it. The radio and literature he had been exposed to had presented the Soviet Union quite differently from the reality of it. When he arrived as a soldier in Ukraine in 1944 he was already disillusioned. He had always tried to find the roads but saw only country tracks. And for 'club buildings' he had looked for big structures but found only wooden hovels. A year ago, while in hospital for a stomach operation, he had been 'progressively' handled – he pulled his hands out of his pockets and showed me a wide scar on his stomach, some twenty centimetres long and eight wide – and now he had to do heavy work again. He need not tell them anything more back home.

There were also some German nationals from Hungary and Romania in the team. They had lost contact with their families and were unable to get any news from home.

As an assistant, Mindak has found a newly important political educator, Eugen Kaiser from Karlsruhe. I believe he will soon have a leading role in the camp.

THE HEROES' CELLAR
The new building is ready in its raw state. As it is quite cold in the tent at night, we have moved into a cellar right next to the newly constructed workshop. Although the room is only 2 by 4.5 metres, it is nearly 2.8 metres high; it has no window, but we have set it up quite pleasantly. We call it the 'Heroes' Cellar' as it reminds us of a bunker. After our time in the punishment unit, Götz, Putfarken, Hindeland and I have already been released for three months, having been reprieved on the Bolsheviks' 'Day of the Great Socialist October

Revolution' on the 7th of November. Only this way was it possible for me to join our comrades in the 'Heroes' Cellar'.

Whatever we lacked in comfort was made up for in our workshop from the material delivered by the Sawod Komunar. Everything is available, from ovens to wall lights. It is astounding to see how the prisoners of war manage to lighten their lives whenever they have the chance. Unfortunately things do not go as well in the camp as they do for us and the accommodation is very crowded. Even with us it is tight but, with only six men sleeping in the cellar, it is not so bad.

We often have friends in as guests in the evenings. The only disadvantage is the dampness of the walls and floor, making it uncomfortable, but as we are otherwise completely undisturbed, this is no real handicap.

Now the accommodation problem in the camp has increased. As the result of a short circuit, a whole barrack block was burnt to the ground. A fire engine appeared but it was too late. As it is already November, the men are unable to sleep in tents and must join the others in the other barrack blocks.

Eichhorn has done it again! Despite his declaration that he would 'no more lead a blind Red Army man to the shithouse!', he is now the head of the WK. Now, without a guard, he himself guards the Germans for the Russians, and feels himself well off with this. He has quite clearly recognised that the responsibility here is much lighter than that with the brickworks, mortar or iron sections.

The NKVD spy Lukviel tries to provoke us. The result was a sound thrashing, which deformed his plump face for a while. Selmer, Götz, Korff, Fischer and I were put in the dark lock-up for this. There we found Sergeant Westerheide from Bielefeld, who was accused of slaughtering a cow during the war and today was condemned by the war tribunal to fifteen years' hard labour. He is waiting for his transport to prison.

Christmas is coming. This time it will be a Christmas that with regard to the provisions will be better than the last few. Each of us saves a contribution of 6 roubles for the festival, but the festival tree is also to be made. As we are unable to acquire any fir or other greenery, we manage here with thin sheets of iron, the angel's hair being made out of glass wool. Fritz gets some clean beeswax to be poured into candles; Günter makes an Advent cross out of tin and hammers out an artistic brass lamp in his spare time. It is good to see how all those taking part do so with zeal, revealing their youthful hearts.

The First Advent is in the afternoon break under the motto 'Mother and Son'. With simple words framed by the appropriate pre-Christmas poems, and with the appropriate songs, we thank the people who gave us life: our mothers.

The days to the Second Advent fly past. It takes as its subject 'Our favourite people'. We think of our wives or our dearest ones. Goethe and Rilke give us resounding songs of love. How different this Advent is to the previous three years! Today we are undisturbed, as no one apart from the eight of us knows about it. We have been fighting for our lives for three years. Heartfelt thoughts of home with poems by Maria Wiedermann, Brüger, Eichendorff and Goethe make the Third Advent a worthy occasion, while on the Fourth Advent tales of Christmas customs prepare us for the forthcoming Christmas festival.

And now it is here: Christmas Eve, 1947. We all hope and wish that it will be our last one in captivity. The indications are there for it. Happy and full of confidence, we celebrate the most German of all festivals. The Christmas stories are recounted, the Christmas songs ring out; Fritz Laschtowitz gives an account of a Christmas celebration in the Glatzer Bergland, and Siegfried Korff describes a Christmas celebration in Hamburg.

My comrades have lain down to rest, but I am sitting at the table. The little lamp is burning. The loudspeaker that we were able to hire for two days is relaying a Christmas transmission from Leipzig. My thoughts are at home with my little wife. My pen scratches over the Red Cross card, seeking to express my feelings in words to my dearest one who has waited so long for my return. I was taken prisoner only six months after we had become man and wife before God and the world. And yet nothing is able to separate us, not even the vast distance! Our souls are as united as they always were, which is only possible in the knowledge of our absolute trust in each other.

I am called back to reality as the sound of church bells rings out here in this godforsaken land. My soul vibrates: how long has it been since I heard the sound of the bells? I cannot hold back my stream of tears any longer. Unobserved, I let all my feelings flow. All the bitterness of the past years flows in the tears from my soul. I know that I would not have come to this state if I had not been sitting here alone. The children's voices of the Thomaner Choir seem like angels' voices from another world. I pray: 'Father, give us all a reunion soon with our loved ones back home. Protect our poor country from even greater distress. Give me back my strength so that I as a German can go free and upright through life!'

On New Year's Eve we shake hands: 'I wish you all the best in 1948 and the return home'. The banner that hangs in the corner in front of the light bulb reads 'Welcome 1948, the year of our return home!' But doubtful thoughts depress me. Certainly the experience of our imprisonment so far justifies these doubts now, but are not the Foreign Ministers of America, England and France guarantors for the observance of this agreement? Has not Soviet propaganda also stressed so far that Soviet Russia has never broken a treaty! So silence your black thoughts, Russia too must stick to this agreement!

Fritz has even been able to acquire a half-litre of vodka in exchange for a really artistic bit of carpentry he made in his spare time. It is the second time in years that I have been able to drink a little alcohol. After we had toasted the homeland with a few short words, through which our hopes for returning home this year resounded, we spent the first hours of the year in happy festivity, determined to forget our surroundings. Franz has made a colourful hat for each of us and, as a special surprise, characterised each individual with an appropriate verse.

There was a happy confident atmosphere in the whole camp that day, the reason being the hope of returning home this year. Even the leading Anti-fascists were confident about it. One particular pessimist was Karl Schnurawa, who worked as a bookkeeper in the factory and whose chief was an old Communist. In a talkative moment the latter had told him that Karl should not fool himself: Russia would hold on to the prisoners of war until 1950 for restoration purposes. We tried to get him to refute this pessimistic outlook.

THE SAWOD KOMUNAR
Our workplace has now been moved into the factory. For several days now we have been marching the 2 kilometres there every morning

with the other five hundred men. The assembly is gathered half an hour before the escort appears at the guardroom. Meanwhile we stand about in the cold and talk about the camp's facilities. We also talk about the news in the German newspapers from the Soviet Zone. General mirth breaks out with the news that a 'House of Soviet Union Culture' is to be built in the eastern sector of Berlin. The performances now taking place there are followed with interest. A wonderful comparison can be drawn between the circus being played out there and the reality that we endure daily. There, like here, the talk is about the main thing that is lacking: culture! We are presented with illustrations of how the people of this country share with our brothers and sisters in the eastern sector their charming 'Jibit paschu mat', and how during their meals they 'elegantly' spit on the ground.

When the escort appears, the gate is opened and three or four men count us through the gate. Often one of them miscounts and we have to go back and be recounted in front of the camp. This compares with the winter in Seloni-Dolsk when the count never lasted less than an hour, but still went well. Then began the slippery march down the kilometre-long hill. As we are all wearing extremely 'advanced' boots, we can hardly keep upright and go through the craziest contortions. The best solution is still linking arms. So Ottel and I or Fritz and I go arm in arm until we reach level ground again. The march is strenuous over the ice. We are counted once more in the factory. Meanwhile 'Herr' Eichhorn's 'Hiwis' take up their sentry posts and finally the teams can go to their work places.

The combine harvester factory is in two parts. Our team works in the big assembly plant on the right side of the factory. About 200 men work on the other side. Along the street are signs pointing to the right and left. Our plumbing team, which is the factory's premier unit and has the best earnings, works undisturbed by the locals in a fenced-off area. There is much theft here, despite the strong controls, and we have to keep a sharp eye on our tools. It is very interesting seeing the local residents and the way they work. I am convinced that a large proportion of these male and female workers have no other clothing than their work clothes. These are full of grease, dirt and stains, and if one looks at their braces closely, one gets the impression that they have not undressed for weeks. I have looked for a washroom without success so far. We give ourselves a brief wash under a hosepipe in the hall. The toilet is an old dilapidated wooden hut, where the men crouch on one side and the women on the other. As the pits are soon full because of the frost, the workers squat down anywhere around, and one can come across these 'anti-personnel mines' everywhere. But it doesn't stop there. For days we have been regularly finding piles of shit on the workbenches or in any part of the workplace. These can only be from the Russian night shift staff who know that prisoners of war work here. We mark these places with signs like 'Watch out, mines!' and so on. Since the youths of this 'most advanced land on earth' were ready to bring these deeds of heroism to our workbenches, Lowag called upon the chief to pay the bill. He vanished with some standard Russian swear words on his lips. Shortly afterwards three old women appeared and cleared up the mess. We had no more problems with this.

There was plenty to see on the way to and from work. Already before seven o'clock in the morning men were standing in long queues in front of the shops to collect their allocation of bread. They must have been standing here already for some time. Many went to work straight from here, often without having got any bread as there was not enough. With lots of laughter we read in the *Täglichen Rundschau* an article by a Russian professor, who depicted in shimmering colours the advantages of the Soviet system, and said, among other things, that 'There is no standing in queues in front of food shops, but one sees long lines of people in front of the theatres, cinemas and museums.' When we go past a bread shop in which the people are fighting over places in the queue, some wit in the column always calls out: 'Look, there's another queue for a museum!' There is begging here, too, but I think much more is stolen.

Yesterday on the way back to the camp I saw a small tattered youth sitting begging. He had a baby on his lap. To increase his takings, he hit the baby again and again on his behind, thus pretending he wanted to quieten him. Naturally the opposite was achieved, the little chap shrieking blue murder.

Often when we return to camp schoolboys are playing games in the grounds of the school near our camp. Instead of balls, here they throw dummy hand-grenades. Whether boy or girl, these little Soviet citizens are being brought up in a military manner that reminds one strongly of the Prussian parade grounds. The referee is a young female teacher.

Our midday meal is brought to the factory in two large casks. I always get soup and porridge in a Romanian mess tin that I have obtained somehow. Despite being called porridge, the food is very thin and if it were not for our wages every month, we would write here the word hunger in large letters. Not all get paid as much as we do, however, and those poor chaps have to starve. Whenever possible we try to help them. Unfortunately it is like a drop of water on a hot stone.

Kaiser has managed it – he has taken over Mindak's job! In his stupidity, coupled with his lack of scruples, he blindly follows all the orders of his Russian controllers. He came to the camp in tattered clothing, but now has all the clothing he needs for his role.

Although the postal censorship is strict, I get more post than most. Even so, I only receive about a third of the letters sent to me, as I can clearly tell from the content. I derive particular happiness from the little pictures my wife attaches to the Red Cross cards. Again and again I pull them out in my free moments and then in my thoughts I am home again. My friends are also pleased with these pictures from the homeland. Today two parcels arrived in the camp. One of the recipients had to go to the NKVD, where he was told to pay customs duty that was so much he was not able to afford it.

It is quite laughable what the Russians put up with in a way. Some prisoners of war who were permitted to leave the camp without supervision were in the bazaar where they saw Red Cross packets bearing the English words 'Only for prisoners of war in the Soviet Union'. They were offered for sale at prices from 30 to 60 roubles. The International Red Cross had also sent us packets of a kind we had never seen before. It would have been wonderful if we prisoners of war had received these packets.

Tired, I sit at the small table that we constructed ourselves. The day has been very strenuous. Yesterday we had all been inoculated, ostensibly against stomach typhus. There were only a few needles available, but they were already blunt and caused pain. Although we had fever, which hit most of the camp, we still had to go out to work, although we could hardly move for pain.

At the beginning of the warm part of the year we had moved out of the Heroes' Cellar into the new building. After months in the cellar we now had daylight and sunshine in our accommodation again. I was dozing with my head on the table top when a knocking at the door made me look up. The office runner handed me a letter which said I was to report to the Joram group at the Gorodok in the morning. I wondered about this as it meant work, and in terms of duties probably a considerable worsening. From my enquiries I established that Kaiser had arranged this transfer. The reason for it was a small picture that I received from home of me wearing a steel helmet during my time as a recruit. Now they can harass me with such things. Eichhorn's friend Werner took my place.

Now I eke out my existence as an assistant in a carpentry unit. Fortunately I was able to remain in the accommodation with my friends. It would have been much worse if I had had to leave them. I got on quite well with my new work colleagues until a presumptuous foreman, Joram, an immature young man, provoked me into taking up an energetic position against him. He was cheating some of the men in his group of their money.

Now I am a member of the Walish Team, which shortly afterwards became the Thalmeier Team. My place of work is again the factory. Here we come under Kupill, a former major in the Red Army and now the director of the reconstruction. Through the manipulation of Thalmeier, who is a clever *Bajoware* and likes to complain, we get a few roubles every month. From knocking down ruined walls to making hole presses, scrap loaders and wooden trays and sweeping up debris with factory brooms, we do all the jobs that come to us. The pay is very little and without cheating we would not get a single rouble in a month. My close work comrades here are Heinz Selzer, Reinhold Dönges and Fritz Neubauer.

In a quiet hour Reinhold tells me of an experience he had in the winter of 1945 that illustrates the inhumanity of the Russians and the creatures that work for them. The Russians had discovered that some prisoners of war in the camp still had watches, fountain pens and such things. An informant, who had told the camp senior that he was an ethnic German called Otto, reported that Reinhold had thrown a watch into the toilet so that the Russians would not get it. Reinhold then had to go before the Russians, where he was interrogated and put in the lock-up. Fully stripped apart from some old, torn Russian trousers and tattered gym shoes that Otto had thrown at him, he had to spend that night in the hole in the ground. The next day Otto forced him to go down into the toilet ditch and spend the whole day looking for watches and other valuable items. Dönges resisted at first but was then forced with blows from the NKVD officers and Otto to comply. As he had not found anything in the toilet ditch in which he had worked all day, he was locked up again. There he reached the end of his tether and was in such a condition that he bit through Otto's throat when he came alone within range. Eventually the German doctor took him out of the dungeon and nourished him back to health. I could understand the grim thoughts of revenge that Reinhold harboured towards Otto.

Few transports have left for home until now. We attentively follow the numbers shown in the newspaper. The pessimists are increasing. It is now almost impossible to send all the prisoners of war home before the end of the year without putting too much strain on the transport system, with serious consequences for the economy.

I had put aside my learning of the Russian language until now. It is clear to me that if Russia does not adhere to the Moscow agreement and does not send us home by the end of the year, we will be here for at least another year. Thoughts of escape still come to me. If I could get to Odessa and swim out to a foreign ship, I had a chance of success. I could make myself understood by the sailors in English. But to get through Russia to Odessa, I must at least have some elementary grasp of the Russian language.

So, on the 1st of September, I began the systematic learning of the Russian language. It is not easy, learning how to write and read it in the room, against the protests of my friends who want to know nothing of this 'cabbage sickness' as they call it. I do not give up, however, and I have a capable assistant in Fritz Neubauer, who already has some knowledge of the Russian language. So during my work with him I am able to learn some vocabulary. I also write down the grammatical rules so that my writing, reading and speaking make quite good progress. That I can see some success, apart from having a firm aim before me, now makes learning this language a pleasure. It no longer seems so hard and unusual any more, and I work at it day and night. I pursue the Russian vocabulary even in my sleep. My friends look at me pityingly, thinking that I am no longer sane, but I ignore them.

I had already put aside some roubles in the summer months. Now that I have 150 roubles, my decision to flee is confirmed. A prisoner of war is not allowed to have more than 150 roubles.

7th November 1948. We have assembled in the camp yard for the celebration of the 'great socialist October Revolution'. The head of all the Saporoschje camps, a colonel, is expected. Before he comes, our company commander goes along our front again and says: 'When the colonel speaks you must clap, and when he calls for applause for Stalin at the end you shout "Hurrah!"' The men in the crowd remain silent at these words, having their own thoughts. The colonel arrives and gives a richly worded speech on the greatness of the October Revolution of 1917. I feel as if I am in a theatre watching a performance and I am annoyed that I have to stand here.

The ensuing propaganda march through the camp was almost like a carnival. The NKVD officers stood on the tribune and let the prisoners of war file past them in their rags and tatters. They were not satisfied with one march through the camp, so it had to be repeated twice. The camp police ensured that no one vanished. Then mottos were called out: 'I love the great socialist October Revolution!' 'I love the friend of all freedom-loving people, Generalissimo Stalin!' and so on. We were requested to finally respond with 'Hurrah!' or 'Bravo!' A prisoner of war raised a laugh as we were marching past the kitchen and smelt braised meat, for today there was to be goulash that had been saved up for days. He called out loudly 'Long live goulash!' And this time all gave a loud 'Hurrah!' amid loud laughter.

Finally there was dancing on the stage by Russian officers and German propagandists, and the prisoners of war were asked to dance among themselves. We have two days free for these highest Soviet celebrations. We had had to work on the three Sundays previously, though, as the additional holidays that we knew in Germany apparently did not apply here. Even the population had to work beforehand for their holidays. Big bonuses were distributed this day. The Stachanovists who had exceeded their norms in the framework of the Five Year Plan obtained bonuses and their pictures appeared in the newspaper. How these bonuses were distributed was explained to me by a Ukrainian with whom I worked together now and then. Before he spoke he looked around to see if there were any eavesdroppers nearby. Then he said: 'I too received a bonus: it was 600 roubles.' I wondered about the amount of the sum, but then he said dryly: '300,000 roubles were allocated to the factory. The director alone received 14,000 roubles. You can guess what then remained for the masses.' To my question how the sum was calculated, he replied: 'Two accountants and a master. As they wanted something for themselves, the director had of course had to allocate a certain premium.' He liked to talk about the time he had been employed as a worker under the previous owner – a German.

In the factory we often have to work next to young girls who are duty bound here for one or two years though they are not local residents. One, for example, is from Sararov, while another lives over 200 kilometres from here. If they do not go to work, they are accused of sabotage and sentenced to up to five years' forced labour. The pay of these people, who live in mass accommodation, is very poor. Several times these girls have borrowed 3 or 5 roubles against their future pay and have had nothing to eat for one or two days. Their standard food consists of bread, gherkins, sunflower seeds, butter and sausage. These poor creatures are paid twice in the month, the first an advance and the second the rest, but they immediately, like children, buy things beyond their means that they like the look of, and end up starving again. They literally live from hand to mouth.

What the situation was like for these compulsory labourers was described in an episode by the odd-job women working in Kupill's construction department. The construction chief for Saparoschje, a civilian named Therekov, who gives a thoroughly European impression and always looks well groomed, appeared in the workplace and saw a girl sleeping. He woke her up and asked her why she was not working. The girl replied that she had not eaten for three days, not having received any money on the last payday because the plaster she had applied had fallen out because of the frost. She did not appear for work the next day. Therekov, unperturbed by her plight, simply commented that she would not get away with this, as not appearing for work was classed as sabotage and was punishable with five years' hard labour. This Therekov bought his children every day a block of chocolate that cost 60 roubles alone!

I heard a good story from my comrade Frosch, who came to us from Camp 7100/1. An NKVD officer going on duty in the summer of 1947 encountered a murderous shrieking and calling for help from a low earthen bunker that was separated from the camp's forbidden zone by barbed wire. It sounded like the voice of a man who had found himself in deadly danger. The NKVD man went to see what was happening and surprised two women in the course of slaughtering a twelve-year-old girl. At their interrogation it was established that these inhuman creatures had already slaughtered several children whom they lured with sweets and then sold their flesh at the bazaar as pork.

The *Daily News Show* brought out an article recently in which the living standards of the Russian workers were discussed. The report was certainly aimed at the German people. The writer wrote in it that a Russian family, consisting of husband and wife, earned on average 3,000 roubles a month. I inquired among the workers in the factory and established that the average pay for an untrained worker was 350 roubles, rising to 600–800 roubles for so-called specialists. In the most unusual cases a husband and wife together might earn up to 1,500 roubles. This was just about sufficient for them to live on, but no more!

In the Sawod Komunar a skilled worker gets the 5th pay grade. The 6th pay grade is the highest and the best paid. Here, 125 per cent of the norm earns a worker a 14.60 rouble supplement. And should he provide twenty-six days of impeccable work he gets 379.60 roubles net. If he wants to earn more he must increase his results. But the costs of living are high: 1kg of bread costs 3.20 roubles, 100g of margarine 3.50 roubles, 100g of butter 6 roubles, 100g of sausage 4–7 roubles. Textiles and shoes are very expensive. And such prices are demanded from the workers although the supplier receives 6 roubles for 1 zentner of grain (wheat) and 2,000 roubles for 1kg of butter. Where is the rest of the money?

IN CAMP 7100/6: THE ASSEMBLING OF THE 'BLACK SHEEP'

Quite suddenly I get the news that I am to be moved to Camp 7100/6. There are about 180 men with me. My friends Götz and Korff, and also Hofmann and Hindenlang from Block VI, are among them. The transfer comes as a surprise for me. Back in the summer I had been on a list with forty other men to go to Stalino for mining work but nothing came of it. Thus, when several days ago a rumour began circulating that the NKVD had a list consisting of uncertain elements and fascists, on which my name was included, I thought little of it.

I only had a little time to say farewell to my friends and comrades in the camp. We know that we will see each other again when we return to the homeland. That this is not likely the Russians had told the Anti-fascist activists several days earlier. Our general indignation could only be expressed in powerless rage. Spies were everywhere to report any utterances against the ruling government. Kaiser, who had said four weeks previously: 'You can hang me if all of us do not go home this year!' is still going about. There have been some violent riots in the other camps but further details have not been given. It is obvious to me that from the 1st of January 1949 I will refuse to do any work. My comrades Götz and Korff independently express themselves in similar fashion.

Once in Camp 7100/6 I meet some old acquaintances I have not seen for over a year, including Otto Doerr, to whose bed Götz, Korff and I are drawn. Prisoners of war are also meeting up from the various Saporoschje camps and it became clear to all of us that the Russians had established a special camp here. The area in which we are accommodated has become like a vast waiting-room with more than three hundred men living in it. We lie on three-decker beds in the vast room not knowing what awaits us in the future. Former big names in the political spectrum, such as Schmidt-Achat, Lörken, Gewiese, Bunder and so on, have also met here.

Under Hindenlang as our foreman we are now working as assistants on the construction of a new building. On the first Sunday of Advent they tried to make us go to work. Most went, but App, Franke, Götz, Korff and I remained in the camp. Kastner, as the dispatcher, is too clever to report us to the Russians.

On the third Sunday of Advent the Russian camp commandant, Gudenkov, informs us that three Hungarian officers have been sentenced to five and ten years' hard labour for refusing to obey orders. We should take this as a warning and not think that the Soviet Union would spare us.

A happy surprise is an accidental meeting with my countryman Heinz Stelter, whom I know from home. Before his arrival in Saporoschje he had been travelling for more than a year.

Unfortunately he was only with us for a few days before being transferred to another camp.

The Christmas festival of 1948 saw among the prisoners of war in the Soviet Union only sad faces and an oppressive atmosphere, as in our camp. The crushing disappointment about the Russian failure to adhere to the Moscow Agreement and the continuing uncertainty over our future did not allow any proper Christmas atmosphere to arise. Among the other ranks, who were accommodated even more tightly than ourselves, their living quarters reminding one of rabbit hutches, not even the saved-up Christmas food could lift their spirits.

On our bed – the upper one – Götz, Korff, Doerr, Breske, Schroeter and I celebrate Christmas Eve. Without letting the dismal atmosphere influence us, our thoughts wander back home. Our old trusted Christmas songs were sung. Like an angel's greeting appears a photograph that I received from my little wife through the post. But even her beaming smile does not hold me back from the coming step of refusing to work.

After a conversation with Second-Lieutenant Dörge, I came to the unequivocal resolution that I will not give up my return home at any price. And if I find myself quite alone on the 1st of January, I will take this step in protest and put an end to all my uncertainty. I know that Dörge is not in full agreement with my flight plan, but I cannot get it out of my mind and I must protest: I am simply not able to remain silent.

My friend Gusti, a Hungarian lieutenant, will be going home after more than a year of delays, and I ask him to write to my wife and describe the true circumstances of our imprisonment. I will do everything possible to escape in the year ahead. If nothing has been heard of me by the end of 1949, she should not expect me to return home.

Our work brigade might as well be on strike, for we do practically no work at all in the last week of the old year. Korff, Götz, App, Franke and I appear formally for work until the 31st of December 1948, but we achieve nothing.

1948 has run its course. Hardly anyone dares to wish his comrades in distress a return home: it has already become too well-worn a phrase. A room in the camp has been established and magnificently called the 'Restaurant' in an effort to lighten the dulled atmosphere among the prisoners of war. There is even beer here and a jazz band does its bit. The prisoners of war sing with a touch of gallows humour: 'Skoro Domoi, isn't that funny? We've already heard that there will still be transport in 1950.'

Those who follow the figures in the *Daily Review* know that there must still be more than 400,000 German prisoners of war in the Soviet Union.

In Lörken at Sylvester, an old NKVD informer and former camp senior has fled with a former member of the SS. He had got into hot water with the NKVD when an attempt to flee with a Ukrainian woman failed. There is no trace of him as yet.

Chapter 4

Under Investigation for Refusing to Work

It is morning on the 2nd of January, the first day of work in the New Year. Sullenly the prisoners of war get up from their beds. Once they have washed and had their breakfast comes the order: 'Parade outside for work!' Without bothering about it, I stay in my bed. I have already told my new squad leader, Bräunlich, that I am not going to work.

The big room is now almost completely empty. Some men on the sicklist sweep out the room, while others, who have the night shift, stretch out on their beds. Götz, Korff, Doerr, Franke, Breske, Mütschele and Schroeter have stayed in the room with me, although they should also have gone to work. The duty German officer writes down the names of those that have not gone out to work.

At 9.30 the whole camp, apart from those now at work, must parade for counting in the camp yard. App was taken off for questioning during the night and is not back yet. We do not know what happened, but suspect that he carelessly said something and it has been reported to the Russians.

I carefully put on my overcoat. Once we are standing in the yard, the duty officer of the day appears. He reads out the names of the eight of us who have refused to work and leads us to the guardroom. There he asks us individually why we have not gone out to work. From each of us he gets the reply that we are not going out to work. The Russian makes a note of our answers and calls the camp commandant. We are led to the administrative offices outside the camp and locked up in an empty room. After some time appears a ninth work-dodger, Second-Lieutenant Hans Menden, from Vallendaer near Koblenz. Grinning, Menden tells us that he was overlooked at first and was then sent after us.

It takes a while before the camp commandant, Major Gudenkov, who had already reported this unusual occurrence to the main administration, lets us one by one into his office, where several officers and female interpreters of the main administration are gathered. I am the fifth to be summoned. It is already noon. Gudenkov, who is sitting at the head of the table, asks me with a grim face: 'Why are you refusing to work?'

'Because Russia has not adhered to the Moscow Agreement! Apart from that, as a German officer prisoner of war, I am not duty bound to work. As Russia has been a member of the International Red Cross since November 1946, the Hague Convention also applies to the Soviet Union.'

Gudenkov: 'You categorically refuse to work?'

'Yes.'

'I order you to go to work!'

'You cannot give that order, for you do not have the right to. The requirements of the Hague Convention state otherwise.'

'Good, you can go.'

I was then taken to join the others who had been to the commandant before me. Once we were all together, we were taken back to the guardroom, where we were given our packs without being allowed to return to the camp. Following a thorough search, we were taken by truck to the headquarters section of the main camp, which was separated from the rest of the camp by barbed wire.

To our surprise we were not alone here. Two Austrians – von Neuroth and Dr Sippel – as well as Second-Lieutenant Heinrich Bauer from Cronnach were also present. The Austrians, who should have already gone home over a year ago, are still fighting for the recognition of their nationality (the Russians counted them as Germans), while Bauer is under investigation because when he was informed that we would not be going home before the 31st of December 1948, he took out his anger on the picture of Stalin on the wall. In fact, he simply put it in a corner without damaging it in any way, but an over-zealous Anti-fascist immediately reported him.

There was sufficient space in the long barrack room for twelve men. Wood and coal were brought in by the German camp senior. We now had to wait for what was to come. Meals were brought to us punctually and correctly. We passed the time with games, discussions, songs and poetry. As before, I continued learning Russian, with Neuroth listening to my vocabulary.

The first hearings started on the 5th of January. Assisted by the female interpreters, three examining officers worked through the written charges against us. I based my case once more exactly on the reason for my refusal to work and only signed it once the Russian text had been translated into German.

The newspaper of the 13th of January brought a Tass report according to which all German prisoners of war would be repatriated from the Soviet Union during the course of 1949. We had a long discussion with a Russian lieutenant from the main administration who was responsible for inquiring into our state of health. It was always the same thing: these people are insincere.

On the 18th of January Breske, who had started a hunger strike, was taken to the hospital, and App, who was also in the cells, accused of being a main conspirator and on these grounds denied rations, was sent back to the hospital.

The indictments were signed on the 21st of January. I demanded a Red Cross representative from a foreign country and, as interpreter, Second-Lieutenant Adam from Camp 7100/2 to ensure an unequivocal translation.

The 25th of January was a cloudy day. The German camp senior appeared very early and ordered us to pack our things and go to the guardroom. We said farewell to von Neuroth and Sippel, and took the same path that Second-Lieutenant Bauer had taken a week earlier. We had heard nothing more about him except from another soldier who had also been in front of the tribunal for an insignificant offence but had been sent back to the camp, who told us that Bauer had been sentenced to twenty-five years' hard labour. The hearing had lasted barely ten minutes. Bauer had only replied affirmatively to the question: 'Have you taken the picture of Generalissimo Stalin from the wall?' The court had then stood and passed sentence.

BEFORE THE WAR TRIBUNAL

At the guardroom we were taken over by three sentries who took us into the town accompanied by the NKVD interpreter, a young second-lieutenant. According to the interpreter, we were going to the courthouse in which the cases against us would be heard today. We made only slow progress along the icy and uneven streets. When we reached the big, dark building in which we would be sentenced, we had first to wait a few minutes until we were led up the steps of the four-storey building. Here we were locked in a room. After we had been waiting for about an hour, we were taken together into the courtroom. There were already two legal representatives (of both sexes) who had been allocated as our defence. I was not very happy about this, and my comrades also did not want to know anything about them. We told them that we would defend ourselves. They countered this by saying that was our choice, but they must remain there in any case as they had been ordered to.

There was no representative of the International Red Cross to be seen. Adam, whom we had requested as an interpreter, was also not there.

We were asked to sit down on the stools in the dock. Behind us sat the four guards. Shortly afterwards, the prosecutor appeared and immediately after him came the judge with two assistants. We were told that the court consisted of the following persons: Judge – Senior Lieutenant-Colonel of Justice Malichin; Assistants – Major Esseljin, Sergeant Schön; Prosecutor – Major of Justice Suchba. The names of the defence representatives were not made known to me. The interpreter from Camp 7100 did the translating.

The judge first established our identities. Once the formalities had been gone through, the prosecution statements were read out, which amounted to a refusal to work by all of us. This offence was classed as sabotage. Next, each of the accused was heard individually. Our points were essentially as follows: the Soviet Union had not adhered to the agreement signed in Moscow in April 1947 with the countries of England, America and France. As German officer prisoners of war we were not obliged to work under the rules of the Hague Convention. We had worked until then in order not to worsen the general pressure that had been brought against us. We were now protesting against the Russians' non-adherence to the Moscow Agreement, demanding immediate repatriation and handling in accordance with the Hague Convention and the Geneva Agreement.

The judge told us that the Soviet Union was a member of the International Red Cross and adhered to its regulations, but we would still be punished. Apart from this, all German officers up to the rank of captain were duty bound to work according to an order from

Moscow. We demanded to see this order, but this was refused. Malichin went on to say that refusing to work in the Soviet Union was sabotage against the establishment of Socialism and was among the worst crimes that one could commit. Our protests and arguments against this found no response.

As witnesses against us appeared the commandant of Camp 7100/6, Major Gudenkov, the duty officer of the day, Senior Paymaster Bräunlich, and Captain Aulich. Except for Bräunlich, who acted very cleverly, they all accused us strongly. Even Aulich made accusations against App that showed his low character. Gudenkov made some false allegations that we refuted. The judge did not respond to our objections. The prosecutor meanwhile sat there untroubled, as we would be condemned in any case.

When I looked at our accused bench, it seemed to me that the prosecutors were sitting here. None of the accused shows any fear nor is impressed by what might happen. Each one of us has acted in his own way so everyone is clear about the possible consequences. When Franke reproaches the court on the Soviet prosecutor's quotation at Nuremburg and compares it to the present situation, it is as if he has poked a hornets' nest. Franke says that the Soviet prosecutor at Nuremburg actually said: 'Germany has left a memorial – the Soviet Union will leave a memorial to itself!' The judge and prosecutor had understood him exactly.

Back and forth the argument raged. I and my comrades understood little of what was said. In his speech for the defence the advocate pleaded for acquittal as it was not proven in the Moscow order if officer prisoners of war had to work.

Towards midnight the judge rose and deferred the session until the following day. We had been sitting here for fourteen hours. I had not expected that it would have lasted so long. The defence gave us hope that we could reckon on a disciplinary sentence. We also had the impression that Malichin had adjourned the session so that not everything remained afloat. The prosecutor's witnesses had been very shaky. Additionally, Malichin had to obtain new instructions. Our guards, who had been present in the room throughout the whole proceedings, are also of the opinion that we will not be sentenced. I have the contrary opinion, for we have set a dangerous precedent and others may follow our example.

We have to smile when we get back to the camp. Even the camp barber had already been summoned to the tribunal to shear our hair. Von Neuroth and Sippel are astounded when they cross over to the isolation compound and listen tensely to our experiences.

Next afternoon we are sitting in the courtroom in the same order as the previous day. The same persons have appeared, only the witnesses have been stood down. Once more the film rolls before our eyes in an abbreviated form. Each one of us gets a last word and the court adjourns. After about fifteen minutes the court returns to announce the verdict. We rise from our seats. In the name of the people of the 'most socialist country on earth', we are sentenced for sabotage contrary to the Ukrainian Punishment Code paragraph 206/P: Lieutenant of the German Wehrmacht Hans Mütschele and Second-Lieutenants Kurt App, Oskar Franke, Georg Breske and Wolf Schroeter to ten years' hard labour; Captains Siegfried Korff and Adelbert Holl, Lieutenant Otto Götz, Second-Lieutenants Otto Doerr and Hans Mendes to eight years' hard labour. Objections are to be raised in the course of the next five days at the Highest Military Tribunal in Kiev.

As the judge announces the sentences I look at him openly without pulling a face. My comrades do the same. The judge seems to find this unpleasant.

Soon we are standing alone in the room with just our guards and the interpreter, and we are given the order to collect our packs. The interpreter gives us a briefing, then we are led below and locked into a prison cell in the cellar. The policemen here are very harsh towards us, but become a bit more friendly when they discover that we are condemned prisoners of war. After only a few minutes we are taken out of the cell individually. Curious eyes look at us through the spy-holes in the other cell doors. All kinds of riffraff are sitting here in the cellar, even women.

The camp barber is waiting for us in the washroom. With a few quick hand movements he shaves off our hair. The female interpreter from the camp is here to help with the writing of the personal files that will be kept about us. It is interesting how well organised the system is here. As the duty policeman paints both my hands with black printing ink and takes an impression of each finger, I hear Schroeter say to the female interpreter in a mockingly scornful tone:

'Dear lady, would you still marry me like this?' I turn around and watch as he takes a small round cap from his head and makes a deep bow to this woman, her face thickly made up with artistic colours. I cannot hold back my laughter; this 187cm tall lad with a completely undernourished body, a thick head and big popping eyes has proposed to a female interpreter in shimmering colours in the outer rooms of the GPU cellar at the war tribunal.

Soon everything required has been done and we are sitting again in a small cell in which there is hardly room for ten men. The bucket in the corner for the emergency use of the prisoners spreads a pervasive stink. On the ceiling and in the corners our predecessors have scratched their names and the number of years of their sentences. But I can only see Russian names.

While we knew each other only distantly or fleetingly on the day we refused to work, in the time waiting for the tribunal we had had the opportunity of getting to know each other better. Here, after the sentencing, we let all conventional formalities drop and now only used the commonly binding '*Du*'.

It is shortly before midnight when the cell door opens and we are ordered to get out. Outside four militia men are waiting to take us to the town prison.

IN THE RAYON PRISON OF SAPOROSCHJE

It is a clear, cold night. The town lies in nightly peace and only the 'Halt! Who goes there?' of the prison sentry standing in the corner tower of the prison shakes us out of our dozing. The small barred window in the big iron door opens briefly. The warder comes and checks the papers of the guard commander, then opens the rattling door and we find ourselves in a small yard blocked on the far side by a trellised gate. Our guard escort has to wait outside the prison; only the sergeant comes with us inside the high stone fencing after leaving his weapon at the guardhouse. A second prison warder leads us to a second door in the building. The building and various doors show us that we are in a proper prison. Despite the darkness I can make out the outline of some parts of the building.

The duty militia officer sits at his desk behind the barrier. We stay in the reception room. The guard sergeant hands over our files and vanishes again. He has completed his task. We are now alone with the lieutenant. In his Jewish language he asks us how many years we have been given. When we answer eight and ten years, he says: 'Miniscule!'

Our personal files are compared. A warder appears and searches our things. Razor blades, knives and needles are all taken away. I try to keep my pictures and my Russian dictionary, but without success. Soon afterwards we are put into a narrow cell without any beds but with the usual stinking bucket. We lie down on the cold stone floor and sleep – more or less – until the morning.

When the little shutter in the door is opened we are on our feet in no time. We are handed warm coffee as well as a piece of bread that we estimate weighs 600 grams. We consume this with real hunger. The bread is hardly better than that of the prisoner of war camp and very damp.

We are discussing our experiences until now when the cell door is opened and a warder orders us to get out. Now out in the corridor, it becomes clear that we are not in the real part of the prison where there are proper cells. That part is separated from our corridor by a thick iron door, and a warder stands there to ensure that no unauthorised person goes through.

We now leave the building by the same way as we came in, and shortly afterwards we find ourselves standing as God made us in the dressing room for the baths and waiting for our clothing, which has been hung on rings for delousing. A hairdresser, who has only a one-year sentence and therefore has not gone to a work camp, gives us hair-cutting implements. When we point out that we have already lost the hair from our heads, he says that we are to get rid of our beards and body hair. From the barber we also discover that Second-Lieutenant Bauer is still here in the prison. However, he was sentenced as a war criminal under paragraph 54, and the war criminals are kept in a separate block with special supervision. With a nail that we found by chance in the dressing room, we scratch our names on the side of the oven.

It has been a long time since we bathed as well as in this bathroom in which there are twelve baths, though they could have given us a little more soap. Our clothing is still very hot when it comes back from delousing, and the wire rings burn red stripes on the skin if one is not careful.

Sweating from the hot water and the hot clothing, we go back through the prison yard into the old building. The clear, clean winter air does us good and we draw it strongly into our lungs. The iron-grilled door to the real prison cells is opened and then the warder opens the door to Cell 12 and shuts it behind us.

A thick stench from tobacco smoke and body smells assaults our senses. The room is crammed full of men and at first glance we do not know which way to turn. Each of us was then surrounded by a crowd of curious people. I establish that here the age group is from fifteen to sixty years. The three sentenced Hungarians are also in this room. As we came from the 7100/2 and 7100/6 camps, there is a warm greeting. The Ukrainians – there is hardly a Russian among them, only one Tartar and one Usbeck – have recognised us immediately from our clothing as German prisoners of war and we are questioned from all directions. In general, they are all friendly; when some youngsters try to annoy us, they are rebuked by the older ones. They have full understanding of our handling and the way it led to our sentencing. A major influence on our treatment by the Russian prisoners is above all the behaviour of the room senior (or *Starschoi*, as the Russians say). As a former lieutenant, he handles us benevolently. The others dare not go against him as he is without doubt the strongest character in the room. The majority follow his lead and are friendly toward us.

We get to know the most unusual people here. There is, for example, a small young lieutenant who was sentenced to six years' hard labour because while he was on leave with his sister he was caught stealing. He was the first to hoist the flag on the Brandenburg Gate and was awarded the decoration 'Hero of the Soviet Union'. Another one was given eight years' hard labour for embezzlement in a shop. A one-legged, one-eyed man, who got around on an artificial leg, had been sentenced to five years for cheating. Others had stolen small amounts of corn from the Kolchose during the hunger period and been given five to ten years. Workers whose machines had been damaged somehow got three to ten years.

The years seem of little relevance here. What by us is punished with months, is punished here with years. A typical case was the sentencing of locksmith Heinrich, who was sentenced to ten years' imprisonment because he did not report the illegal sale of petrol by a director who was sentenced to fifteen years. In comparison, the little Ukrainian with the flickering restless eyes is given six years because he hit his mother-in-law during a quarrel. There are very many young lads here that didn't go to work. They get six months' hard labour.

The impressions that I get in such a short time here are numerous. Lying in the corner on the ground under the bed, I get no sleep and spend the time thinking over my experiences. There are ninety-eight convicts here this evening as reported by the room elder to the duty officer. Lying on the floor with me are five of my friends as there are insufficient beds for this number of prisoners, even though the two-storey bed frames run right up to the wall and the doorway with its two observation holes. High in the wall are three small barred windows, and in the middle of the room stand two small tables with two benches each. Directly next to the entrance is the toilet bucket.

A former major, who was sentenced in Hungary back in 1944 for some racket or other and got ten years, recounts his story to popular demand. The story begins just like a fairy tale with: 'Once upon a time . . .'. The location of the deed is Paris, the characters a rich young aristocrat and a poor but pretty sales girl. I can understand the content quite well and learn some new vocabulary from listening. Ottel and Siegfried, who had called me crazy three months ago for studying Russian so hard, are now pleased that I can understand it and can speak for them. I fall asleep from the speaker's monotonous account.

Already several days have passed. The routine hardly differs from day to day. Before reveille at five o'clock in the morning the early risers are ready to have their morning wash with the first batch of water brought to the washroom. At the same time they take the opportunity to use the toilets. We are taken to the washroom room by room. We do not look like the other prisoners. As a rule the supervisor has to bring three batches of us to the washroom until our whole room has been through it. The old prisoners have their hiding places in the toilets or the washroom, which they use to exchange news with other prisoners, as every prisoner uses the washroom at least once a day. Despite constant supervision by the warders, they are always able to exchange messages. After we have washed, the room is swabbed down by the two room orderlies, who get a second helping of food for their work. Then comes the order: 'Get ready for counting!' Shortly afterwards the duty officer appears. Those who can sit down on the beds, and the remainder stand. Once the count is complete, the duty officer asks if we have any requests. Paper and writing materials can be requested, or prisoners can ask for an interview with the prison governor.

Once the counting is complete, breakfast is served through a small hatch in the door. It consists of a thin soup, 600 grams of bread for the whole day and a small lump of sugar. The fish is either in the soup or distributed by hand. From 1000 to 1020 hours we have access to the prison yard, which is about 20 x 20 metres and hermetically sealed. Lunch consists of about 500 grams of soup similar to the morning one. Up until 1800 hours we can play domino or chess or other games, or do various activities. In the evening there is more soup and after the evening count everyone has to lie down to rest. No one may climb into the upper bunks. Every week we are taken to the baths, which is connected with a delousing of our clothing.

On the second day of being here we were photographed for the criminal record.

There is always coming and going as new prisoners are inducted and old ones released. My ear has grown accustomed to the voices of the speakers. Many discussions with the natives were conducted and I learned things from bystanders that I, as a prisoner of war who had never lived so closely with the inhabitants, could never otherwise have been able to learn. I gather from the talking among the prisoners that one can purchase one's freedom from the state prosecutor with the appropriate sum of money. They tell me that the state prosecutor informed them at the beginning of their case how much money it would take for their release. But I also learn here the true attitude of these people to their government and Communism. It naturally happens that everyone talks a lot about it, even in front of the room spy, about whom we had been warned on the very first day by the well-meaning Ukrainian.

The people here that are going into exile for several years, and do not know when and whether they will ever go home again, are awaiting liberation from Bolshevism by the Americans. The name of the president of the United States of America has a special resonance for them. They see in Truman a demi-god who will bring them freedom. They follow political developments with special interest and speak a lot about the new war that they see coming. As they tell me, they would not fight any more. The way these people speak amongst themselves is anything but polite. But they try to be loyal to us.

There are other cells in which professional criminals conduct a truly shocking regime, without those afflicted daring to report them. Food, and anything else that the recipient gets from his family, is simply taken from him and he is happy if a few crumbs come his way.

Cells with reduced rations are not used for punishment, and should a prisoner repeatedly offend against prison discipline, then he goes into the *Rubaka*. Not only that, he is stuck in a rubber sack for a length of time, and his legs are tied to his back.

It is interesting to see how the Russians trade with the adjoining cell, in which the women are. They hold a cup against the wall, press their mouths to it and shout loudly into it. Their partner the other side has pressed an ear to the wall to listen. Then they change round. In this way they maintain contact.

Every day relatives living in the neighbourhood bring packages to the prison, which, after careful checking by the guards, are passed on to the prisoners. They are mainly the same things, from which I gather that the Jews in our cell live substantially better than the others. While the Ukrainians' packets contain mainly bread, machorka, potatoes and milk, the Jews also have butter, eggs and bacon. The dozens of condemned men watch the mouths of those eating with hungry eyes.

Now and again we are given the left-over remains of their prison food from those receiving packages. We divide these items equally between us. The food is not sufficient to live on, but we vegetate.

I am the only one to have a voucher for 135 rubbles. As the hunger among us all is so great, and smokers are fully dependent upon what a Russian gives them, I declare myself agreeable when Ortel suggests to me that the money intended for our flight be used for buying bread and tobacco at the camp. It takes days before we receive the first items ordered, although the shop is in the same building.

Our appeal to the highest military court in Kiev has already been under way for days. We have also submitted an application for the paying out of our account money in Camp 7100. We are sceptical, but an attempt should do no harm.

A really hearty relationship exists between the Hungarian comrades and ourselves. They report that a statement made by their comrades led to their conviction. They are now waiting to be transported off once their conviction is confirmed by Kiev.

The number of Germans in our room has now been increased by four men. Some of the work teams sold wood in order to supplement their food a little, and one of them stole a corn cob to cook for them. The Russian response to this was five to ten years of hard labour!

On my birthday this year I did not get the rest period that I got the previous year. I did not have to work, but we still had delousing and a big cleaning of the room. Afterwards I let my comrades take me into the waiting room, which was full of people, to sing the hymn *Deutschland heiliges Wort*. Puzzled, the Russians listened; some of them who had been in German captivity understood our language quite well.

The Hungarians have gone. Our appeal has come back from Kiev and the sentence is confirmed. We are now waiting daily for our onward transport. But another positive thing has happened: the main administration of the prisoner of war camp has actually transferred the remains of our money to the prison. In total, there is more than 600 roubles for us all. Truly it seems a wonder. The whole sum will be a communal treasure once more.

The March sun is already showing that spring is about to chase away winter. The roofs drip water very strongly at lunchtime and we take care to let the sun shine on us when we take our walks outside. Through a Czech, who is to be shipped to Russia and is sitting here in the prison at the moment, we learn that those who have been sentenced to twenty-five years' imprisonment have gone to an unknown destination. They include Bauer. Our hour too has arrived. The warder reads out our names and we take our last bath in the *banja*. Here the transferred money was handed to us by the female accountant. We immediately share it out evenly. As we are led to the gate, I ask the warder where our packs are. He wants to see our receipts. But as we have been given no receipts, we cannot show him. He says that means we will not get our packs back. The guard who is to take us to the station in the green *Minna*, as the prison vehicle is called, is already waiting. Time is limited, as we are to be taken by the Sevastopol–Moscow train to Charkov, and it leaves Saporoschje on schedule. I translate clearly to the warder our determination not to go without our packs from the prison, and say we would rather be shot. Swearing terribly, the warder goes off and returns in a short time with the packs. Wolf's and Oskar's things are missing. I bring this to his attention but the driver acts stupid and we are manhandled into the green *Minna*.

IN CHARKOV TRANSIT PRISON

Six well-armed militiamen and a guard dog ensure that we are brought to Saporoschje-South railway station in the shortest time. The right-hand factory of the Sawod Komunar goes past like a ghost. Room has already been made for us at the station. The people appear to be familiar with this practice, as they immediately jump aside as we come along. In threes we move at a fast pace to the train already standing at the platform, which has a prison wagon. Here we are handed over to the officer responsible and NKVD guards lock us into a cell with a civilian who comes along with us.

In three stages the twelve of us now lie like sardines in this cage. Our astonishment is great when in this cage we meet another condemned prisoner of war who had been with the Waffen-SS. His name is Butterweck, and he comes from Vallendar near Koblenz, as does our Menden. They did not know each other before, but the world is just a village.

Butterweck tells us the following story. As a prisoner of war he had worked in a normal camp in Nikopol. There he got to know a young Ukrainian girl who fell in love with him. He used this opportunity to run away with her. With the use of several thousand roubles that the girl had obtained, they first went to Moscow. As he was wearing civilian clothes and bribed the responsible train guards and controllers with suitable sums of money, they got there without trouble. They stayed with relations of the girl for several days and then went on to Riga, their actual destination. From there they intended to try to get away by sea. The girl hoped to find accommodation with an aunt living abroad. As the journey to Moscow had gone so well, they became careless the nearer they got to their destination. Shortly before Riga, they were found asleep by a militia patrol. As Butterweck could not produce his identity documents, and was not Russian, they were both arrested. When they arrived at the old camp the real suffering began. Under special interrogation he was made so irresolute that he agreed with everything the NKVD wanted from him. He signed up to things that he had never done in his life. The NKVD derived a special amusement from having a member of the SS in front of them. In court Butterweck rejected the statement he had made under force and mistreatment. The judge took no notice of this and sentenced him to twenty-five years' hard labour. As we worked out, this was the same judge who had awarded us eight or ten years' hard labour: Lieutenant-Colonel of Justice Malichin.

It is already midnight when we are unloaded in Charkov. Butterweck is travelling on to Moscow. We wish him all the best for the future, but it looks really bad for him.

Militia soldiers are waiting for us on the station platform with two Alsatian dogs. Accompanied by some male and female Russians, who have difficulty managing their heavy packs, we are led through the streets of Charkov at night. Fortunately the way is not too far and soon we stop in front of the thick, high walls of Charkov Transit Prison.

We still have to wait a while before we are led through the long gate entrance, which has two heavy gates reminiscent of a medieval castle. Here in the prison we are put in a cell that has no windows, merely an air vent in the roof six metres above us. Not knowing where we are, we lie down on the damp ground. While I am tossing and turning restlessly, it occurs to me that this is the 9th of March.

Is it day? Is it night? We do not know. Shivering from the cold ground and the dampness of this dark hole, we stumble across the yard into a room in which a woman is sitting in a white smock. It is about 0800 hours. We have to strip completely and this woman turns out to be a female doctor taking the well-known 'flesh show' and lazily entering our work capability on a list. I have grown accustomed to this theatre and am not troubled by it any more. From here we are taken for delousing, and endure another shaving with a knife. A warder finally takes us to Box VI.

In the yard leading to Box VI we see several cells have already been opened to air. The occupants are walking around in single file, one after the other. It is a sad picture with these figures wrapped in pathetic rags and wearing footwear that any beggar in central Europe would have burnt. Noticeable among many of these young people is the cheeky, bold look from deeply set eyes lying in their baldly shaved, pale heads. Some are quite well fed.

We are led to a low corridor where our baggage and clothing are undergoing a thorough search. All metal objects are removed from us, including the spoons that we eat with. With difficulty I manage to persuade the officer responsible that the photographs the Red Cross sent me do not endanger the Soviet state. I can also keep my sketches and my Russian-German dictionary. The suitcases, containing whatever we cannot take to the cells, are handed in to the baggage room.

After the search we come to Box II and discover to our delight that the responsible senior, a sergeant, has allocated a small cell for us Germans. It is the last cell but one on the right side on the first storey. We can appreciate this, as all the other cells as small as ours are occupied by at least thirty Russians, while there are only fourteen Germans. We meet up here with another four prisoners of war who have been sentenced like us to six or so years' hard labour. The reason: stealing because of hunger.

In the cell next to us is Arthur Marx from Cologne, with whom I had worked in the Lowag Brigade in Camp 7100/2, together with Götz and Korff. He has a fifteen years' hard labour sentence. He had apparently been involved in anti-partisan operations. Lörken came against him as a crown witness and confirmed the Russian statement that the young man from Cologne had fought against him.

Our cell is 4.5 metres long and 2 metres wide, and 2.5 metres in height. Ten men can sleep on the double iron bunks, with the other four lying on the stone floor. We get light through a small semi-circular window that is particularly prominent in the thick wall. We have no freedom of movement at all in this small cell, but we are happy to be among ourselves here. The four new comrades tell us about the conditions in the other cells and paint a picture of homosexuality, thieving and beatings such as we have not experienced so far. When we are let out for our daily half-hour walk we meet the company of such a cell and are happy not to have been subjected to such conditions.

The food here hardly differs from that in Saporoschje, except that the bread ration is 150 grams more at 750 grams, for being on the transportation list and liable to be called any day.

Korff, Götz and I receive receipts for the wedding rings that were taken from us here. I handle mine with care as we should get our rings back at the end of our banishment.

Heroes' Memorial Day, 1949. We do not know whether the authorities in the homeland today think of our fallen. The millions left behind will certainly be thinking about their dead, who fought for the well-being of their people and were lost on the battlefields or fell victim to the enemy bombs falling on their home towns. We too in our narrow cell think of them, and neither the enemy's hatred that still strives to destroy us physically, nor the powerful prison regime with its metre-thick walls, nor even the uncertainty over our fate can prevent us. Is it the unusualness of the situation that makes us susceptible? We are not ashamed of the tears that roll down our cheeks from singing the songs of good comrades. They apply also to our fatherland that now, torn and bleeding from innumerable wounds, has become a football to be kicked around between East and West.

The calm in the cell lasts only another two days. Kurt App is suddenly removed. The next day it is Mütschele, Franke, Doerr and Menden who leave the cell in the morning. Only a short time later follow Götz, Korff, Breske and me. Schroeter is the only one of us remaining in the cell.

The warder leads us to a cellar room where the window is open. Russians come in who have clearly been politically punished and sentenced to twenty-five years because they had fought on the German side against Bolshevism. They are very friendly towards us, some even giving us machorka and a little dried bread to eat.

Night brings me little sleep. The cold stone floor and the open window make it uncomfortable. The next day the cellar becomes even more crowded. To our delight, Schroeter also appears. The adjacent cellars are equally stuffed full. There is talk of a batch of 1,200 persons leaving, including also women who had worked for the Wehrmacht.

There are days of waiting in which we move from room to room, are sent to the bath and back again, and then left in a cellar waiting for what was to come. To the uninitiated it seemed an unhealthy confusion but in fact it was organised.

When we collected our bags, a warder informed us that we were going to the Lena area in Siberia. Others had hoped we would be sent to Alma Ata, which would have been preferable as the border of Alma Ata was not so far distant.

New sentries appeared. The old hands knew that we would soon be on our way. The whole of the 20th of March we had to endure a thorough search of our baggage. As a group of ten men we came to a cellar in which our escort was waiting. A young soldier wearing a Komsomol badge searched me. I looked on naked, my teeth chattering, as he went through my clothing. When he saw my little photo album in which there were forty photographs that my wife had sent me via the Red Cross, he called his supervisor. This one, a sergeant, rummaged through them with curiosity and wanted to take them from me. I kicked up a racket, my knowledge of Russian coming in useful. The now decisive captain commanding the transport gave them back to me. My dictionary, on the other hand, he held on to, but with the promise that he would return it at a certain place. All other writing was also taken from me. Fortunately I was able to save a book of poetry that I had composed myself and an English-Russian reading book that had been published in Moscow. Bereft of most of my valuables – I had even had to give up my wooden suitcase – I went back to my comrades who had been handled in the same sort of way.

ON THE WAY TO SIBERIAN BANISHMENT

Shortly after midday our names were called out in alphabetical order and we were brought to the prison yard. Here already stood individual columns with their baggage. Some of the condemned ones wore inadequate clothing, having lost everything else in games of chance. It took some time until half the transport, about six hundred men, stood ready to march off. Under careful supervision, we were directed through the gate that we had got to know on the night of our arrival.

We had to form up in fives. My astonishment was large when I saw the gigantic contingent of soldiers. There were even some mounted ones. I estimated at least a company of them. We were now formed into rows of ten. To the right and left of us stood the soldiers in double rows three paces apart, armed with machine-pistols or carbines with fixed bayonets. There was a guard every ten metres or so. They had great trouble controlling their bloodhounds, with their slavering mouths and loud barking.

Great numbers of people have assembled to watch this spectacle and they come as close as the cordon of sentries allows. Their faces express sympathy for our plight and several mothers or wives dab away their tears with a handkerchief. Some of them have travelled several hundred kilometres by railway to get here: it is a mystery to me how these people knew that we would be transported today.

Today is the beginning of spring. After the long winter months, spring life begins again. Few of those in our ranks share this hopefulness today. Which of us will return from the uncertainty that awaits us? Does uprooting millions, putting them behind barbed wire and leaving them there for years and years under the hardest slavery sit with freedom? Perhaps we previously defined freedom falsely in the homeland. According to reports by the prisoners, between twenty and thirty thousand Soviet citizens are living in banishment.

Some of the Russians in our ranks recognise relatives. They are unable to suppress their emotions and have to wipe away their tears. It is a farewell for years, perhaps even for ever.

The last prisoners are now standing outside. Slowly the gigantic column sets off. The second half of the prisoners will be brought along this evening. To the constant shouts from the guards, which is largely a waste of their breath, we hasten forwards, taking care to keep in line with our row of ten. We are on the road, but it is very bad in parts and often there are big puddles that we have to go through; it is not easy to stay upright, for we are carrying our packs in one hand and holding on to our neighbour with the other. The word Siberia weighs heavily on these banished men, staggering along with their heads hanging. My friend and I bump up against them. With a clear conscience, and the belief that one day the door to freedom will open again, we hold our heads up high. We look people firmly in the face as they look at us from the trams and make ourselves known immediately as Germans.

It is also interesting to observe the behaviour of those standing on the roadside. An old woman standing near a picture of Stalin points her finger at us as we march past. Behind a window pane I see a man photographing this column of prisoners. Everywhere I can see nothing but a deep and silent sympathy. What could the thoughts be behind these faces? By the morning it could be any one of them marching along here.

We are marching at a brisk speed through the town's neglected streets, but the wooden buildings let us know that we will soon be outside the town. Where are we going now? Railway wagons can be seen in the distance – could they be our destination? A scrap heap reminds us of times past, with German and Russian tanks and trucks waiting to be scrapped. We have long since given up trying to keep our feet dry. Our feet are wet and covered in mud up to the ankles.

Finally we reach the loading place and the last preparations are made by the escorting troops. Several civilians who have been following us until now stay at a secure distance and try in vain to hand over gifts to their family members.

We halt alongside our railway wagons. There are sixty-two of us standing in front of a Pullmann car, and once our names have been called out, we can climb aboard. We establish from our friends that Kurt App, who had not been seen until now, is here, so all ten of us condemned men are on this transport. In our wagon, apart from me, are Götz, Korff, Mütschele, Doerr and Menden. I follow the example of several Ukrainians, writing a letter to my family in the last of the dimming light. I was told that immediately the train started off the letters would be pushed out through the gaps in the doors. Locals would immediately search the area and any letters they found would be thrown into the letter box. The same sort of thing had happened in Charkov Prison, where the prisoners, at an unguarded moment on their daily walks, would wrap their letters around a stone and throw them over the five-metre high prison wall to the street. Passers-by then picked them up and forwarded them on.

I wrote one letter to the wife of my fallen commander in the East Zone, another to my friend Karl in Saporoschje. Although I was not convinced that the letters would reach their destinations, I threw them through a crack in the door in the darkness of the night as the train moved off. Once more I was travelling in a barred and heavily guarded wagon through the endless expanse of Russia.

Heavy banging on the wagon door woke me up. It was dark. With the help of the duty doorman the door was opened by the guards outside. A torch flashed. Through its half-covered beam I made out two guards. All the prisoners in the wagon had to move to one side, and we were herded together like sheep as the empty half of the wagon was carefully knocked and checked by two guards with long wooden hammers. Once it was ready, we were counted across into the checked half of the wagon. The guard counting us shouted 'March, march!' When this did not work, he enforced it with his long hammer handle. Finally they checked out just as carefully the other half of the wagon. To the guards' loud shouting we had to run to and fro like recruits several times. Finally they disappeared. Midnight must have passed already. I fell asleep thinking over the experiences of the day.

Early next morning the same game started as we had experienced at midnight. This time the counting went better.

Days went past, with our train often remaining stationary on one bit of track or another for long periods. The guards were very sharp. We were counted two or three times a day, and the wagon repeatedly checked. Sentries ran about on the roofs and ensured that none of the prisoners went to the window without permission.

The food was like all the rest until now. Prisoners with only short sentences have come with us from Charkov Prison and cook soup for us or bring us water. They will be returning to Charkov with the guards.

In our wagon were several condemned persons who had fought on the German side against the Soviet Union. Except for one Russian, who nevertheless lived in the Ukraine, all the occupants were Ukrainians with sentences of between five and twenty-five years. Many of them had been in Germany and were enthusiastic about the general standards of living there. And these men had supported Germany in the fiercest fighting in their lives. We still do not understand today why they had believed the announcements of their government and returned to their homeland. Some were already in America or elsewhere on the globe away from the reach of the Soviets. But love of home overcame them and they believed Moscow's promises that they would remain unmolested. Now they were paying for their gullibility with twenty-five years' hard labour and further years of being deprived of the right to vote. Their families were punished with confiscations, of houses, cattle, and so on, and they themselves were not allowed to return to their place of birth at the end of their sentences.

In long talks, which were very interesting for me and also educational, I obtained an impression of the character of the

Ukrainian. They all had a deep national feeling and did not speak well of the Russians. Even with the youngsters, despite a unified Soviet education, I was able to establish that they had not lost their national instincts.

Two Ukrainians especially stood out because of their education: Buburenkov, a former Kolchose supervisor who had studied theology but had had to change after the revolution, and Poronovsky, a bookkeeper. They told me about the history of Ukraine when it was still a principality with its capital in Kiev. In time the country became dependent upon Moscow and the revolution did not change things. With deep sincerity they both spoke of the famine that in 1932, according to their accounts, claimed more than two million victims and how the government, in order to diminish the vast extent of the death figures, paid the worth of 1 kilogram of corn for every dead person buried. When a person became weak from hunger and fell over they threw him on a cart and buried him even though he was still alive. In their hunger-madness some even became cannibals. I would not have believed it had I not myself lived through it in the months of February, March and April 1943.

And then they started talking about the death figures of the hunger years 1946/7. It is extraordinary to learn from the mouths of Kolchose workers that people were starving in Europe's bread-basket while deliveries of corn were being sent out to Australia.

They asked questions about Germany in the period after 1933, and I answered them as far as possible. They wanted to know about the handling of prisoners on the German side. As I did not know, I could not say anything about this. Buburenkov told me: 'When the German Wehrmacht came to Ukraine the whole of the Ukrainian people were delighted, as they regarded the German Wehrmacht as their liberators. Within half a year this smiling had turned to tears. And do you know what it means when a whole nation cries? Our men did not then come to you, but rather went to the partisans because they did not have to starve there!'

Another Ukrainian reported about wartime conditions. He had been wounded in the fighting and went to the Irkutsk area to recuperate. Food was scarce and very poor. The old people suffered especially and were little more than skin and bones. Suddenly it was announced that an American commission was to visit the little townships and Kolchoses in the area and almost overnight all the shops were filled with foodstuffs that the starving people knew only from their dreams. The old and undernourished were driven far away to another place so that the Americans would not see them. Those remaining at the place were asked to go to the food shops when the commission was present, but they were warned of the strongest punishment if they did not take everything back afterwards. Should they be questioned by the Americans about their state of health, they must not complain, but rather declare that they were well and could buy everything necessary. It sounded unbelievable, and yet everyone knew who saw the arbitrary way in which things happened here, that these people could not have been handled otherwise. They were never in the position to liberate themselves by their own strength.

We have long been travelling on Asian soil. Shortly before the Volga we met a homeward-bound train that was apparently carrying mainly sick. Our wagon stopped on the track right alongside and we were able to explain by signalling through the tiny window that we were sentenced prisoners of war. Hopefully they will report this back in the homeland.

The next big station will be Novo-Sibirsk, where guards tell us, we will be deloused. We have already been on the way for eight days. In six batches we are taken from the train to the bathing place about 800 metres away. It was, by European standards, primitive, but we were bathed and deloused within a few hours. In the course of this one of us had 25 roubles stolen from him.

A long, narrow footbridge runs over the track. Some passers-by gather and look curiously down on us as we get back aboard. From what I hear, their sympathy is on our side.

We are still going east, and soon we are standing at Taishet station, with yet another 600 kilometres to Irkutsk. Will we be staying there, or going further on? From here to Vladivostock is another 2,500 kilometres at least.

To our astonishment the train now turns off the main track and heads in a northerly direction, gradually turning east. It is clear to us that our journey cannot be much longer, as on the map that we still have in our minds there was no railway line here a short time ago.

IN THE BANISHMENT CAMPS OF THE 'ANGARLAG' WEST OF LAKE BAIKAL

We drive through the taiga for three days before the train stops at its destination, Bratsk. The terrain here is cut through by valleys and ravines and is very hilly. Several times we stopped on this stretch near camps. We even saw some Japanese prisoners. Back in November 1948 the Japanese had already been loaded onto wagons with the apparent intention of returning to their homeland. The Ukrainians lying by the window called out twice to them when the train was stopped. About 200 metres away we saw a prisoner of war camp. The occupants – of whom we saw several – were wearing SS camouflage uniform tunics and gloves. We were unable to attract their attention.

We had long discussions about the likely fate of these men, who were strongly guarded. Were they also unable to write home, as at every camp in the Urals in which there were only members of the SS. A Russian prisoner in a Saporoschje prison said that he had worked quite close to a member of the Wehrmacht who was allowed to write home, while SS troops working in a woodland camp and carrying out wood-felling tasks were not allowed to.

From the railway wagons we went in smaller columns to the individual camps of Bratsk. All such movements were carefully guarded, including with tracker dogs. We were, according to those who brought us, to be divided up among the town's transit camps, so that those with political convictions and the criminal elements are kept apart. The whole town seemed to consist of these camps and the personnel belonging to them. I did not see a single factory, only the great wooden watchtowers so characteristic of the Soviet Union.

The transport commander who took the German-Russian dictionary from me appears and gives me, instead of the dictionary, a Russian-English textbook on the grounds that the dictionary had been retained at Charkov. In fact, I think that he had kept it for himself. Anyway I am content to have some reading material at least.

The camp that we have been brought to is overcrowded. As preliminary accommodation we are allocated the dining room, in which people are already housed. Such overcrowding reminds me of the time shortly after I was taken prisoner. We put our bags on the little stage on which the camp inmates live. I go to the toilets for a moment. During my absence of about ten minutes my bag is taken. I do not know what to do and am upset, as most of the books that I have been able to save until now have gone. All of the papers that I have been working on in order to learn the Russian language are also in my bag. I can get over the loss of everything else, but this loss cannot be replaced in the taiga. Such a thing has never occurred in the years until now, while I have been living with my comrades, but it has occurred here within minutes of my arrival.

Even the pack from Breske has vanished. The Russian duty officer tells me that he can do nothing about it and that I should take better care next time. There will be no next time - I have now nothing to lose. I am angry with my comrades for not watching my bag, although I had asked them to. But which of us central Europeans could imagine that such theft takes place here like this?

The night passes very slowly, as it always does when one has a poor sleeping place and people are so closely packed together. Everyone that has to go out must climb over the mass of bodies and listen to all sorts of complaints. My thoughts are still busy with the stolen items. Fortunately I still have the Fournier wooden-bound diary and the *Drift der Papanins* in English. If I want to learn more Russian I will have to use both these books as writing aids. I will cut out all the unpleasant things. I must escape during the summer and until then I must study.

Early in the morning we are driven out into the yard to be counted. This is always a very disorderly process. My comrades stand forward in the first rows of six. The commandant complains a lot about having to translate things that are not understood. I step forward to try to translate for him, but I have hardly opened my mouth when I get struck in the neck from behind, followed by a hard kick. I am pushed back with the most horrible swearing, with which this country is so richly blessed. With my teeth clenched together, holding back the tears of pain, I stand there looking into the hate-filled face of this fellow who looks so subhuman. For hours after the counting I am still in no state to talk with my friends, who leave me alone. I will not forget the face of this NKVD agent.

Luckily we were moved on the next day, the 8th of April, on trucks that drove up in front of the camp for this purpose and were specially equipped for it. We had to share with thirty other prisoners, while two sentries with machine-pistols saw to it that no one tried to escape. On the principle that it is 'better to be driven badly than to walk well', we were happy to save our legs.

Our destination was Kaimonovo, a village lying far out in the taiga on the planned railway line. The distance to it was about 150 kilometres. We were driven a long distance on the ice of the Angara. This was already showing some very wide cracks that the hidden stream would soon sweep away for a few months. Sitting became even more uncomfortable. My friend Ottel, who was sitting with me in a truck, had an especially uncomfortable place, so we changed places at one halt. The villages here lay very far apart, and their huts illustrated the poverty of the inhabitants. The Russians were frightened of the fast driving of the truck drivers. One truck had already overturned. My friends Mütschele, Korff and Doerr were on it. Fortunately nothing serious occurred, with only a few Russians getting soaked.

As night sinks down over us the driving becomes more difficult. We often have to climb off and push the trucks out of mud and holes in the snow. We stop on the edge of a village for a long time. Our truck driver has driven into a hole in the ice and the truck is now hanging with only the front axle secure. Here too it is a wonder that nothing happened.

It is cold. The veins on my hands are frozen from the frost. My gloves were among my stolen things. Ottel gives me one of his. We have already been on our way for more than fourteen hours. The guards are becoming ever more unpleasant. My legs ache from the tight seating. Wherever one looks, there is nothing but woodland. The taiga is unending here.

At dawn we come through a small village. Kaimonovo at last. Another 3 kilometres and we stop. How our legs ache after such a strenuous journey. We are taken over by another guard and march from the road down a short hill to a camp. The surrounding fence puts an end to all doubts. A short stop before the camp gate and then we are called forward by our personal files and let into the camp.

As I soon discover, this is the 206th Column 'Angarlag': a women's camp. Apart from Kurt App, who we had seen from our truck on the way – he was with a column that was continuing on foot – we are all together. Apart from the kitchen hut and the bathhouse, there are only two barrack blocks. Our provisional accommodation is a summer barrack that had been used as an isolation barrack until now. One could almost compare it to a cave, and had I not already experienced similar holes I would have believed it impossible to sleep here with so many people. However, it suits us and we are especially pleased to have a roof, even if it has holes in it, and it also has a petrol can that serves as a stove. It is inadequately supplied with water, so snow is melted. There is no toilet available. I have the impression that this camp had only been set up the year before.

Russian sentries ensure that the young prisoners do not get into the women's barracks, but some still manage it during the night. They report on their experiences with the usual smiles.

To my surprise there are female sentries in the watchtowers. It is explained to me that these are condemned prisoners with only short sentences to complete. The same thing happens in the men's camps.

Despite my fatigue I can hardly get any rest. The lack of room in the barrack prevents me from sleeping. There are bugs here, too.

On the morning of the 10th of April we were deloused and examined by a doctor. The doctor himself did not speak a word to us, but his companion was full of hate towards us when he discovered that we were German. Then at midday we had to assemble at the camp gate and form up in our allocated work teams. To my regret we were separated. Mütschele, Korff, Breske, Doerr and Menden went to the 209th Team, which was based about 12 kilometres from here. Götz, Franke, Schroeter and I had to go with the prisoners in the 208th Team. As the sentry told us, this is quite a new camp.

With us come those with political sentences. The track that we are marching along is saturated. It was first made several months ago, and until then hardly any human foot had trod this ground. Silently, each one of us considering his own thoughts, we go through the endless taiga. I visualise once more the map I had seen hanging in an office in Bratsk. According to that, we are now some 600 kilometres northwest of the northern edge of Lake Baikal. If I am going to flee, then my only option is to try to get to Irkutsk and from there via Schita to Manchuria. But how to achieve this, I have not yet worked out.

There are women there! Suddenly, at a turn in the track, about two hundred female prisoners come into sight. Silently we look at each other, the guards having forbidden any talking. All races and nationalities are represented. Old and young, with more or less tattered clothing or padded suits. Most seem careworn, but some of the younger ones give a carefree impression and ask us where we come from. Despite the ban on talking, some men speak to them as they go past. Immediately the guard commander jumps between them like a bulldog. Are there also German women with them? We cannot establish this from their dress, since they all look the same.

At last we reach the camp. In fact, it is quite a new camp. There is no fencing and apart from the guardroom, in which the camp commandant lives, only two tents have been set up. In the first tent there are already about a hundred men who arrived yesterday from Charkov. They were not, however, political prisoners, much to our regret, as it seemed to us that those imprisoned for political offences were rarely also thieves. There are three Germans among them (one of whom, Hans Rempelt, was abducted from the Siebenbürgen to Russia), making seven Germans in the camp altogether.

The living conditions here are very bad and are typically 'in progress'. There is no kitchen, its function being replaced by a cauldron standing in the open air. There is no toilet, so we use anywhere outside that is suitable. There is no bath, so we have to content ourselves with washing with melted snow. The water for the kitchen is brought in by cart, but it is hardly sufficient. There is no bakery, the bread being brought from a neighbouring camp.

Apart from the guardroom, everything has to be planned and erected. Our first job is to fence ourselves in, erecting a 3.5-metre-high fence around the whole camp complex. It is a difficult and tiring task, as the melting ice is very obstructive. All four of us – Götz, Franke, Schroeter and I – work on the holes that have to be dug for the posts. The ground is frozen down to a metre's depth and hardly thaws at all in the summer here, where the woodland closes in and the sunlight cannot penetrate. Often stones make it difficult too. As tools for the workers there are only crowbars, hammers, hoes and spades. The food here is also completely insufficient and our strength soon diminishes. As our foreman, a Russian called Schlakov, cheats on our provisions, we soon come into conflict with him. We are able to move to a carpentry brigade, but here too the work norms are very high in order to obtain additional food.

Despite the strenuous work and the poor food, I keep up my language studies. I try to write down every new word that I hear, together with the German translation, so as to at least learn something. I am pleased with my success. A young Ukrainian who had fought with the Waffen-SS and had been sentenced to twenty-five years makes friends with us. His father, an officer in the Red Army who was connected with the Bucharin affair, vanished and since then he has not heard any more of him. He has nothing particularly good to say about the system. I am especially astonished again and again to find that a great many of those who do not come under the political heading speak badly about their government.

The bread deliveries from the neighbouring camp are wholly inadequate. Until now, we have not had the correct amount on a single day. The hunger is overwhelming. We are supposed to get it all later, but I do not believe this. We worked feverishly on making an oven so that the camp could be independent for bread. The old ones among us are the most pessimistic and believe that they will not live much longer. There is a 58-year-old among them who has been given a twenty-five year sentence.

Something out of the ordinary has occurred. Three young Russians from the neighbouring tent have escaped. For me this is proof that it is possible if one so wishes. But how far will they get? Their disappearance was discovered at this morning's head count and within two hours there were people here from the main administration with tracker dogs. If the fugitives are caught then they can expect the same treatment as was meted out to then men from the 209th Column who were on the run for three days. When they were caught, one was shot, the second was badly wounded and was taken to hospital, and the third came back to the camp. I saw him standing in front of our camp with a battered face describing himself as an idiot and giving us the advice not to make any attempts at escape. Nevertheless I will try should a suitable moment occur.

Easter 1949. In the remotest part of the camp we seven Germans have got together to celebrate Easter. With the 'Easter Walk' from Faust and some spring poems we return in our hearts to our homeland and try to forget our surroundings and our difficult situation.

UNDER FALSE SUSPICION

It is a lovely day in May. The sun is shining and we are already quite warm by midday. The short noon break is already over. Another two-fifths of the present area and we will have fulfilled our norm.

A Russian appears and says that Götz, Franke, Schroeter and I have to go to the guardroom with our baggage. Not knowing what it is about, we go back to the tent and collect our belongings. With the contributions from my friends, I have again acquired some rags, which are valuable items here. Three Asiatics are waiting for us at the guardroom. There follows a basic body and luggage search in which both my diary and the *Drift der Papanins* are taken off me. Even my photographs, which I always carry with me and until now have been able to keep, are taken from me by these slit-eyed Asiatics. I keep quiet. Once the rest are done comes the order: 'March!'

With us come three men from the 209th Column, who tell us that our friends are still there. We dare not leave the centre of the track and are constantly chased forward by the barking and aggressive tracker dog. Although a few days before we had received new summer shoes, they are made out of cheap leather uppers and rubber soles and the melting snow and marsh quickly permeate through. We follow the same route that brought us here. On the way we meet our former camp commandant, who grins scornfully when he sees us. As one of the guards told us, we are going to the punishment column. The reason for this transfer is not made known to us.

It is already beginning to get dark when we reach our new unit. It lies near the 206th Column, which was our last post before we went to the 208th Column. In front of the wooden building that apparently serves as the guards' accommodation, we have to sit on a fallen tree trunk. A captain soon appears – he has only one ear, the other side being covered by a black flap – and asks us if anyone speaks Russian. I report that I do. He then orders me to follow him into the building. In his office I remain standing at the door while he takes a place at his desk. The captain asks me my name and rank, where I had fought and for what I had been sentenced. Once I have answered his questions, he asks if I know why we are here. I reply in the negative. He snaps back: 'You have made preparations to flee and apart from that you are carrying Fascist propaganda!' The captain looks sharply at me while speaking these words. I counter his look and ask with a contemptuous smile: 'And where would we then flee to, captain? Apart from that, I am the only one of us who speaks any Russian and you yourself must realise that by the second word it is obvious that I am a foreigner. We have all been in the Soviet Union for years as prisoners of war and know all too well that we can only harm ourselves by escaping.'

'We will see. Only don't believe that your agitation will work here, or you will experience things to wonder about!'

The hearing appeared to be at an end, as the captain called in the guard. I asked once more for my handwritten vocabulary and the pictures that had been taken from me. The first was flatly refused, the second allowed. Ottel's mirror, which I had had since Stalingrad, remained with the captain. Mirrors are very rare items here and very highly prized as they belong to the 'Kultura'.

The guard brings us, together with the three Russians, to a dark cell. Before we seven men are shut in the small 1.5 by 2 metre cell, we have to undergo another thorough search. Ottel and I still own a comb each that we acquired in Saporoschje. The warder finds some fallen hairs and we keep quiet as both combs vanish into our pockets. Since I lost my pack in Bratsk it is all the same to me. And we still possess something that these people find attractive.

It takes some time for all of us to squeeze into the extremely small cell, which is intended for two or three persons. We all have to make ourselves as small as possible. I make it clear to the Russians that we would prefer to have no problems with them, and, as we are in the majority, they agree.

Two hours must have passed already. Our limbs ache from the uncomfortable conditions in which we half-crouch, half-lie. Near our cell is a second one with women in it. The Russians use the time to start talking with them as their deprived circumstances leave hardly anything else to wish for. The abusive names they use on both sides are very numerous, the least harmless being 'dog', 'bitch', and 'whore'.

IN THE 205th COLUMN

The cell is opened quite unexpectedly. It is dark outside. We have to get together all our things that are strewn around in the anteroom and climb on a truck. We go like the wind through the night. We disembark at the entrance to the village of Kaimonovo and are directed by the guard through open country that we are unable to recognise in the dark. I do not feel well, and seem to have a fever.

We proceed over boulders, grassland and through a stream, followed by the two swearing guards, who hit us with their rifle butts if we do not move fast enough. The glow from an open fire serves to guide us and a few minutes later we are standing before the camp guardroom. On all four sides outside the camp four great fires are being maintained so that the darkness cannot be used as cover for fleeing.

The guards are particularly alert of late since twelve men escaped from the 203rd Column, including a former tank major and a submarine commander. They took the guards by surprise and disarmed them before taking the first good truck on the road, which happened to be full of food, and setting off in a generally western direction. Anyone who offered any resistance at the road-blocks every 4 or so kilometres was shot down. So far no one has heard that they have been killed. We did learn that the three men who had escaped from the 208th Column were caught, though. One of them was left on the track.

We went through the usual search at the guardroom. Why do they do it? Is it just curiosity? My photographs aroused considerable interest, and the purses containing about 40 roubles were retained by the guards. Experience reassures me that they will be returned the following day.

It is already midnight when we are locked up in the isolation block. Water is brought from the kitchen for us to drink. We lie down on the cold ground floor in the anteroom of the little blockhouse, but no one can sleep properly as the night is too cold and there is a draught coming under the door. My head wants to burst with heat.

We are up before the warder arrives. It is already daylight outside and we can make out where we are. It is a small depression in the dark woods of the taiga with a shallow stream running through it. On one side lie the few partly collapsed and windblown houses of Kaimonovo village. Opposite them stand the new-looking prominent blockhouses of the prison camp, which bears the number of the 205th Column. Here we are to learn our fate.

We are allocated to an already overfilled barrack for our

accommodation. The prisoners within receive us with shouting. Most of them are between sixteen and thirty years old, with only a few older men. I get the impression of living in a primitive jungle. We lie on the floor at the rear of the barrack. Every moment some person or other comes to relieve their curiosity about us.

We discover that there are already three other Germans here, as well as a Volga German. The latter soon appears and asks in an unrecognisable Swabian dialect where we come from. His name is Caspar Leisle, whose antecedents had come from southern Germany at the time of Catherine the Great. But he does not differentiate himself from the others and gives the impression of being cunning.

Shortly afterwards we get to know the three other Germans, who are prisoners of war like ourselves. There are two Silesians, Ruprecht Scholtissek and Theo Murawiets, and a Dortmunder, Erich Sommerfeld.

That evening I go to the hospital at the appointed time. I am running a temperature of 39.2 degrees. I will not have to go to work tomorrow.

Next morning my friends have to go with the Voronin Brigade to work on the railway line, but the camp nurse has ordered bed rest for me. Tired and washed out, I lie down on one of the bunks and soon fall fast asleep. I wake at noon, my head still feverish. I climb off the bunk to put on my shoes, which I had placed under the bed. I ask the room orderly, a large, rigorous bull of a man, if he had seen who took my shoes. He says not. I clasp my head and think I must be in a madhouse. This is simply not possible. Who could possibly be interested in my shoes?

Barefoot, I go to the guardroom and report the loss of my shoes. The duty officer is the one who had received us in the night, and he now returns my photographs and the purses with the money. Then he came with me to the barrack but he too was unable to find my shoes. I then discover from the other Russians that one must never leave shoes or other items of clothing lying around as they are immediately stolen: 'There are professional criminals in these camps who steal everything they need, or even take them forcibly. Your shoes will soon have been turned into boots, as now the summer is beginning and the brigadiers allow boots to be made out of shoes. The soles of the boots will be made of leather while sailcloth is used for the uppers. Whoever stole your shoes will sell them to a brigadier, who then gives him supplementary food to eat for several days or gives the shoes to a racketeer who will sell them openly in the village. You must put your shoes under your head and sleep on the other things.'

That evening I take note of the footwear of the brigadier and several prisoners who enjoy a special status in camp life. They have better footwear and also clothes that stand out from the rest. Although their clothing is not up to European standards, it is far better than the rags and tatters of the majority. Here the strong live at the expense of the weak, enforcing their rule with brutal force. Should anyone oppose the despotic system of the brigadiers, beatings and deprivation of food ensue.

These professional criminals are known as *Bladnoi* and all over the Soviet Union they stick together like pitch and sulphur. They regard work as dishonourable and acknowledge no authority, so they are seldom challenged. A life counts for nothing here! None of the supervisors dares to go against these lads, for fear of retribution. Even those who have left the Bladnoi have put their lives at risk, as every 'law-abiding' *Bladnoi* is duty-bound to kill such apostates. Even if they have been outside for ten years or more already, there is no end to the chase. 'Who knows what tomorrow will bring?' is often heard. So these criminals have to rely on a war to bring them freedom, and many want to get to Germany as soon as possible as they have heard that one can live well there. Everything is available in the shops and the citizens are not as closely watched as they are in the Soviet Union.

My comrades return late in the evening from the worksite. They are tired and shattered. Their physical weakness is visibly more apparent. They had to move earth in very primitive wheelbarrows. They tell me there is no proper work supervision in the brigades other than that of the brigadiers. And they have already lost favour. From lack of knowledge of the customs or – as the convicts say themselves – camp rules, we have turned some of the brigadiers against us. As Ottel went to the workshop to get something repaired he met a *Bladnoi* on the way who was a brigadier. He called Ottel to him, but Ottel, in his ignorance when he was before him, replied that if he wanted something he should come himself. The brigadier punched Ottel in the stomach. Immediately Ottel aimed a blow at his head but missed, and other criminals hurried to help the *Bladnoi*. Ottel told them that if they wanted something from him, they should meet him alone behind the barrack. An overseer agreed with Ottel and took him away. There was nothing to be seen of the brigadier on the way back to the barrack. As we later discovered, the *Bladnoi* was called Miroshnitshenko.

God be praised, we were able to transfer to another brigade, where the brigadier is a former captain who had attended the Russian War Academy. He is very friendly towards the Germans and keeps a protective hand over us. He also keeps away from the other brigadiers. The reason for his sentencing he keeps to himself. I assume it was for a military offence. He agrees that we have been too harshly punished with eight or ten years under Paragraph 206, for which the highest punishment is five years. Under his instructions we have to dig boreholes. It is an arduous job as the scaffolding is insufficient and unprofessionally laid out, but at least we get a little extra bread for it.

Early in the morning we go to the workplace, which is about a kilometre from the camp. There is a hill here that has to be demolished. With crowbars, hammers and spades we dig bore holes four or five metres deep into the cliff. The deeper we go, the more dangerous the work becomes, because the scaffolding is most insufficient and also unprofessionally erected. Those working below have to beware of stones falling from the shovels of those working above them. There are relatively few accidents. The loose stones that we dig out are hauled up on wire and wooden ropes in wooden buckets made in the camp, and heavy enough when empty. There is very little pay for all this hard work.

No longer do we have the pleasure of working in a brigade with our friends. The new camp commandant, a captain who had been a prisoner of war of the Germans for some time, as I was able to interpret from some remarks, ordered that no more than one German should work in a brigade. This is very bad for my comrades as they cannot understand Russian without my help. I was moved to the Klutshnikov Brigade. This is a carpentry brigade which is based in the women's camp of the 206th Column, some three kilometre distant from here. The brigade consists mainly of criminal elements. It is twenty-four men strong, of whom between fifteen and eighteen work at a time in most cases. The others spend their whole time in the women's zone. Every day the camp experts change some of the brigade to enable men to let off steam.

On the way to the women's camp we have to go past the workplace where the women are employed. While we are marching past conversation starts up between them and the Bladnois that concerns the lowest, animal-like desires and is conducted in a general and ordinary manner that would make even prostitutes blush. The children of the guards' families, aged around six or eight, hear these conversations every morning on their way to school. They laugh about them because they know nothing else. Overall, if one looks at the children's faces, one can see a certain precociousness that is not on the whole visible in our children back home. It is the knowledge of reality that our youngsters acquire later. I regret these creatures that mar their children's paradise. Do they also know the excitements of Christmas, Easter or their birthday?

Having arrived at the women's camp, we work animals are immediately chased to work while the do-nothings lurk about, waiting for an opportunity to slink into the women's huts. One man keeps lookout so that they are not taken by surprise. If there is any danger, such as an overseer on the way, then these lads are immediately at the workplace, grabbing the tools out of the working men's hands and digging like mad. This way they displace the men who have already been working away for hours, so that the overseer concerned gets the impression that they are the best workers. Of course, the instant that the overseer is out of sight again, they throw the tools into a corner and vanish again.

Those of the robots who will not work are beaten down and get less to eat. The percentages, however, are in the hands of the do-nothings and *Bladnois*, and on payment days they of course get the highest sums. As there is little money overall, the *Bladnois* and brigadiers also take part of the workers' money. Most workers donate money willingly just to keep on good terms with the brigadiers.

Anyone who sees these emaciated figures knows without being told that hunger plays a great part here. They are all physically too weak to be able to speak out against this criminal injustice. The brutes rule here with fists, and I am relieved that the Bladnois generally handle us Germans somewhat more carefully. They know that we are spiritually superior to them and have heard much about our fatherland so they have a little respect. It is naturally often difficult to give them the answers they want to their sometimes naïve questions about Germany. With those who have had a little more education it is quite a different matter. With them one can discuss matters that are relevant. They mainly occupy positions in which there is no physical work to perform and they can therefore live better. I am certain that, in contradiction to the statistics that I have seen until now, there are still very many illiterates. Even my limited knowledge of Russian grammar is still better than that of many country children.

One day I met in the camp the chief of the camp guards, the captain who had questioned me and had arranged our transfer to this camp. Once more I asked him for the vocabulary that I had written out. He refused to give it back, saying: 'Study our solution to the fulfilment of our Five Year Plan, which is here in this yard, and you will learn enough!' He then pointed to the signs standing on both sides of the camp road calling for the early fulfilment of the Five Year Plan. 'If you get back to Germany once your sentence is completed, you can still learn enough Russian!' He left me standing there with a cynical laugh.

STRANGE ENCOUNTER IN THE TAIGA

The month of May has almost ended. For more than two weeks now I have been working with the Klutschnikov Brigade in the women's area. The northbound truck convoys, heading for the Lena, are still stopping here with their Lithuanians, Latvians, Estonians and West Ukrainians from the former Poland, with their few belongings. These groups were given about twenty minutes to decide whether to adopt the Kolchose system or not; those who were reluctant were then regarded as dangerous elements living too near the border and were shipped out. Ammunition, fuel and food transports have also been rolling north for about fourteen days without a break. The trucks, mainly three-axled, are from the Red Army, like their drivers.

Our work is very hard, especially dragging up the large tree trunks required for building the blockhouse. It has already gone noon. As always we are immediately driven back to work after eating. With my axe – it is the bluntest one, as I was not at the morning struggle for the best tools – I hack at a trunk.

I am already thinking about the vast difference between the

women at home and the creatures that go about here. A few minutes ago one of the women made an indecent proposal; they seem to be only on the search for men. She had previously discovered from the Russians that I am a 'Nemetz', i.e. a German. I continued with my work without reacting in any way until she left. How repulsive can such a person be!

Other images run through my head. One only has to look at the people who have been here for years, some living behind the wire for a decade or more, and the question arises: 'Are they men or animals?' My conclusion is that they are 'animal-like people'. One can then also understand why these unfortunate creatures, if they are a little less robust, would one day be prepared to put an end to their lives, as was the case yesterday evening with a female guard on the watchtower of Camp 206. She shot herself through the head, although she had less than five years' imprisonment to go. Grossmann's book, *These people are imperishable!*, describes how he came to a place in which he found German prisoners of war at a meal. From their slurping he obtained the impression that he was in a pigsty. Grossmann was right, erring only in that he came not to German prisoner of war accommodation but to the canteen in some Russian factory or perhaps a dining room in a Russian prison camp.

The incidents that we see in the dining room every day – including the brawling at the kitchen serving hatch – are indescribable and incomprehensible to a normal European. I had not experienced such scenes even in the prisoner of war camps where great hunger reigned. And how is it at the construction site? Not a jot better! The brigadiers and *Bladnois* get double and triple rations that the cooks pass under the table to them, as they get their money from the brigadiers for the gas that comes to the camp in mysterious ways. We working animals often do not even get what is due to us. Not everything goes into the cauldron that should! Quite often the camp's experts receive meat, fat, oil, fish, noodles and various high-grade items from the kitchens. The final result is naturally that the broad masses see nothing of it. No one dares raise a storm against this or they would be done away with. Despotism rules here! The work norm setter is a prisoner, as are the bookkeeper and the master and all those concerned with our supervision. As they earn just about nothing, they have to obtain their money by other means and so their demands are relatively high –

vodka is not cheap! The broad mass of the working animals are hungry and want to live, and their focus of attention is directed only at food. It lies in the hands of the brigadiers to allocate them a larger percentage than they can actually obtain from the state norms. The master, however, must approve the whole work and check it. The brigadier pays him only a set sum, confirming also the work not carried out, so that more income can be allocated. The slave is happy if he receives up to 450 grams of bread a day, and is quite ready to hand over the biggest part of his money to his brigadier as he otherwise would get nothing at all in the coming month in either money or supplementary food! This way, as a rule, the monthly income does not exceed 40 to 50 roubles.

The majority are happy if they can buy a loaf once a month. This bread is smuggled in by the bakers, who work outside the camp. A 3 kilo loaf costs between 10 and 20 roubles and so takes half the money earned. In every brigade there are those who give the whole of their money to the brigadier. In turn, every day they receive most of the supplementary rations, although they have done no work. They are the special darlings of the brigadier; often homosexually inclined, they remain at his disposal. These lads do not work; they do nothing all day. Even the guards can do nothing about them.

If only there were none of these damned small midges. It is impossible to chase them away and they creep into every gap in one's clothing in order to suck one's blood. The Russians call them 'Moschkach'. They swarm around us in their thousands. It is simply impossible to work in the open air without wearing scarves that have to be secured under the neck, or the insects creep into the mouth, eyes, ears and nose. It is enough to drive one crazy: our hands are bitten and full of small bumps. But no one asks the foremen for relief – the answer is always the same: 'You have to work, you dog!'

At midday the temperatures average between 30 and 40 degrees. Then in the evening it cools down so quickly that one is happy to have a padded jacket.

I am jerked out of my thoughts. A West Ukrainian, formerly a Polish citizen, who worked in Austria during the war and would love to go back, calls out to me: 'Comrade, there is a German here!' I suddenly see a blond woman opposite, of medium size and blue eyes. From her appearance she could be in her mid-thirties.

'Are you German?' She looks at me questioningly.

'Yes, I am from Berlin.' I present myself. 'But how did you get to this godforsaken place?' With a sad smile that shows quite openly the pain and harm she has endured, she replies: 'I am called Lisa Nickel and I was arrested in the street near Schloss Bellevue in 1947. I am married and have always lived in Berlin. They accused me of being a Russian citizen who had first seen the light of day in Kiev. I was indeed born there, as the child of German parents, and I went to Berlin with my parents as a two-year-old child. I grew up there and got married. But it was confirmed in the official registry there that I was born in Kiev and because of this I was sentenced to ten years' hard labour for being a traitor. Now I am here and have to work like the others. I can barely understand even the most important Russian words.'

The fate of this woman impressed me a lot, but I did not let her see this. The Russians watching us made salacious remarks and asked me why I did not vanish with the woman into the barracks. In reply, I tell them that in Germany other customs apply and not all men are animals like them. A braying laugh was the reply. They had not understood the sharpness of my ripost.

Frau Nickel told me that she was not the only one. Other German women and men had been taken from the Soviet Zone after the end of the war. But there were also *Volksdeutsche* women from Ukraine and the Volga Republic here. They had either worked for the Germans and been banished at the end of the war, or, like Lisa, had been in banishment camps as enemy aliens since the beginning of the war.

Back in the camp I described my meeting with Frau Nickel. My comrades were also touched by her story. We knew what this woman must have already gone through and what lay ahead of her. How many other German women and girls could have been taken away? I thought of the report of my comrades who worked in the Electricity Works. While emptying railway wagons, they found that German women had written on the walls while loading the wagons. This was their work now.

A FRIEND FALLS BY THE ROADSIDE

Ottel is giving me cause for concern. He is still working as a carpenter with a brigade whose brigadier is an especially disgusting creature.

Ottel is too proud to reject the work allocated to him. I was deeply shocked when I last saw him in a bath. He is now nothing but skin and bones, just like Schroeter, and yet he was the strongest one among us until now. It is perhaps understandable – for a man 187 centimetres tall the food here is far too little, even were he not working. Ottel lies on his bed with a very flushed face and takes no part in the evening conversation. He has a temperature of 39 degrees. He should go to the sickbay in the morning – hopefully his temperature will have gone down by then.

To our regret, Ottel has to go to the hospital, as his fever has increased. But it is better for him to go there for a few days than to lie here in the barracks. We say goodbye to our friend before going off to work. Days pass without our being able to discover anything about Ottel. He is in the 204th Column's hospital 4 kilometres away.

Meanwhile I have got to know a Latvian who served as an SS man in German service. He is a tall chap, with open, clear eyes and a pleasant manner. He speaks good German and confides in me that he wants to escape, having no wish to spend another nine years in this hell. He loathes the Russians who have oppressed and looted his homeland, as he says. I am also constantly thinking of escaping, and we agree to flee together. We will try first to get through the taiga in a northerly direction to reach the Trans-Siberian Railway and then go on by train to Manchuria. The border is some 2,000 kilometres distant. As long as we are on Soviet territory he will use his knowledge of the language to safeguard our interests, while I will use my knowledge of English in Manchuria. We both know that it will be a very difficult adventure and it could easily go wrong.

Our intention is not to go on the roads and only to march by night, as long as we are in the border area. For the time being it is still too early to make the attempt as at the moment it is impossible to obtain fruit from the wilderness. We make our preparations slowly and carefully, concerning ourselves with such matters as what we will need for catching fish. It all has to be done with extreme caution, otherwise our escape plans will come to nothing.

Luckily I am able to join the Latvian's brigade. This is important because we want to flee from our workplace. But unfortunately my stay with the brigade is very short: my left knee has been causing me pain for days, and now I can hardly walk. It is very swollen, and the pain and the swelling are extending to my foot. Every step brings tears to my eyes. The Russian woman in the ambulatorium says it is the *Zinga*. What that is, I have no idea. Prisoners who have already had it say it is due to a lack of vitamins and is brought on by the bad and unbalanced diet.

My friend Oskar, who found himself a job as a laundryman in the camp and is now working with Ruprecht Scholtissek, has also fallen ill with this Asiatic sickness. His leg displays swelling as thick as mine. There is no medicine in the ambulatorium for this sickness, but we constantly hear the same thing: 'Drink chvoi!' This is a drink made from the chopped leaves of the Listviniza, a needle-like Siberian tree. After boiling the leaves, the water looks green. We drink the chvoi, but it is little better than nothing.

I have been within the camp area for several days already. Every movement gives me indescribable pain, such that it takes me a quarter of an hour to hobble the fifty metres to the ambulatorium. No brigade will have me, as I am a burden. Food has to be brought to me, and I can only conduct my necessary functions with the greatest pain because I cannot bend my leg. There is no question of escaping under these circumstances, but I have to get better again before the time of year makes flight impossible. It is now the middle of June and I have to be better by August. Ivan the Latvian will wait until then. I lie down in the barracks waiting for my comrade Wolf, who should appear back from work at any moment.

Today is the 15th of June. The day, like the previous ones, was very hot. The first men are coming into the barracks. They are dirty and sweaty, moving tiredly. Some have swollen faces from the bites of the small blood-thirsty midges that drive men mad.

Wolf comes in. He looks tired and exhausted. His face is also swollen – he has difficulties with the flies because he has to wear spectacles.

'Good evening, Wolf!'

'Good evening, Bert!'

'God be thanked the day is over. Anything new?' He looks at me with his big blue eyes. I then notice for the first time that he looks particularly serious.

'What's the matter, Wolf?' I ask him. With a tired, sad voice he replies: 'Bert, Otto is dead.'

'That cannot be!' I cry out. 'How do you know?'

Wolf sits down opposite me. 'Today at the workplace I met a new chap who had left the hospital yesterday. When he discovered that I was a German, he came up to me and said that a German had died in the hospital on the 9th of June. He could not give me the name exactly, but when I said Otto's name, he confirmed it.'

I sit as if stunned. That simply cannot be true. Otto had been taken prisoner with me at Stalingrad on the 2nd of February 1943. We had been together since March 1944, with the exception of a few months, and had shared happiness and sorrow together. At age seventeen he had already been a soldier and had overcome everything until now. Telling lies was unknown to him. His way was straight ahead, without compromise, and now he is no longer alive. I think of his wife and his children who long for him.

'We must go to the female doctor. She is the only person who can give us a precise explanation. Perhaps it was another German that died.'

I carefully make my way to the ambulatorium, suppressing my pain. The little doctor asks what I want. As we are always very quiet and withdrawn, we Germans enjoy a more advantageous handling than the broad mass of prisoners.

'Excuse me please, madam, but our friend Otto Goetz is said to have died. A convalescent who came to the camp yesterday told us. We are greatly upset and would like to know for certain whether the news is true. We ask you, next time you have an opportunity, to ask at the hospital whether the dead man is really Otto Goetz.' The little doctor promises to ask at the next opportunity. I thank her and hobble back to Wolf. With him were Oskar and Ruprecht, who could hardly take in this sad news. Oskar said: 'As long as we have nothing official, I do not believe it.'

The awfulness of the news, and not knowing the truth of it, was like a nightmare for us. But the next day I was called to the ambulatorium. 'Your friend Goetz is alive. It was another German who died, whose name we do not know. I met the doctor from the hospital who told me personally that Goetz is alive.' I thanked her with much joy and hurried as fast as I could to my friends, who as usual at this time of day were having their evening chat: 'Ottel is alive! I have come straight from the doctor, who confirmed it to me.

Unfortunately another of our countrymen died whose name is not known.' They all heaved a sigh of relief. We were delighted at this news.

Two murders have occurred during the short time we have been here. The first was when a former *Bladnoi*, who had become a camp elder, stabbed another *Bladnoi*. He was quickly removed by the NKVD as he was difficult case, or so I was told by another *Bladnoi*. The murderer had already taken two other men's lives in this way. As punishment for this he was taken to another camp and given the job of camp senior. We have not heard anything about an official sentence.

The second must have happened yesterday evening. This time it was the camp senior who stabbed the work assigner. The camp senior was an old *Sakoni*, a professional criminal, while the other was a renegade.

It is cruel to see how such creatures behave when they argue. Crowbars and axes are their favourite weapons. The one caught stealing lies on the ground and the other jumps on him as if he were a rubber mattress. When others take part, it becomes more savage. The thief is bound hand and foot and thrown high into the air, the impact rendering him unconscious. To me these sights revealing the animal nature of these creatures are utterly repulsive.

I myself have been badly handled three times in this camp. The first time, my brigadier, Klutschnikov, in a drunken state hit me without reason with an arm-thick birch branch on the right forearm; my arm swelled up and gave me severe pain for several days. On the second occasion a *Bladnoi* of this brigade jabbed the thumb and forefinger of his right hand into my eyes because I would not carry his tools back to camp. The third time another *Bladnoi* gave me some strong blows in the kidneys because I had allegedly left a hatchet lying behind. It is a simple matter for these bandits. If they lose something or make a mistake, they simply blame the German. He is alone and cannot defend himself – apart from which, it is more sensible to keep his mouth shut. If he tries to say something, then it is: 'Shut your gob, Fritz! Fascist! Damned dog!' With inexpressible anger and fists clenched in his pockets, he keeps his scorn under control.

A week has passed since we were informed that Otto was alive.

Today I am summoned to see the Russian woman doctor, who tells me that she had been given false information. Otto is dead. This morning she was in the hospital herself and asked about Goetz. This way she discovered that Goetz had died from pneumonia at 6 o'clock on the morning of the 9th of June. It took days for us to return to a normal existence in the camp. Otto was my best friend in captivity and was liked and respected by all of us. Fate is unfathomable and sometimes also incomprehensible. So many rogues return home and the best men remain by the roadside!

AN UNSUCCESSFUL ESCAPE ATTEMPT

After four vitamin injections the sickness in my left leg eased off for a while. Oskar also improved a little. Nevertheless, work still made me very tired. Because of my sickness I was put in a brigade that worked within the camp and was busy preparing the camp for winter. For the next few weeks I made mixtures of water, sand and clay to plaster the wooden walls of the barracks. Now and again I had to help with the erection of trellises. I am convinced that our forebears knew this 'advanced' working method more than 150 years ago. In Germany a person would hardly have survived on this kind of work. However, this work in the camp is good for me, although I have to walk around a lot each day.

As before, the few roubles that we earn every month are thrown into a pot. The distribution of the money reminds me that I still have my purse and the appropriate pockets in which to conceal it. We have learned that we are surrounded by thieves and not to let others see anything lying around for a split second. The worst thing is Wolf not doing anything about it, and once my nerves almost got the better of me when some money was stolen through his lack of attention. I think that this pressure is not worth it.

Now it is Wolf's turn to go to the hospital. He has a high temperature and the nurse suspects pneumonia. I hope this does not get any worse, as happened with Ottel! We say goodbye to him with great concern; we can only hope that he will recover. Wolf is as thin as a rake and we can count every one of his ribs, but he is still sharp.

The camp experts' initial dislike of us diminishes as time goes by. They can see that we do our work as well as possible. We also keep ourselves neutral as to do otherwise can only do ourselves harm. I still definitely want to escape, but my leg is not yet sufficiently restored for that.

There are only a few men in this camp who have been sentenced under political paragraphs. They behave very cautiously and only act otherwise when they believe themselves to be unobserved.

Wolf returns to the camp in the middle of August. Quite by chance he had the opportunity before his departure to visit Ottel's grave, which has the number A.36. There are still some Germans in the hospital, including Major Friedrich Mueller, an engineer with the Oak Leaves to the Iron Cross, who comes from Solingen, and Captain Reingraeber, an East Prussian. Both have been sentenced to twenty-five years under Paragraph 58. Of the German doctor, Dr Mueller, Wolf reports that, in contrast to the Russians, he is not good. Mueller refuses to have any Germans in his barrack and keeps well away from them. He was sentenced to twenty-five years for dealing in medicines at a prisoner of war camp.

My pack has been ready for our escape for several days already. Despite the misgivings of both Oskar and Wolf, I am going to flee with the Latvian. It must be done! I have been away from home for seven years now. I have put up with a life of slavery until now in the hope and belief of seeing my homeland again. But I cannot hold back any longer or I will go as crazy as many of my comrades.

The night of the 23rd of August seems especially suitable for our plans. I wake up at about midnight. It is raining heavily outside. Almost every second the darkness is lit with a flash of dazzling lightning, and after each flash the night seems even darker. It is so dark that I cannot even see my hand in front of my face. I have never experienced such a storm as this. Inconspicuously I get up, take my coat and go through the sparsely lit room. Everyone in the barrack is fast asleep, even the duty orderly. Refreshed, I breathe in the exquisitely fresh air. Behind the barrack door the smell hits you like a wall. I hasten through the rain to the neighbouring block in which Ivan sleeps. I am feverish with excitement. Here too the man on duty is asleep at the table. I gently rouse Ivan, who wakes immediately. I leave the room and wait for him outside. Flashes of lightning rip through the night. Suddenly I hear footsteps and step into the dead angle of the door so as not to be seen. It opens and the room orderly steps out. Ivan follows him on foot. I am noticed. The orderly asks me what I want here. I reply that I have been assigned to the kitchens with Ivan for night duties. Not to arouse any suspicion, I leave my sack standing behind the door. Ivan and I go to the gate. Under its left side is a depression that has become even more washed away by the rain. If we keep quiet, we can get out through here. Now, though, the glare of the searchlight is directed on the gate. We can do nothing. As quickly as we can, we vanish back into the barracks. One thing is certain, as this effort has shown, we are unable to get out of the camp. The guards within and outside the barracks are too alert.

The night orderly in Ivan's barrack is suspicious because he found the sack. However, Ivan took it back and gives it to me in the morning. That morning Ivan is examined by the NKVD. The night duty man has reported both of us. Fortunately the orderly does not know my name, and the NKVD runner is now searching for a small German man with a limp. As I am not limping at the moment, the runner takes Sommerfeld, who has the same illness as I had. Sommerfeld truly knows nothing of my plans as for several weeks already we have been excluding him from our company for stealing. I keep quiet, and so does Ivan. Both of us are kept under special supervision when working outside the camp. After a short while Ivan unexpectedly admits that he has been detained under the political paragraphs and he is suspected of fleeing. I have no chance of saying goodbye to him.

THERE IS NO EXPLOITATION OF PEOPLE BY PEOPLE IN THE SOVIET UNION

At the next parade I am assigned to Work Group 2 and so have to work outside the camp again. I am allocated to the Dolgushen Brigade, a wild crowd consisting mostly of young lads aged between eighteen and thirty. Only a few are older. The brigade is thirty-six strong and we are working on the foundations for a railway bridge to be constructed over the little valley stream. To my pleasure Ruprecht Scholtissek is also with this brigade, so at least I am not so lonely. We always work together. The work is very hard and defies description. Cleverly, the supervising engineer understands that in return for small allocations of food and some handfuls of machorka, the men will do their utmost. It is not unusual for us to be at the workplace from 7 o'clock in the morning until the next morning.

With an especially crazy work commitment, the brigadier wants to drive his men hard, even at the cost of their bones. He drives the men on without a pause. They follow him because crumbs fall from his table. Food is brought to the site by vehicle in the evening.

I discover a particularly obnoxious practice when I see how the prisoners smoke cigarette butts. Such a butt goes through five to six hands and each makes yet another one. The last remnants of crumbling machorkas remaining from the butts are then collected to produce another small cigarette. Tobacco is more precious than gold for the banished here.

The days are still hot, but as soon as the sun sinks it is suddenly cooler. We had almost finished the big hole for the foundations in the stream bed when a commission arrived. The responsible sector commander, a general, decided that no bridge should be built here, but rather a concrete pipe with a dam. The whole job was in vain. What we had dug out yesterday we shovelled back today. Afterwards we dig in the stream bed again. The stream is diverted but the mass of water does not drain and the ground water keeps coming back. It is just as well that some of us have rubber boots, but these have holes in them and one can be sure that the water will rise above our artificial leather shoes. We try to keep the stream dry with two or three pumps, but it is futile. Sometimes the pumps are not used at night, because the risk of flooding is so great, and then the next day the whole stream bed is under water again. Until it has been pumped empty again, we are set to breaking up stones. The norm here is so high that one cannot achieve it without deception. At unobserved moments we bring across the already crushed gravel on stretchers to a new heap. Thus the piles of gravel often change and there is more on paper than in reality.

Once the engineer has made the all the preparations – the cement brought out, sand brought and washed, prepared gravel lying in sufficient quantities there – and the sinks for the foundations are sufficiently deeply excavated, then the work of pouring concrete can begin. The mass of men are then committed in a constant process. In Europe such a process has been done with technology and the appropriate machinery for years. One group washes the components and takes them to the concrete mixer, a product of the Molotov Factory, while others bring the mixed concrete from there in the tipper. In addition, men with wheelbarrows are ready to do the mixing on the spot. The concrete layers are worked on next. If the mixing machine goes wrong, a 'specialist' comes and brings things back to order, using mainly hammers and crowbars. It often takes a considerable time before the mixing machine is working again, further mixing being done by hand. The water is taken from a source about fifty metres away.

Ruprecht and I had the task of carrying gravel. This is the least popular job and everyone shirks it. It is a real bone-breaker and we are thinner from day to day, although Ruprecht has some reserves from his work in the baths. We return fatigued to camp late in the evening, but never fail to meet again at some place or other. Pleasures and sorrows are shared. Our constant concern is food. We are as hungry now as during the worst times in the prisoner of war camps. Fortunately now and then we meet a person who gives us something, but for the four of us it is always too little.

Sommerfeld is not quite sane. We have tried to stop him, but all appeals and admonishments have been for nothing; his hunger is driving him ever deeper and he has sunk to the same level as the most dissolute individuals in the camp. Even when he was caught stealing by the Russians and was repentant, he was stealing again the very next day. Now the Russians come grinning to us and report that he is a homosexual and involved in homosexual orgies. In payment for this he gets bread and the beloved porridge. The matter is so serious that we decide to ostracise him as all attempts at reforming him have been in vain. When I see these starving men in the camp crawling around, I always think of the predators prowling in the zoo. They have the same characteristics.

The Red Army truck convoys keep on coming. As I discover, their loads are taken to Lena and transported from there to the far north. Of late they have been mainly fuel convoys.

In October Ruprecht and I together earned 34 roubles. The brigadier demanded 5 of them and we gave them to him without a whimper as our peace is precious to us. Until now we have had Dolgushen giving us a protecting hand and preventing the bandits from bothering us. We want to buy bread and tobacco with the remainder but obtaining foodstuffs from outside the camp is very difficult. Several times already we have entrusted people with money, believing that they would not let us down. It has been a disaster until now. Even the friendliest men in the camp here are unpredictable when it comes to money. Which of these people can one trust to distinguish between mine and yours? The only option left to us now is Sasha Melnikov, an air force lieutenant from Dnjepropetrovsk. He has been friendly towards us until now and helps where he can. We have not given him any money until now; if he too betrays us, we will have no one.

Sasha is immediately prepared to look for bread, tobacco and even oil. He says he will bring them another day. Unfortunately he also lets us down. Not the next day nor on the following days did we see anything of the promised items or the money. We can only write it off and for the whole of the remainder of the month we have no chance of buying bread.

The atmosphere in the Dolgushen Brigade has become unbearable. Ruprecht and I are transferred to the Sainulin Brigade, which consists, apart from one Ukrainian, entirely of non-Russians such as Usbecks, Kazakhs, Turkmenen and Tartars. The brigadier himself is a Kazakh. We often talk about why non-Russians of all colours are more friendly as a rule than the Russians themselves. The Jews are also very forthcoming towards us, although they must harbour some spite for Germany. Their behaviour causes me to revise my prejudice. We understand each other well because here we all belong to the repressed nations. These nationalities are great lovers of a free life. Nevertheless any efforts in that direction are vigorously suppressed because the informer system makes any resistance impossible.

Working conditions in the Sainulin Brigade are somewhat easier. I have come to an agreement with the brigadier for him to ascribe us to the highest percentage, in return for which he will get half of our earnings. In this way we get the 350 grams of extra bread per day. Our work? We again dig boreholes all day, or break up stones.

Overnight it is winter. At first it is not so cold, and snow comes. The individual brigades have received winter clothing following urgent demands. Almost all of us have received padded clothing from a specially erected tailors' workshop. The old prisoners use this as grounds for concern in the maintaining of the workforces. If we fall out through freezing, it will spoil the unity of the workforce.

Soon after receiving it, Ruprecht's padded jacket – a half-length steppe coat – is stolen. He gets nothing else, but is charged 300 roubles for the replacement. This money will be deducted from his pay. There are thieves everywhere, and I think we will never learn and will always fall for their tricks. While I was putting on my shoes, my 400 grams of bread was snatched from the windowsill. It was only out of sight for a brief instant as Ruprecht stood in between to pull something out of his bed space, but the bread was gone. Four Russians sitting there denied having seen anything. Even a search by the guard was unsuccessful.

Many are now going around without winter clothing because they were not careful enough with their coats or felt boots. The stolen items are immediately smuggled out of the camp as fast as possible and sold for a cheap price to the people.

We have two days off on the 7th and 8th of November, which had already been worked for as usual. With a big banging of drums and speeches in the month before the revolutionary celebrations, we were expected to compete against each other in honour of the 'Greatest Socialist October Revolution' which was to be fulfilled ahead of the 'Stalinist Post-war Five Year Plan'.

Even the big concrete tunnel intended to carry the stream under the railway tunnel had to be finished for the celebrations. Although this was not accomplished, a completion report was passed on to the supervising office so that the people in charge of the job would not be subjected to reprimands. Only a week later could one really say that the job had been accomplished.

Sainulin let me remain in camp today because I had been working constantly and needed a rest. A film is being shown today; I will go and see it with Zubeck, who has been in the camp for some days and comes from Upper Silesia. Unfortunately I cannot see much of the film as the room is overcrowded and I am obliged to crouch on my knees with my head bowed to the ground: if I raise my head any higher, it blocks the screen and hides the picture. Immediately the mob shouts: 'Head out of the way, you dog!' I console myself with the fact that several others must be in the same situation.

For days already we have been working on the excavators. These machines are products of the Molotov Works. They load earth for the railway embankment on trucks at a location about 2 kilometres south

of the camp, in day and night shifts. The mass of men work here
ceaselessly as the Russians want the line completed and the first
trains running. Here and elsewhere the prisoners are engaged in
clearing the ground. If the machines cannot accomplish it, we have
to make boreholes in the difficult terrain – which is very difficult with
the lack of tools – so that the excavator can get on with its work.
Thirty Siss-Ural trucks – some of them new tippers – drive
continuously, working day and night. With them come two more
Germans: Ludwig Zubeck from Upper Silesia and Heinz Becker from
Westphalia. Both, like us, were sentenced under Paragraph 206 of
the Ukrainian law. Their workplace is in the workshop company, as
they are good with their hands.

58 DEGREES COLD

The cold now sets in hard. It is suddenly down to a degree of cold
that even the old prisoners have hardly experienced. Already when
we get up in the morning to get our sparse breakfast, we can see from
the window whether there is more than 50 degrees of frost. The dark,
dirty barrack, the walls of which are already collapsing because of
the damp, is overfilled.

Already for a long time we have had to sleep on the floor and not
infrequently we discover in the morning that one of those living on
an upper bunk has urinated over us. All rubbish here is thrown on the
ground. For several nights Ruprecht and I had a place in the upper
bunks, but the bunks are so narrow that one can only sleep on one's
side. Should one of the sleepers change position, the others are forced
to change their position too. If you get up to go to the urine barrel,
which stands right beside the door, it is difficult to get your place
back again. Hence we are trying to sleep on the ground again.

In the morning I feel washed out, and Ruprecht is the same. The
hoarfrost on the windows tells us the approximate temperature, it
being 30, 40 or 50 degrees according to the thickness of the frost. In
the open air the cold hits you and immediately takes your breath
away. As fast as we can we run to the cookhouse, where the food
servers of the individual brigades are already arguing. After breakfast
we all lie down again on our beds and wait with trepidation for what
decision the officer of the day or his assistant brings regarding the
work. A howl of pleasure goes up when we do not have to go out

because of the cold, which is usually the case when it is more than degrees of frost. Swearing and complaining arise when it is: 'Get out to work!'

When that is the case, many try to dodge the work. They do not appear at the guardroom, but rather keep themselves hidden. However, after the camp is counted, a search begins for the shirkers. Most are soon found and driven to work with blows and prodding. In response, for the next two days they receive the daily punishment ration of only 350 grams. Nevertheless sometimes some of them manage to remain in the camp. They think the punishment ration less harmful than the cold. Those who gain a reputation for being shirkers eventually end up in a punishment unit.

As we know that shirking work can only bring more harm and is pointless, Ruprecht and I always go out. I am already so frozen through at the guardroom that I am simply no longer able to think anyway. It is as if my brain is frozen. Despite the winter clothing and the padded gloves, which are not very good, I am frozen to the bone. The cold gnaws at my body and I realise that I have never been so run down as now since the time I had the fever. I haven't felt so bad since the time in the Xiltau Woodland Camp.

Quite automatically I clasp the spade under my arm, or hang the pickaxe over my shoulder, and trot after the others. At the workplace I am worthless for the first few hours. Only when one of the prisoners lights a great fire and I can warm myself for a while do I discover that I am still a human being. The contrast between the fire and the cold is so strong – especially with the wind – that one's skin is singed in front while the part away from the fire is ice-cold. The Japanese winter gloves prove to be good, and better than the Russian ones. They are also preferred by the Russians. Nobody wants to leave the fire, and we all huddle as close to it as possible until the brigadier drives us back to work. Our hands are stiff and ice cold, hardly able to hold the pickaxes. I am also not in good enough condition to work intensively enough for my body to warm itself with the movement. My strength is insufficient. It is the same with the others. I freeze too often.

Even if a prisoner proves that he has been frozen, he gets an increased sentence for sabotage. For me these hours of 30 to 40 degrees below freezing are absolute hell. Ruprecht is no different.

Again and again we run back to the fire for a moment to warm ourselves. Even if the brigadier and his assistants, who crouch around the fire, chase us away from the fire with curses, we reappear after a few minutes. Exhausted and dog tired, we creep back to camp in the evening, but the few hours of night in the densely occupied accommodation give us no respite.

Our camp is now overpopulated as never before. Some 1,200 prisoners now live in the three and a half barracks. The railway track layers of the 208th Colony have appeared here and are to lay the lines in our sector in the next few days. Rüping and Plinta, our comrades from Charkov Prison, are among them. They bring us news that we can hardly believe, but is of considerable significance if I is true. Plinta says that a Russian, whom he takes to be utterly reliable, had heard a radio message in November at the 206th Colony whereby all German prisoners of war who had not been sentenced under the political paragraphs would be given amnesty. Our two comrades are so convinced about the truth of this news that they expect to be home by Christmas. I am basically more sceptical, as this news is being circulated by a Russian. Our camp also has a radio and we have not heard any such report. For us it means waiting and not relying too much on optimistic hopes. Nevertheless I can imagine how it would be.

The first train has driven past our camp. More are following. Even wagons with supplies have arrived. In the supply camp, which lies outside the camp zone not far from the railway line, the supplies for the 2nd, 3rd, 4th and 5th Detachments of the 'Angarlag' have been stored. From now on the individual detachments will receive their supplies by truck, as the railway line in their sectors is not yet ready. Only after a few weeks do the 4th and 5th Detachments change location.

Our brigade has the pleasant task of unloading two wagons loaded with flour. I am able to get some flour and take it back to camp. But where can I rest my swollen leg? When the medical orderly, an emigrated Jew from Romania who is very friendly, sees my leg and takes my temperature, he writes me off work. The nights are terrible as the pain does not ease off. In fact, it gets even worse. My legs are thickly swollen and I can hardly walk. In a visit to the barrack, the medical orderly orders my transfer to the sickbay of the ambulatorium. It is the 16th of December.

The little sickbay has five beds. In comparison to the beds in the barracks, they look clean and have blankets as well as straw mattresses and pillows. I have not known such luxury for months. I have been lying fully clothed on the floor or on the wooden planks of the bunk beds because I did not want to lose my clothing. After delousing, it is a relief for me to lie in clean clothing in the whitewashed room and fall asleep. Fortunately the fever soon dies down, but the swelling remains.

There is a 'flesh show' on the evening of the 17th of December. When my brigade is mustered, I am taken to the examination room. I am written down as unfit for work for a month.

I quenched my desire to sleep in the first few days. Now I work on my recorded vocabulary. It is very cold outside. As bed neighbours I have two prisoners who like me are happy not to be chased out into the pitiless cold. Mornings and evenings we can hear the moaning and groaning of the sick who appear in the treatment room, often exaggerating their symptoms to deceive the medical orderly. But he knows his way around. With other means too the Russians try to avoid having to work in the cold. With ham, tobacco and other desirable items, but also with money that some get sent from home, they try to persuade the medical orderly to write them off as sick. The longed-for success is not impossible, for what Russian can resist?

Ruprecht now has my headgear while I am in hospital. I am sorry for the young chap. Even Wolf has it better because he is in a brigade working in the potato cellar.

Some days later the Russians are released from the sickbay while I remain in the room. Through the window I can see how cold it must be outside. Here inside one notices little of it except when one leaves to go to the toilet, wearing shirt and underpants, plus felt boots and headwear. The swelling makes me think that I must have the only frozen clubfoot.

The wood supply for the heating is irregular, however, and so it happened that on the 22nd of December, when it was 40 degrees below zero, I was lying in a cold room. Because of this the male nurse, a Tartar, covers me with all available blankets (five) and two straw sacks. So I survive, thankful that I do not have to be in the barracks.

On this day the whole camp does not have to work because of the cold. On the 23rd and 24th December the cold is so intense that, except for a small brigade collecting wood for the heating, nobody has had to go out to work. It is as if nature has died. Thick fog lies over the valley so that even at midday the sun is unable to break through. Everything lies in the deepest silence. The smoke from the chimneys is kept low by the fog.

From our money, which we got in December and have kept until now, despite the danger of theft, we have been able to buy some flour, sugar and fat. In the laundry Oskar baked some little flour cakes that he sweetened. I cannot go to the Christmas celebrations in the barrack, but at least Oskar, Ruprecht and Wolf sit there together to chat over old times.

That evening Wolf appears and reports that my brigade now has to go out on a catastrophic duty. Ruprecht is also outside. I shiver as today we have the severest frost yet – 56 degrees below freezing. Poor Ruprecht, how endlessly long this night will be. Hopefully he will not freeze. This is typical of the Russians. First they insisted that the railway line must be completed, but now there has been an accident and the trains are iced in.

For the next two days Ruprecht again has the bad luck to be on night duty with our brigade at the accident spot. He gives quite a depressed impression. I thank God that I am lying here sick in the hospital and so exempt from this martyrdom. A new record: the lowest temperature reached was minus 58 degrees last night, and those poor men had to go out in it. If I had told this in central Europe, no one would have believed me.

New Year, 1950. I am still lying in the sickbay. The swelling has gone and bodily I am quite well recovered, because my Tartar sickbay attendant looks for food in the kitchen for me. I am very grateful to him as my body takes everything in and looks full, like a dried-up sponge that has been thrown into water. Fortunately I am a good food consumer and have a healthy stomach. The frost period continues, but less severe. We now have between minus 35 and 40 degrees, much to the disappointment of the prisoners, who would prefer more than 40 degrees. In fact, one hardly notices a difference between 35 and 40 degrees of frost.

AS FACTOTUM IN THE AMBULATORIUM

On the 13th of January I am deemed to be recovered and am released from the sickbay and assigned to Working Group 2. A little stronger, but with a greater fear of frost, I return to work with my brigade. My brigadier, who in his own way has considerable respect for the Germans, is very lenient about my work. Our brigade is still breaking up gravel and demolishing an embankment so that the railway track can be widened by two metres, but the work proceeds only slowly because of the frost. The stones and clumps of earth are taken on a tipper to a narrow dyke about 300 metres away and shaken out.

The 15th of January sees a small change in the camp as a group of undesirable elements go off to a punishment column. Two men go from our brigade. For the last two days Ruprecht and I have gone to the ambulatorium to saw wood. In payment, the sickbay attendant brings us a bowl of porridge, which we eat together. Our astonishment is great when a little time later we discover that this attendant is no longer working in the ambulatorium. Pavlik, the nurse from the Donez area, asks me if I would stand in for him, as I probably already know what the job entails. I gladly agree. I do not have to be outside in the cold, and I will receive better food and thus can support my friends. The job is not easy because Pavlik is a very difficult person, for whom one can hardly do anything right. But nevertheless I will try. Every day that I spend here brings me closer to the spring and can be regarded as a success.

On the morning of the 16th of January I stay in the camp. I had previously told my brigadier, who had nothing against it. As a nurse I remain out of sight and concern myself with the cleanliness of the small barrack and its catering facilities. Now I get a proper picture of how well the camp experts live at the expense of the broad masses. What I had previously only suspected I could now see for myself. Besides my job of tending to the sick, making the beds and controlling the traffic during working hours, especially ensuring that nothing was stolen, I have to go to the kitchen once or twice a day. Here I get for the doctor the food that the workers should have. That he gets the choice items such as fat, meat, fish, noodles, sugar, meal and dried potatoes is obvious enough. Only a fraction of the stipulated norm is actually received by the workers, the largest part going to the small gang of camp experts. But it is also shared with free persons who have dealings with the camp. Among them is the free doctor, a young lad about twenty-five years old, who comes from the Gorki area and has been sent here on compulsory duty. Every day he appears at the camp and takes part in the meals, during which the senior orderly and the nurses give all their attention to what he has to say, as their jobs depend upon it.

It is informative to discover how many of these individuals there are, who have already lived in banishment for years and even attained a position. They have become slaves of their passions. Daily they appear to obtain opium, caffeine or narcotic injections in their veins. Men who were once very brutal and unscrupulous behave like small children here if they do not get an injection one day because there are no more ampoules available. They give everything in order to indulge their passion. It is disgusting to see when they become drunk from this, and any means are justified to get them into a drunken state. Here I first discovered that one can get intoxicated on Eau de Cologne or other perfumes. The individuals drink it from a beaker diluted with water. For preference tea extract is used with 50 grams to a litre of water. The nurses and Pavlik are slaves to these vices. Now and then, when the guards are bribed, they are also able to smuggle women into the camp from the women's camp situated 3 kilometres away. Then the 'expert' concerned spends the night with the prostitute in the ambulatorium's little galley.

Despite the strenuous duty – often I get no rest for thirty-six hours and then can only sleep for a few hours – I feel well. It would be somewhat different if we were only given watery soup and poor bread, but here my body is given food rich in proteins, which it definitely needs for improvement.

Whatever I can slip away I give to my friends, who also need it. Ruprecht looks the best of them, remaining all day in the camp and washing for the ambulatorium. Within fourteen days I had made myself indispensable. Nevertheless, because of Pavlik's consistent grumblings, connected with the worst insults, I lost my patience and answered back. But he called me back again that evening. Sheer anxiety makes this work a burden for me, but I have to carry on, not only for myself but for my friends. How the times have changed. I was running about like a recruit in basic training.

In the evenings, after the treatment hour, begins my real work as a cleaner. With cold or, with luck, hot water from the laundry I wash the floors of the four rooms of the ambulatorium barrack. At first I scrape the floors clean with a cleaver or glass shard. Then I start working with a rubber scrubbing brush that I had first to acquire. Whatever I do, Pavlik is never satisfied. I have already become used to this, although it has not been easy, and now I continue scrubbing until I am chased away.

News. It seems somehow to have something to do with our return home. The camp's cultural worker, who was in the ambulance this morning, told me that Moscow had demanded an assessment about us Germans and that we would soon be going home. I did not want to believe it at first but then the clerk of the cultural section told me that he himself had written the assessment of all who fulfilled 144 percent of their norm on a daily average and were politically faultless. This news triggered off my hopes, although the Russian State has not announced anything yet. It seems almost inconceivable to be going back to a civilised environment, to be able to live again like normal people.

The days are long for us. My birthday, already my eighth as a prisoner of war, allows me to prepare a small snack for my comrades thanks to my connections with the ambulatorium and the kitchen. At the centre of my good state of health is the question: 'Will we really be the next to go home?' We are now all optimistic and believe that our homeland has not forgotten us and is busy preparing for our return home by all possible means. An important factor for all of us is the behaviour of America, England and France. If they combine to demand our liberation, the Russians cannot keep us here for ever. It would not be clever and would only arouse new hatreds.

On the evening of the 16th of February Pavlik tells me that I will have to return to work in the morning. My successor is a small Tartar from Stalingrad called Kaloma, who looks like a gnome.

Early in the morning I see to the sick for the last time. After four weeks working as a nurse in clean surroundings, the dirt in the barracks repels me more than ever. The brigade is still working in the old place. Discontentedly I look for the stones that I can best smash in the snow on the slope. Every few minutes I abandon my place to warm myself. It must be 30 or 40 degrees below zero. Is it ever going to get warm? Hopefully the month of March will be a bit warmer.

Chapter 5

The Journey Home

I enter the lobby of the ambulatorium. 'Good evening. Have you any work for us?' Kaloma comes towards me. 'Ah, welcome Holl! You can saw up the tree trunk lying outside. You know the lengths. By the way, you are going home tomorrow.' I look at him suspiciously, but his face is expressionless. It could be a joke, but I am wise to such tricks. I laugh. 'Very funny! We are going home tomorrow! Ha, ha, ha!' Kaloma looks at me earnestly with his big eyes. 'It is no joke, the runner from the guardroom told me so himself. He overheard a telephone conversation between the camp commandant and the detachment. You can believe me, it is really true!' I still don't believe it. In the small room nearby are the free doctor, the medical orderly and the nurse; they have overheard our conversation. Pavlik gets up and says to me: 'Yes, it is true, you will travel to Germany tomorrow!' The medical orderly nods in confirmation.

The door opens and a baker steps in. He works outside the camp but is a frequent guest here. As he sees me, he asks: 'What is wrong with you, your journey home? There is someone waiting for you in the guardroom; he comes from the 211th Column and is also travelling to Germany.'

'That's me!' With a leap I was outside and running to the guardroom. Through the tiny window in the door I looked inside. Immediately in front of me stood Wilhelm Rueping, who had been here in the camp eight weeks ago and had left with the track layers. I start to speak but my words are broken and I cannot think what to say. Soon the door opens and Wilhelm enters the camp, escorted by the assistant work director. 'Good evening, Wilhelm, what are you doing here?' Curiously my eyes watch his mouth. 'Good evening, Bert! This evening I was suddenly marched off here, we are going home!' Full of happiness, we shake hands. It seems that it is true.

Now the assistant work director says I am to inform all the Germans in the camp that tomorrow none of them will have to go to work. How willingly I do that!

Wilhelm tells me that on his way he saw our friends in the 209th Column, who would be joining us here tomorrow morning.

The night passes in happy expectation and with the prickling feeling of inner excitement, in which I could hardly close my eyes. Already early next morning the first comrades convicted for various crimes gather in the camp. Prisoners of war assemble here from all the camps in the area. Soon we are able to greet our friends Mütschele, Doerr, Korff and Breske. Still absent are App and Menden. About Kurt App we have had no definite information so far, but Hans Menden has been in the punishment camp of the 203rd Column since May 1949. According to the opinions of my friends, who had been with him originally, the Russians had denounced him. We enquire whether there are any men from the 203rd Column present. Viktor Hildebrand, who was with Menden for several weeks, reports that Hans was taken to hospital on Christmas Eve with jaundice. Impatiently we wait for the arrival of the sick from hospital. Koloch, who was a nursing orderly, and Dr Mueller, who carried out amputations, finally appear. To our questions about Menden we receive the sad reply that Second-Lieutenant Hans Menden died in hospital on the 8th of January this year from jaundice and the freezing cold. This bitter news dampens the pleasure of our impending journey home. We must leave behind us, lying next to our friend Otto Götz on the roadside, our youngest colleague Hans Menden. He was not yet twenty-four years old. Within just seven months two of the ten of us to be sentenced have died. And we still do not know what has happened to Kurt.

Another bit of news troubles us. Ludwig Zubeck from Gleiwitz is not on the list of those going home. Already this morning they wanted to chase him out to work. He is forty-two years old and ailing. He sat on his bunk and quickly falls apart under the weight of this hard fate. The best and most well-meaning words fail to comfort him. I do not understand the harsh decision. Zubeck was punished under the same paragraph as us and was given only five years' banishment, of which he has already done half. The responsible office in the camp insist that he is not on the list. A telephone call to the detachment is also unsuccessful. An old acquaintance, who has always been very friendly towards us, says that Zubeck is not a German but a Pole. I do not believe it and ask Ludwig whether during his imprisonment he has been indiscreet. He declares to me that he has never done anything wrong. I promise him that I will take his case to the main administration of the 'Angerlag' if I have the chance.

On the 19th of February we twenty-six 'home-comers' drive off in two trucks towards Sajarsk. Shortly before our departure the accountant appears and pays us the balance of our accounts. I received 14 roubles, Korff and Mütschele something over 80 roubles, as they had worked as locksmiths in the repair workshops. We leave Ludwig a small sum for tobacco. Back in the barracks crying eyes watched us drive away.

The trucks travel quickly to Sajarsk in the winter sunshine. At the woodland edge we pass the 204th Column's hospital, and as we drive past we salute with bare hands our dead friends, whose wooden crosses sticking out of the snow bear their names and numbers.

It all seems like a dream. Ten months ago we drove along this road in the opposite direction, uncertain of our future. Now we can entertain hopes about our journey home, although with the bitter aftertaste that two of our best men will lie here for ever.

To our great pleasure we are met at the gate of the Sajarsk Transit Camp by Kurt App. Artur Sauer, who shared a cell with us in Saporoschje, is also there. Kurt straightaway warns us of the bandits in the transit camp as we are searched at the camp gate. 'If you have money on you, then conceal it well! They have already taken everything from me. I was completely helpless against them!' The reunion with him is very hearty. We have been apart since Charkov. He tells us that the Hungarian horseman Tschermak, who had represented Hungary at the 1936 Olympiad in Berlin and had sat in a cell with us in Saporoschje, still remains in the 4th Detachment. Kurt is also saddened to learn of the deaths of our two friends.

We now go to our allocated accommodation: a dark barrack full of people. We are immediately surrounded by a swarm of young bandits who want to search us. Warned by Kurt, we press close together and go back to the door. The bandits try to stop us, but they are unable to do so. Oskar is already outside. A young lad blocks my way to the door but I push him aside and he runs off. As I am going through the door, Oskar calls out a warning. I turn around and see the bandit coming at me with a drawn knife. But I am already in sight of the sentry standing on the watchtower, so he vanishes again back into the darkness of the barrack.

Emile Holler, one of the homeward bound, who has already lived in the camp for a long time, finds us better accommodation in a building that had previously served as a workshop. We will only be here for two or three days, so we can be content with our temporary accommodation. The main thing is that we are among Germans and not bothered by the bandits.

All day men going home are brought here from the various camps of the 'Angarlag'. There are some men who have become so acclimatised to the conditions that they have lost all sense of property and can no longer distinguish between 'mine' and 'yours'. They will find it very difficult when they get back to a normal life. I even think it possible that some of them will find themselves in a German prison sooner or later, although previously they were upright and honest men. The years of imprisonment and constant hunger have forced them to sink to this. They can think only of themselves. God be thanked, most of us are still sensible and normal people.

I learn from a Berliner who was in a prison of war camp with Zubeck that Ludwig had tried to be repatriated to Upper Silesia during the repatriation of the Poles in 1946. However, the Russians had not recognised him as Polish. Now everything was clear to me. In truth Zubeck was not a Pole but a German citizen, but in 1946 he had claimed to be a Pole and therefore could not go home as a German. Truly this was a boomerang that had returned with the worst consequences. I have no chance of speaking to Zubeck to explain.

Our accommodation is without a stove and thus very cold. We will get an electric one.

Just as I had always taken an interest in our old 205th Column, so I concern myself here too in pursuit of my friends' requests. I return late in the evening from my unsuccessful search for a stove, which was as urgently necessary as the lighting. My friends then tell me that, despite the guards outside, we have been visited by the bandits. Quite unexpectedly they had suddenly appeared in the room, each armed with a knife. One of them blocked the exit. Carrying an oil lamp, they had gone straight to those who had money. Resistance was pointless as we had no weapons. Siegfried refused them, but when he felt a knife, despite the thickness of his clothing, he gave his money away.

It was obvious to us that the few roubles we had were not worth someone being stabbed. We learned from this experience that these creatures were capable of anything and would murder a man without hesitation. Indeed, Kurt App had survived a serious incident in his camp which left several men dead. These bandits had even taken our food from us. I was very angry but could see that resistance was really pointless. There were more than seventy of us in the room, but we did not know each other. No one trusted the others, and anyway most of us were physically very weak.

The night passed very slowly, and we got up early in the morning to get the blood flowing again and warm our stiff muscles. The day passed with measuring for clothing that would be provided that night or in the morning.

We then discovered that the bandits were planning to pay us another visit in the coming night. I went to see the camp commandant, a captain, and told him what had happened. I added that we were not prepared to hold back from the robbers, and any Russian prisoners who entered our room in the dark would be beaten up. The camp commandant promised to provide a guard on our accommodation.

To our delight we were issued with our new clothing that night. Next morning we were ordered to march out to another place. Two men who were apparently Volksdeutsche, one of them a policeman, were not issued with the clothing and, like the four Hungarians, had to remain behind.

The station is 4 kilometres from the camp. The route is very icy and for some of our men who are still sick it was quite a strenuous journey because of the freezing conditions. The guard is very strong. Even a guard dog accompanied us and it does not look like we are going home. At last we reach the station and see the Pullmann coach in which we will be travelling.

When the train conductor sees our guards he asks what this means, as we are going home and are free men. He has the escorts immediately return to camp.

It is an unusual feeling for me, after more than seven years, to be without a guard again. Happily I discover the joy of not having a machine-pistol aimed at my back. In the Pullmann coach assigned to returning prisoners, we were taken from Sajarsk via Bratsk to Taishet. The journey takes two days, and our conductor allows us full freedom of movement and does not treat us as prisoners.

At Taishet transit camp we are treated very kindly by the commandant. It is as if they want us to forget all the bitterness and awfulness of the previous years. We have to wait three days here.

In the women's part of the transit camp I meet a German woman from Riga, who had moved from Latvia to Berlin soon after the 1945 Polish campaign. She is about forty-five years old and was sentenced by the Russians in 1947 and brought here because her place of birth was in Latvia. A Czech who had been taken from Czechoslovakia tells me that he had been in a camp with Generals Sixt von Armin and Heinrici, both of whom were given twenty-five years' forced labour sentences. He further reports that along the Taishet–Bratsk line there is a row of prison camps in which there are more than fifty sentenced German generals. This confirms the observations that we had made on the journey from Taishet to Bratsk in April 1949, when we had ourselves seen two camps whose occupants were wearing Waffen-SS uniforms. I also have the opportunity of speaking with a twenty-year-old Spaniard who had been brought to Russia during the Spanish Civil War of 1938 and has no possibility now of returning to his homeland. The Soviet Union is holding him against his will and he is not particularly happy with the current system.

New comrades join us. Again there is a general checking of clothing and old items are exchanged. We are deloused on the 25th of February. The camp doctor wants our hair to be cut. He says it is the rule, but some refuse. I allow this last cut in the secret hope that it will ensure our return home. I am not going to fall out with the authorities now through resisting or other reasons!

As we march through the camp, the commandant asks us to sing a German marching song in thanks for our forthcoming release. Happily we fulfilled this request, now really feeling that we were going home. But here also two comrades are struck from the list by some authority or other and have to remain behind.

We take seats on the Taischet–Krasnojarsk train. Our escorts – a second-lieutenant and his assistant, a Red Army soldier – are very friendly and we hardly feel that we are still prisoners of war when we travel in a normal passenger train. As far as Krasnojarsk the journey goes smoothly. By ten o'clock in the morning we are already alongside the station. The next train towards Mariinsk goes that evening. Today is Sunday. Our escorting officer leaves us with his assistant at the station while he goes off to the Kommandatura to obtain a further travel permit. He returns late in the evening without success, as all the offices are closed on Sundays. We now have to wait until the following evening, as without the Kommandatura's permission we cannot travel.

Our group, which was twenty-six men strong in the 205th Column, has now already increased to 105 men, who all come from the area west of Lake Baikal. I have trouble keeping them together and the Red Army soldier keeps coming to ask if we are all there. This is not the case, because several disappeared hours ago. However, I calm him down as I do not accept that anyone would miss the train through carelessness. I myself do not take the risk of being arrested by a militiaman. Instead I remain with the crowd and do not go far from the train.

That evening I can confirm that a whole number of men have sold some of the items of clothing that were almost completely new. They have given up old clothing and obtained money in exchange. But a lot have simply sold dispensable items as a form of insurance. For the first time in years they were in a position to be able to purchase things in the station hall that many of us have only dreamed of for many years. Here again I did not allow myself to take part in such experiments, as I did not know whether something serious was about to happen. But as always, Russia is the land of 'boundless impossibilities'.

Next day the dealings are eagerly pursued. That evening we travel on, arriving in Mariinsk at midday. A large number of men who received new items of clothing in Taishet have foolishly sold them. Now comes the result: a report has been written about it and we do not know what the consequences might be. The sellers are of the opinion that Moscow had given the orders for our transport home and nothing will happen. I hope they are not wrong!

IS THIS REALLY THE JOURNEY HOME?

The camp in Mariinsk is a transit camp like the previous two. More than two hundred prisoners of war have already been here for several days, brought here from all parts of Siberia, from Karaganga, from Vladivostock, from the territory west and east of Lake Baikal, even from the gold mines on the lower reaches of the Jenissei, and from the high north. My surprise is great when I meet the former Flak Lieutenant Heinicke, whom I knew from Jelabuga Camp. It is even greater when Heinicke tells me that my old comrade from Block VI at Jelabuga, Captain Fritz Schmeizer, is also here. I immediately make my way to him and we fall into each other's arms with delight.

Fritz tells me that in 1948 he was sentenced to ten years' hard labour for industrial sabotage in accordance with Paragraph 47, although he had declared himself a keen Anti-fascist.

The long-established Russians in the transit camp are ordered to give up their barracks for us and move into the earthen barracks. Mattresses, pillows and blankets are issued to us. We did not really want them but the camp commandant says that we will have to wait here for several more days, as more home-goers are expected to arrive. 'Several more days' turns into four long weeks and our patience is tested. Rumours about our eventual transport onwards come thick and thin, but there is nothing definite yet.

A heavy depression curbs our optimism when twenty-six men waiting for the transport are moved to another camp. With heavy hearts and their hopes dashed, they say goodbye to us. They are men who were either in the police or were sentenced under Paragraphs 58 or 54. The NKVD Operational Detachment stands like a frightening ghost in the background and we none of us know whether we will be called to the guardroom at any moment.

We pass away the time with home-made card games that have never seemed as slow or snail-like as now. Some countrymen of ours who have lived here for years, making their own living, join us. They have all kinds of things to report about what occurred here. They encountered civilians from the Soviet Zone of Germany who were brought here in 1947/8. There is, for example, a district judge whose chief after the capitulation had been a concentration camp inmate for fourteen years. The judge ended up in Siberia.

With the last women's transport to arrive in the camp were two

German women. One was a 20-year-old from Koenigsberg who had been a hair dresser, the other a 26-year-old Berliner. It is interesting to see how the years of banishment in Siberia have affected these women.

The journey home now seems to be certain. We have been dressed since this morning, but things are now going slowly. The reading of the home-going list takes a long time as the number has now increased to 909. But twenty men still remain behind as their names are not on the list and their cases have to be checked by the lawyer responsible, a justice colonel. After a last thorough search, in which all our old clothing has to be given up and we are given in return cheap, factory-made items, comes another endless night. Except for my unmarked photographs and the purse with the receipt for my wedding ring, which was taken from me on the 12th of March 1940 in Charkov Prison, the controlling officer takes everything away. Any pictures in which German Wehrmacht uniforms can be seen are taken from me. It is curious about the receipt for my wedding ring. None of the officers to whom I have mentioned it until now will acknowledge any responsibility. Now I must ask at the last Russian station at Brest-Litovsk. Siegfried has not had his receipt for a long time now, and Ottel's receipt too has gone which he took with him to hospital. I am curious as to what they will say in Brest-Litovsk. In any case I must try to bring the receipt back to Germany if I do not get the wedding ring back.

THE BIG LEAP!
And finally the time has come! Under the charge of a Russian lieutenant, our train, consisting of thirty-eight wagons, including the administrative wagon, sets off. It is 04.30 hours on the morning of the 12th of April 1950. On the 10th April – the first day of Easter – we spent all day being fitted out with clothing, and loading began on the 11th.

We have now been rolling in a westerly direction for hours already. It is an indescribably happy feeling, although there is still mistrust concealed in our hearts. Three of the twenty who were held back have made it, the others having to look on with heavy hearts as we marched to the station. One final man joined us on the way, having just passed through his camp's controls. We now amount to 913 home-goers.

The transport commander's adjutant, a young second-lieutenant, wants to appoint me as the German transport commander and thus put all the responsibility on me. Using all kinds of excuses I get away from him and for several days avoid seeing him at the stopping points so as not to get involved in any duty. I have no intention of going home as a transport commander after having been a working animal for years and perhaps being filmed in Moscow. I want nothing further to do with these people!

For days we travel through Russia's unending wastes. At Novo-Sibirsk station we stop quite close to a bridge under which we were unloaded a year ago for delousing. We travel on through the Urals on a local line, stopping exactly where we stopped in March 1943, half-starving, with the remnants of the two thousand men who had been loaded on at Beketovka, on the last stage of the journey to our first permanent camp at Jelabuga. Then we pass the two camps of Seloni–Dolsk, before crossing the bridge over the Volga. We are now heading directly to Moscow, but the track is partly iced over, so that we have a long delay.

In Moscow we go from the eastern part of the city on the bypass track to the western part, From the centre, the five-pointed star of the Kremlin Tower is visible. Nearby stands the steel framework of an incomplete tall building. We were deloused at a station near a prison. I am surprised at this good and smooth operation, with the cleanliness of the facilities such as I had not as yet encountered, and which reminded me of the German baths. However, there were only showers available.

And once more the train rolls on to the west. The rattling of the wheels sounds very friendly but I can still detect the traces of the invisible fist of the NKVD in the background.

THE LAST STAGE

On the morning of the 25th of April we arrive at Brest-Litovsk. It is a sunny Sunday morning. After a brief search, in which I was able to conceal and thus keep the receipt for my wedding ring, we are loaded into the waiting German goods wagons that provided a shuttle service between Frankfurt/Oder and Brest-Litovsk. Even here eight prisoners of war experienced the power that the NKVD still held over us. They were isolated and taken away in a green *Minna*. I knew that I would only feel truly safe once I had crossed the border near Göttingen.

With about 1,400 prisoners of war we travelled across Poland on the morning of the 26th of April. The journey lasted three days and took us by the shortest way via Warsaw to Frankfurt/Oder. Some of the home-goers soon forgot their care regulations and even sold the items of clothing that they did not want to take back to Germany. But the Russian escorts were only interested in taking us to Frankfurt. The behaviour of the Polish people towards us was in general very friendly. Some even asked when we would be coming back. They had learned the difference between the German and the Russian soldiers of occupation.

Early in the morning we arrived at Zielenzig station, the first German place that now belonged to Poland. Polish border officials checked our wagons and finally gave the train permission to carry on. We soon reached the Oder and tore open the doors that had had to be kept closed until then. On the Polish side stood a Polish guard, on the German side a Russian one. Oskar pointed out his home to us.

ON GERMAN SOIL

After more than seven long years I am back on German soil. The train slowly goes round the curve into the main station. I am overwhelmed and my throat is dry. My first picture of German soil with German people makes a big impression on me. On a big heap of coal stand twenty to thirty women in men's clothing, with careworn discontented faces, watching the passing train, which is decorated with garlands and pictures of Pieck and Grotewohl. Scarcely a hundred metres further on I see an old woman with a pickaxe and a spanner dressed as a Red female worker, also in men's clothing. As we drive into the station we see an old woman sitting on a rail eating a piece of bread.

Meanwhile youths from Frankfurt have climbed into our wagons begging for food and cigarettes. Unfortunately we cannot give them these things as we have none ourselves. Hunger has remained our constant companion until now. They tell us some of the jokes that have developed among the Frankfurt city people and conceal a bitter irony. It is shattering when one sees what the distress of the past has left in the faces of these children.

In Gronenfelde we also notice that the Germans have already

completed their organisation but the Russians have not. They no longer appear. We are deloused for the last time, and given money and food. Before the release papers are distributed, the camp commandant, a representative of the German Socialist Unity Party, uses the opportunity to make a speech. He praises the merits of their party's progress and urges us to do the same in the west, especially telling the truth of what has been achieved in the eastern zone!

Together with those being released to the French and American Zones and travelling to Thüringen or Saxony, we go in a collective transport to Leipzig. In Kottbus I send off a telegram to my wife: 'Will be home soon, calling at the next opportunity.'

In Leipzig I have a night in which to see the distress and unhappiness of the population, as people stop at the station to ask about conditions in the Soviet Union. Early in the morning we go on through Thüringen to Heiligenstadt. There we get food for the journey again, although we have already been given ample for the three days in Frankfurt, so that we will not arrive in the west without food. But most of my comrades give the food to the children of the refugees from the east waiting for travel permits to go to the west. East German policemen deployed in large numbers escort us to the barrier. Red Army soldiers are deployed on the roof of the building immediately on the Zone boundary looking at the west through binoculars. As I cross the zone border a feeling of relief sweeps through me. Now at last I am safe! Life can carry on!

'TELL THE TRUTH'

After more than seven years' imprisonment in the Soviet Union I am again a free person. My pleasure is saddened by some news passed on by some friends who have returned from the Soviet Union – that 'Workers' and Farmers' Paradise' – but are now lying ill in hospital, having not yet recovered from their time of slavery. My comrades Colonel Wolff, Lieutenant Colonel G. von Gueldenfeld, Captain Schmidt, Captain Knauff, Lieutenant Gerischer, Captain von Wenczowski and others are being arbitrarily retained in the Soviet Union and being kept in custody contrary to all peoples' rights.

They have only done their duty as soldiers, like everyone else who, as a son of his people, fought the enemy on the battlefield. They are no more guilty than any other soldier in the world who did not betray his country. And this is the real reason why they have to eke out an existence somewhere in the wastes of Russia under the worst of conditions. They are being kept as prisoners only because they remain the true sons of their people and are not traitors! And with them are still hundreds of thousands of Germans!

I can still hear the words of the SED speaker at Gronenfelde: 'Tell them in the west the truth of what you have seen under the signs of progress!' Yes, I will tell them the truth: that hundreds of thousands of our brothers are buried there in the endlessly wide expanse of Russia while their relatives wait in vain for news, and that several thousand more – who knows the exact number? – are still scratching out an existence under conditions of slavery and yearning to be given back their lives.